Chinese Primer

(Hànyǔ Pīnyīn)

中文入門

臺靜農題

陳大端　臺益堅

林培瑞　唐海濤

CHINESE PRIMER

Notes and Exercises

SECOND EDITION

Ta-tuan Ch'en

Perry Link

Yih-jian Tai

Hai-tao Tang

Princeton University Press

Princeton, New Jersey

Library of Congress Cataloging-in-Publication Data

Chinese primer. Notes and Exercises / Ta-tuan Ch'en . . .
[et al.].—2nd ed.
     p.   cm.
     Previously published by Harvard University Press, 1989.
     Includes index.
     ISBN 0-691-03695-0 (Pinyin)
     ISBN 0-691-03696-9 (GR)
     1. Chinese language—Textbooks for foreign speakers—
English.
     I. Ch'en, Ta-tuan.
     PL1129.E5C4225   1994c
     495.1'82421—dc20   93-45905

This book was prepared at the Chinese Linguistics Project,
Princeton University, with the aid of a grant from the Geraldine
R. Dodge Foundation.
The title page calligraphy is by Professor

Ching-nung T'ai（臺靜農）.

The cover design is by Daniel Shawjing Lee（李小鏡）.

Audiotapes and videotapes are available for use with the *Chinese
Primer*. For further information, contact: Chinese Linguistics
Project, 231 Palmer Hall, Princeton University, Princeton, NJ
08544. Phone: (609) 258-4269. Fax: (609) 258-6984.

CONTENTS

UNIT I

LESSON 1

NOTES ON CONVENTIONS:

Quotation marks indicate approximate English equivalents: e.g., *rén* "human being". When a dash separates two different glosses, the first is a literal rendering and the second a derived one: e.g., *diànyǐng* "electric image—movie".

In the Grammar Notes, "WARNING" indicates a point that frequently gives trouble to beginning students. Both student and teacher should pay special attention to such points.

As in the lesson texts, a period indicates a neutral tone (*Zhōng.guó* "China"; *xué.shēng* "student"; etc.). Third tone sandhi is indicated by italics throughout the first four units, for example: *wǒ* xǐ.huān "I like".

Vocabulary

WARNING: The English glosses provided here are intended only to help you identify which word you are looking up. THEY MUST NOT be taken as "equivalents" of the Chinese words they appear with. To learn the uses and meanings of the Chinese words, refer to the lesson texts and the notes. This warning will not be repeated before every lesson, but you should always remember it.

rén	人	man, woman, person, human being, people	kè	課	lesson
			péng.yǒu	朋友	friend
dì	第	ordinal prefix: -st, -nd, -rd, -th	guìxìng	貴姓	your (honorable) name
			wǒ	我	I, me
dānyuán	單元	unit	xìng	姓	surname; have the surname of
nán	男	male			
			Dīng	丁	common surname
nǚ	女	female			
			nǐ	你	you (singular)
xué.shēng	學生	student			

Zhāng	張	common surname		xiǎoxué	小學	primary school
.de	的	particle of sub-ordination and modification (see Grammar Notes)		xiǎoxuéshēng	小學生	primary school student
				hái.shi	還是	or (for choice)
wǒ.de	我的	my		zhōngxué	中學	'middle school', high school
míng.zì	名字	given name, full name		zhōngxuéshēng	中學生	high school student
jiào	叫	be called		chūzhōng	初中	junior high school
Zhāng Rúsī	張儒思	full Chinese name		gāo	高	high, tall
Dīng Xīn	丁新	full Chinese name		gāozhōng	高中	senior high school
shì	是	be, is, etc.		wǒ.mén	我們	we; us
bù	不	no, not		dōu	都	in all cases
shì, shì.de	是 是的	yes		gēn	跟	and, with
yě	也	also		suǒ.yǐ	所以	so, therefore
yī	一	one		kě.shi	可是	but
.ge	個	general auxiliary noun (AN) (see Grammar Notes)		nǐ.de	你的	your, yours
				nǚpéng.yǒu	女朋友	girlfriend (as against nǚ péng.yǒu - female friend)
Měi.guó	美國	(United States of) America				
.ma	嗎	interrogative particle		nánpéng.yǒu	男朋友	boyfriend (as against nán péng.yǒu - male friend)
bú.shi	不是	no; is not				
Zhōng.guó	中國	'middle-country' China		zá.mén	咱們	we (including the person addressed)
xiǎo	小	small		xīn	新	new

Vocabulary Classified by Type

Nouns
rén
dānyuán
kè
péng.yǒu
xué.shēng
míng.zì
xiǎoxué
xiǎoxuéshēng
zhōngxué
zhōngxuéshēng
chūzhōng
gāozhōng
nǚpéng.yǒu
nánpéng.yǒu

Proper Nouns
Zhāng Rúsī
Dīng Xīn
Měi.guó
Zhōng.guó

Pronouns
wǒ
nǐ
wǒ.mén
zá.mén

Adjectives
xiǎo
gāo
nán
nǚ
xīn

Verbs
xìng
jiào
shì

Adverbs
bù
yě
dōu

Conjunctions
hái.shi
gēn
suǒ.yǐ
kě.shi

Auxiliary Nouns (ANs)
.ge

Particles
.de
.ma

Idiomatic Expressions
guìxìng

Numeral
yī

Prefix
dì

Grammar Notes

1. *Rén* "human being". The English appellation for the dog as "man's best friend" poses a problem of sex-free reference. Professor Y.R. Chao once remarked that this problem can be solved by using the Chinese term *rén*, because it applies equally to men and women.

2. *Dì-*, prefix for ordinal numbers. *Dìyī, dì'èr, dìsān, dìsì,...* "first, second, third, fourth,..." *Dìyī dānyuán* "first unit", "Unit One".

3. *Guì* "noble"; "expensive"; "your" (honorific form). *Xìng* "surname". *Guìxìng* is a polite expression applied only to others, never to yourself. Never say *Wǒ guìxìng* "my (honorable) surname". (See Culture Note 1, Unit I, Lesson 1.)

4. *Xìng* here is used as a verb "have the surname of". *Wǒ xìng Zhāng* "I am surnamed Zhāng". Note: ALL CHINESE VERBS ARE TENSELESS. *Tā xìng Zhāng* means "He (or she) is (or was, or will be, etc.) surnamed Zhāng". Usually you can tell what time is referred to from other words in a sentence, or from general context.

5. *Dīng* is a common surname. It is also one of ten words which serve as arbitrary counters in much the same way as the letters of the alphabet do in English. The first four counters are *jiǎ* (A), *yǐ* (B), *bǐng* (C), *dīng* (D).

6. The particle *.de* is used between a modifier and a noun. The modifier plus *.de* precedes the noun. Modifiers can be other nouns, pronouns, adjectives, or whole clauses. Thus *wǒ.de míng.zì* "my name"; *lǎoshī .de péng.yǒu* "the teacher's

friend". Note that when the modifier is a noun, it too can be modified, thereby creating a string of modifiers. Thus *nǐ.de lǎoshī .de zhuō.zi* "your teacher's desk".

If you have studied French, note that the word order using the French *de* is the *reverse* of that in Chinese. **CHINESE MODIFIERS ALWAYS PRECEDE WHAT THEY MODIFY.**

N.B.: In this note we have used *lǎoshī* ("teacher") and *zhuō.zi* ("desk, table") in our examples, although they do not appear in Lesson 1. They were introduced in the Foundation Work (see blue book). The notes will continue to draw occasionally on Foundation Work vocabulary.

7. *Jiào* "call" or "be called". To tell one's full name, or one's given name only, the expression is *wǒ jiào X* "I am called X". (See Culture Note 1 for details.) The ability of Chinese verbs to serve either actively or passively will be discussed in Unit III, Lesson 1, Grammar Note 18 (III.1.18).

    N.B.: In this book we will refer you to other grammar notes using abbreviations such as III.1.18 to refer to Unit III, Lesson 1, Note 18.

8. Chinese nouns do not need articles like "the" and "a" in English. *Wǒ shi xué.shēng* "I am (a) student".

9. **V-not-V questions** are questions that offer the listener a choice between something and its negation. To answer this kind of question, you must make a choice between "V" and "not V". You cannot simply agree or disagree. Consider the two questions, "Are you a student?" and "Do you like dogs?" along with their possible answers:

    Question: Nǐ shi .bú.shi xué.shēng?
                You are (or) are not (a) student?

                            Answers:

to choose "V"	to choose "not V"
1. Shi, wǒ shi xué.shēng. Am, I am (a) student.	1. Bú.shi, wǒ bú.shi xué.shēng. Am not, I am not (a) student.
2. Wǒ shi xué.shēng. I am (a) student.	2. Wǒ bú.shi xué.shēng. I am not (a) student.
3. Wǒ shi. I am.	3. Wǒ bú.shi. I am not.
4. Shi. Am.	4. Bú.shi. Am not.

In answers 1 and 4, V (*shi* in this case) is the equivalent of "yes", and not-V (*bú.shi* in this case) is the equivalent of "no".

    Question: *Nǐ* xǐ.huān .bù.xǐ.huān gǒu?
                You like (or) not like dogs?

Answers:

V	not V

1. Xǐ.huān, *wǒ* xǐ.huān gǒu.
    Like, I like dogs.
2. *Wǒ* xǐ.huān gǒu.
    I like dogs.
3. *Wǒ* xǐ.huān.
    I like.
4. Xǐ.huān
    Like. (Or "yes" in English.)

1. Bù xǐ.huān, wǒ bù xǐ.huān gǒu.
    Don't like, I don't like dogs.
2. Wǒ bù xǐ.huān gǒu.
    I don't like dogs.
3. Wǒ bù xǐ.huān.
    I don't like.
4. Bù xǐ.huān.
    Don't like. (Or "no" in English.)

V-not-V questions have two forms:

    Closed Form: Nǐ shi .bú.shi xué.shēng?
                   Nǐ xǐ.huān .bù.xǐ.huān gǒu?

    Open Form: Nǐ shi xué.shēng .bú.shi?
                   Nǐ xǐ.huān gǒu .bù.xǐ.huān?

In the closed form, the V and not-V alternatives are always right next to each other. In the open form, the not-V alternative is always at the end of the sentence, with other things possibly coming between it and the V alternative.

10. *Yě* "too, also" is an adverb. Since Chinese modifiers always precede the words they modify, adverbs always precede verbs. *Yě*, therefore, cannot move around in a sentence as the English words "also" and "too" can. "I too am a student" and "I am a student, too" both must be *wǒ yě.shi xué.shēng*. Also, note that adverbs cannot appear **without** a corresponding verb. Thus there is no equivalent of the shortened English form "Me too". The closest Chinese equivalent is *Wǒ yě* + Verb".

11. **Auxiliary Nouns (AN).** To say "one student", "two books", etc. in Chinese, you cannot put the number directly before the noun. You must "measure" the noun, somewhat as when we say "one sheet of paper" or "two lumps of sugar" in English. The words that do this measuring are called "auxiliary nouns" (AN). Many nouns require specific ANs and cannot use another AN (just as in English we do not say "two lumps of paper" or "two sheets of sugar"). It is best to learn the AN with the nouns for which it is used. *Gè*, which is written *.ge* when in the neutral tone, is the most common AN and can be used with most nouns.

There are a few nouns in Chinese that do not require use of an AN. In this lesson, the word *kè* "lesson" is the only example.

12. *Guó* "country". *Měi* "beautiful" is here used to represent the *me* in "America". Thus *Měi.guó* is "*Měi*-country" or the United States of America. Chinese nouns can modify other nouns that follow them, as in *Měi.guó xué.shēng*, "American student". (See Culture Note 12, Unit IV, Lesson 1.)

13. The particle *.ma* at the end of a sentence changes the preceding statement into a question. Although this may seem an easy way to ask questions in Chinese, you should not use it all the time, because Chinese people use V-not-V questions (see I.1.9) more often than *.ma* questions.

The answers to *.ma* questions are given in different ways from answers to V-not-V questions. The answers to V-not-V questions must be either V or not-V. But the answers to *.ma* questions are either 1) one of the words for "yes" (*shi* or *shi.de* or *dui.le*) or 2) one of the words for "no" (*bú.shi* or *búdui*). Note, however, that these Chinese words for "yes" and "no" are sometimes used differently from "yes" and "no" in English. The confusion does not arise so long as the verb is positive. For example:

	Question	Answer
Chinese:	Nǐ shi xué.shēng .ma?	Dui.le, wǒ shi xué.shēng.
English:	Are you a student?	Yes, I am.

But when the verb is *negative*, the Chinese and English answers behave in opposite ways:

	Question	Answer
Chinese:	Nǐ bú.shi xué.shēng .ma?	Dui.le, wǒ bú.shi xué.shēng.
English:	Aren't you a student?	No, I'm not.

The English "no" here matches the sense of the negative verb. But the sense of the Chinese answer is to say, "That's correct, I am not a student." The best way to master this small point is to forget about English and just remember that *shi*, *shi.de*, and *dui.le* mean that you agree with the statement in the *.ma* question, while *bú.shi* and *búdui* mean that you disagree with that statement.

14. *Xiǎoxuéshēng* means "small (i.e., primary) school student". To say "small student", pronounce *shēng* in the neutral tone: *xiǎo xué.shēng*.

15. *Hái.shi* "or" is used only when asking someone to choose between alternatives. The English sentence "Are you a primary or a high school student?" is ambiguous. It can mean either 1) "Which of the two are you (primary or high school)?" or 2) "Are you one of the two (or not)?". But our Chinese sentence here definitely means 1), not 2). You will learn how to say 2) in Unit II, Lesson 1.

16. The subjects of Chinese sentences can sometimes be omitted when they are understood. (Here *wǒ* has been omitted.) Although this is uncommon in English, it happens frequently in Chinese. Such sentences are called "minor sentences" (see I.4.6).

17. *.Mén* is a plural suffix for pronouns. Thus *wǒ* "I, me"; *wǒ.mén* "we, us". *Tā* "he, she"; *tā.mén* "they, them". On rare occasions *.mén* can be used with other nouns that refer to people, e.g., *xué.shēng.mén* "students". Normally Chinese nouns have no distinction of number, however. While *xué.shēng.mén* is definitely plural, *xué.shēng* itself can be either singular or plural, and is much commoner than *xué.shēng.mén*. In the early stages of your study, use *.mén* only with pronouns.

18. *Dōu* is an adverb meaning "in all cases". Although it can often be translated using the English word "all", it behaves very differently from "all" grammatically. Because *dōu* is an adverb, it must always precede a verb. It can never precede a noun as "all" can.

19.   *Gēn*, originally "follow", usually means "and" or "with".

WARNING: Although "and" in English can connect nouns, verbs, adjectives, or whole clauses, in Chinese *gēn* can connect nouns or pronouns ONLY.   The word "and" in "You and I are both students" is *gēn*: *Nǐ gēn wǒ dōu.shi xué.shēng.* But the "and" in "You are a student, and so am I" corresponds to no word in Chinese: *Nǐ shì xué.shēng, wǒ yě.shi xué.shēng.* To put *gēn* between the two clauses in this sentence would be a spectacular mistake. Similarly, the "and" in sentences like "she is both intelligent and good-looking" or "Sam goes fishing and catches nothing" CANNOT be expressed by *gēn*.

20.   There is no difference in Chinese, in either pronunciation or written characters, between the words for "boyfriend" and "male friend".   The different spellings *nánpéng.yǒu* and *nán péng.yǒu* in our romanized text have been invented simply to help you see the pun.   The same is true of *nǚpéng.yǒu* and *nǚ péng.yǒu*.

21.   In the dialects of Peking (*Běijīng*) and certain other places, there are two words for "we".   *Zá.men* "you and I" or "you and we" includes the person addressed, while *wǒ.men* "he (or she) and I" or "they and I" excludes the person addressed.   When speaking to an audience from other parts of China, a Peking speaker will usually use *wǒ.men* for all cases.

Culture Notes

Language and culture are inseparable, and the more you can integrate your learning of the two, the more solid will be your eventual mastery of both.   With the Culture Notes provided in this text we attempt to introduce you to some basic connections between language and culture in China.

You should be aware, however, that Chinese culture is vast and extremely varied. Customs differ considerably from region to region, place to place, and among different generations.   They also change as time passes.   Thus, in offering you these notes, we can promise only that they describe very common patterns; we cannot promise that every Chinese person you might meet will observe them.   Your general approach to Chinese culture should include a considerable tolerance for variety.

Culture Notes are generally added to the lessons in which they first become relevant. On some large and complicated topics (such as Chinese names), the notes have been spread out so that they do not all appear in one lesson.   When you are referred to a Culture Note that appears in a future lesson, you may look ahead to read it, or wait until the lesson arrives, as you like.

Culture Note 1:   Chinese Names

Xìng. Every Chinese has a *xìng* "surname", which is inherited from the father.   In Chinese names, the *xìng* comes first.   This is, of course, the opposite of Western names. Most Chinese surnames are monosyllabic.   (Four or five commonly encountered surnames are two syllables.)   Although the characters used in Chinese surnames have meanings, when used as surnames they usually are not thought of as having meanings.   This point is similar to English. (No one would be concerned about Dr. Slaughter's qualifications as a physician because of his surname.)

Míng.zi. Chinese also have a given name, consisting of one or two syllables, called a *míng.zi*. As you know from Unit I, Lesson 1, the *míng.zi* comes after the *xìng* in Chinese: Zhāng (*xìng*) Rúsī (*míng.zi*). In common usage, however, the term *míng.zi* can also refer to one's "whole name", including both *xìng* and *míng.zi*. Thus if someone asks your *xìng* ("*nín guìxìng?*") and then follows up by asking your *míng.zi* ("*míng.zi jiào...*"), you would simply answer by giving your *míng.zi* only. But if someone simply asks *nín jiào shém.me míng.zi?* without first asking your *xìng*, you would reply by giving both *xìng* and *míng.zi*.

A child's *míng.zi* is chosen by his or her parents, and the meaning is highly significant. Whereas Western parents generally choose a name from an existing pool (Jane, John, etc.), in Chinese the naming of a child is a creative process. Traditionally, two kinds of considerations have been brought to bear in the selection of a *míng.zi*.

First, a name often expresses the parents' hopes for the kind of virtues the child should develop. These typically include honesty, sincerity, great learning, and other essentially moral virtues. The virtues typically differ somewhat for boys and girls. Boys' names tend to include the ideas of brave, brilliant, strong, etc., while girls' names frequently refer to purity and refinement, and are often names of flowers or jewels.

Second, names frequently are chosen so that siblings (brothers and sisters) will share similar or identical elements in their names. Typically the shared element is either the first or second character of a two-character *míng.zi*. For example, five siblings might have names like *Péirén* 培仁 , *Péiyi* 培義 , *Péili* 培禮 , *Péizhi* 培智 , *Péi yīng* 培英 ; or, if the second character is the shared one, names like *Wéndé* 文德 , *Zhèngdé* 正德 , *Yǒudé* 友德 , *Yídé* 懿德 , and *Xiándé* 嫻德 . In some cases the first character will be the same and the second will share a radical in common, for example *Réndòng* 仁棟 , *Rénzhí* 仁植 , *Rénkǎi* 仁楷 , etc.

In cases where siblings have a shared character in their names, the character is often determined by a poem that is kept in the family from one generation to the next, following the male line. Each generation takes, in order, the succeeding character in the poem. For example if the poetic line is *Dà xué yǔn cháo zōng* 大學允朝宗 , siblings in the first generation would use *dà* 大 in their names, those in the second generation *xué* 學 , in the third *yǔn* 允 , and so on. Hence a two line couplet of five characters per line would supply characters for the names of ten generations. (When the poem is finished another needs to be chosen.) If the various branches of a family all observe the poem faithfully--which traditionally they did--it is therefore possible to know, for all males in a family, which generation a person belongs to among second, third, or even more distant cousins. In modern times, although the custom of observing a family poem is dying out, it is still common, especially in Taiwan, Hong Kong, and overseas Chinese communities, to give siblings names that share a character in common.

NOTES ON EXERCISES:

Four types of exercises are listed below, and at the ends of all lessons:

1.   Recitation.   This traditional-style Chinese exercise continues to remain extremely useful. You should cover the romanized text and learn to recite it with accurate and natural pronunciation. You can glance at the English version on the opposite page, but only as a reminder of the content, never as a guide to grammar and usage. **Although we list recitation as an exercise only in Unit I, Lesson 1, you should do this important exercise for every lesson.**

It is best to spend some class time on recitation, and your teacher may well schedule it. Some teachers find it is better to assign only parts of the text rather than all of it. In general, it is better to do an excellent job with a smaller piece of text than a mediocre job with all of it.

2.   In-class exercises.   This kind of exercise is meant for oral practice, in class, under the supervision of a teacher. For example, in 4A below, students should quickly take turns saying what their names are in response to appropriate questions from the teacher or from other students. In fill-in-the-blank exercises, students should repeat the whole sentence, not just the word to be filled in. Some of the exercises offer "clues" to help get things going, but students should also try to think of their own responses beyond the clues.

The point of in-class exercises is to internalize basic patterns through frequent repetition. They should be done without referring to the textbook. They should not be used as out-of-class written homework, for which they would be far too easy.

3.   Homework.   These are written exercises that should be done outside class and presented to your teacher for correction. There are two important stages in homework: 1) doing the homework, 2) studying the corrections the teacher has made. Do not neglect stage 2. Examine every red mark until you fully understand why it is there. Then review the corrected version several times in your own mind. All the written exercises should be done in *pīnyīn*, **not** in Chinese characters. The purpose of these exercises is to build up students' oral proficiency. Doing them in characters will defeat the purpose. For reading and writing characters, there are special exercises in the Character Workbook (yellow book).

4.   Classroom/Homework exercises.   Some exercises are suitable as either classroom exercises or homework. Teachers can assign these to be used either way, or do certain examples in class and assign others as homework.

Exercises

Recitation:

1.   Memorize the Chinese text of the lesson, and prepare to recite it in class. You may use the English translation as a reminder.

In-class exercises:

1.   Fill in the blanks.   Read all of the sentences aloud, using the English in parentheses as a clue.

A.   My name is ...

    1.   Wǒ xìng ... .   (surname)
    2.   Wǒ jiào ... .   (full name)
    3.   Wǒ.de míng.zì jiào ... .   (full name)
    4.   Wǒ xìng ... (surname), míng.zì jiào ... .   (given name)

B.   V-not-V questions

    1.   Dīng Xīn ... .bú ... nǐ.de péng.yǒu?   (Is Dīng Xīn ... ?)
    2.   ... ... , Dīng Xīn ... ... wǒ.de péng.yǒu.   (No, Dīng Xīn is not ... .)
    3.   Nǐ shi gāozhōng xuéshēng ... ... ?   (Are you ... ?)
    4.   ... ... , wǒ ... gāozhōng xuéshēng.   (Yes, I am ... .)

C.   Choice type question and answer

    1.   Nǐ shi ... hái.shi ... ?   (primary school student, junior high school student)
    2.   Wǒ shi ... bú.shi ... .   (junior high school student, primary school student)

D.   Noun with Modifier

    1.   Nǐ shi ... xué.shēng .ma?   (American)
    2.   Nǐ shi ... , *wǒ* yě.shi ... , nǐ gēn wǒ dōu.shi ... .   (female student)

E.   You are ... , I am ... , we both are ... .

    1.   Nǐ shi ... , *wǒ* yě.shi ... , wǒ.mén dōu.shi ... .   (American)
    2.   Wǒ shi nǐ.de ... , Dīng Xīn yě.shi nǐ.de ... , wǒ.mén dōu.shi nǐ.de ... .   (friend)
    3.   Nǐ.mén shi ... , *wǒ* yě.shi ... , zá.mén dōu.shi ... .   (students)

F.   Is Zhāng Rúsī also ... ?

    1.   Zhāng Rúsī yě.shi ... .ma?   (your new friend)
    2.   Zhāng Rúsī bú.shi ... , Zhāng Rúsī shi ... .   (my new friend, Dīng Xīn's new friend)

G.   We (exclusive vs. inclusive)

    1.   Dīng Xīn gēn Zhāng Rúsī shi gāozhōng xué.shēng, *wǒ* yě.shi gāozhōng xué.shēng, ... dōu.shi gāozhōng xué.shēng.   (we)
    2.   Nǐ shi wǒ.de péng.yǒu, wǒ shi nǐ.de péng.yǒu, *suǒ*yǐ ... dōu.shi péng.yǒu.   (we)
    3.   Nǐ bú.shi xiǎoxuéshēng, *wǒ* yě bú.shi xiǎoxuéshēng, *suǒ*.yǐ ... dōu bú.shi xiǎoxuéshēng.   (we)

H.   *Suó.yĭ*   therefore

    1.   Xué.shēng dōu.shi péng.yŏu, nĭ gēn wŏ gēn Zhāng Rúsī dōu.shi
        xué.shēng, *suó*.yĭ zá.mén dōu.shi ... . (friends)

    2.   Dīng Xīn shi nŭ xué.shēng, yě.shi ni.de péng.yŏu, ... Dīng Xīn shi
        nĭ.de nŭ péng.yŏu. (therefore)

    3.   Nán xué.shēng shi péng.yŏu, nŭ xué.shēng ... péng.yŏu, *suó*.yĭ,
        xué.shēng dōu.shi péng.yŏu. (also are)

    4.   Nĭ xìng Dīng, wŏ yě xìng Dīng, ... zá.mén dōu xìng Dīng.

    5.   Wŏ shi chūzhōng xué.shēng, Zhāng Rúsī shi gāozhōng xué.shēng, ...
        wŏ.mén dōu.shi zhōngxuéshēng.

2.   Complete sentences without clue and read aloud.

A.   Wŏ xìng ... .

B.   Wŏ jiào ... .

C.   Wŏ shi ... .

D.   Nĭ shi xué.shēng, wŏ ... xué.shēng, *suó*.yĭ, zá.mén ... xué.shēng.

E.   Dīng Xīn shi nĭ.de nŭpéng.yŏu, shi ... ?

F.   Búduì, búduì. Dīng Xīn shi wŏ.de ... , bú.shi wŏ.de nŭpéng.yŏu.

3.   Change the following statements into questions.

Example:
    Wŏ shi xué.shēng.

    1.   Nĭ shi .bú.shi xué.shēng?
    2.   Nĭ shi xué.shēng .bú.shi?
    3.   Nĭ shi xué.shēng .ma?

A.   Wŏ.de péng.yŏu shi Měi.guó xué.shēng.

B.   Xiǎoxuéshēng gēn zhōngxuéshēng dōu.shi xué.shēng.

C.   Dīng Xīn shi Měi.guórén.

D.   Dīng Xīn .de xīn péng.yŏu shi wŏ.de nánpéng.yŏu.

E.   Zhāng Rúsī .de nŭpéng.yŏu shi Zhōng.guórén.

4.   Read the following questions aloud and answer them.

A.   Guìxìng?

B.   Nĭ shi xué.shēng .ma?

C.   Nĭ shi .bú.shi Měi.guó xué.shēng?

D.   Nĭ shi zhōngxuéshēng .bú.shi?

E.   Zhāng Rúsī shi .bú.shi ni.de xīn péng.yŏu?

F.   Dīng Xīn shi Měi.guó xué.shēng hái.shi Zhōng.guó xué.shēng?

Homework:

1.   **Mark the whole romanized text for this lesson using the tone
signs ⌐ ⌐ ⌐ ⌐ ⌐ and ·| .**

2.   Translate the following sentences into Chinese.[1]
        A.   Are you a male student or female student?
        B.   Is Zhāng Rúsī's new girlfriend a Chinese or an American?
        C.   You are Dīng Xīn's new friend, and you are also my new friend.
        D.   My last name is Zhāng, but I am not Zhāng Rúsī. (My full name is not Zhāng
                Rúsī.)
        E.   You are my friend, and you are Zhāng Rúsī's friend, too. Therefore, you are
                our friend.

---

[1] For the English-to-Chinese translation exercises, we have given examples in natural
English rather than "Chinglish" (Chinese-English). But you should remember that
natural English is a very bad guide to Chinese grammar. So for each example, try to
think of how a Chinese speaker would express the same idea. Occasionally we provide
"hints" to point you in the right direction.

LESSON 2

Vocabulary

nà, nèi-	那	that, those (see Grammar Notes)	bǎ	把	AN for chair and for things with handles
shéi	誰	who	yǐ.zi	椅子	chair
tā	他	he, him; she, her; it	něi-	哪	which
dà	大	big	.ne	呢	particle for follow-up question
dàxué	大學	college, university	É?	世	interjection of surprise
dàxuéshēng	大學生	college student	shém.me	甚麽	what?
wǒ.mén.de	我們的	our	zhī	隻	AN for animals or for one of a pair of things
lǎo	老	old (referring to age); long-standing	gǒu	狗	dog
lǎoshī	老師	teacher	shéi.de	誰的	whose
lǎo péng.yǒu	老朋友	old (longstanding) friend	hǎo	好	good
zhè, zhèi-	這	this, these (see Grammar Notes)	duì	對	right, correct
zhāng	張	AN for flat things	búduì	不對	wrong, incorrect
zhūo.zi	桌子	table, desk	suírán, suīrán	雖然	although
tā.de	他的	his, her	dàn.shi	但是	but
			hái	還	still

Vocabulary Classified by Type

Nouns		Adjectives
dàxué	yǐ.zi	dà
dàxuéshēng	gǒu	lǎo
lǎoshī		hǎo
lǎo péng.yǒu	**Pronouns**	duì
zhūo.zi	tā	
	tā.de	

Adverbs	ANs	Determinatives
hái	zhāng	nà, nèi-
	bǎ	zhè, zhèi-
Sentential Adverbs	zhī	něi-
(Moveable Adverbs)		
suírán, suīrán	**Particles**	**Question Words**
	.ne	shéi
Conjunctions		shém.me
dàn.shi		
	Interjections	
	É?	

Grammar Notes

1. **Determinatives.** Determinatives are a special group of words including *zhè* (or *zhèi*) "this or these", *nà* (or *nèi*) "that or those", *nǎ* (or *něi*) "which", and *měi* "each". Numerals (or numbers), of which we have so far learned only *yī* "one", are also technically members of this group. The group has the following characteristics:

   (a) They combine with ANs to form substantives (Det. + AN): *zhèi.ge* "this (one)", *něi-zhāng* "which (desk or other flat thing)?", etc.

   (b) The determinative + AN combination can be followed by a noun (Det. + AN + N): *zhèi.ge rén* "this person", *něi-bǎ yǐ.zi* "which chair?". etc.

   (c) Two determinatives may be used together if the second is a number and the first is not (Det. + No. + AN): *zhèi-sān.ge* "these three", *nèi-sì-zhāng* "those four (flat things)", etc. A following noun can be added to make Det. + No. + AN + N: *zhèi-sān.ge rén* "these three people", *něi-sì-bǎ yǐ.zi* "which four chairs?", etc. (Note: the forms *zhèi*, *nèi*, and *něi* were originally created through phonetic fusion of *zhè* + *yī*, *nà* + *yī*, and *nǎ* + *yī* respectively. After the phonetic fusion the idea of *yī* "one" no longer matters. *Zhèi-sān.ge* "these three" is perfectly correct.)

   (d) *Zhè* and *nà* are exceptions to rule (a) above because they need not be followed by ANs, but can be followed directly by nouns: *zhè rén* "this person", *nà zhuō.zi* "that desk".

   (e) *Zhè* and *nà* can also be used with *.shi* to form *zhè.shi* and *nà.shi*, which are two of the very few cases where subject and verb are bound together in Chinese. The reference can be either singular or plural: *zhè.shi yì-zhāng zhuō.zi* "this is a desk"; *nà.shi sān-zhāng zhuō.zi* "those are three desks"; *zhè.shi shém.me?* "What is this?" or "What are these?".

   (f) *Zhèi* and *nèi* are not used in the way *zhè* and *nà* are used in (d) and (e) above. Correspondingly, *zhè* and *nà* are very seldom used before ANs, as in (a), (b) and (c) above. Therefore you should make it a rule to use *zhèi* or *nèi* when ANs follow, and *zhè* or *nà* when they do not.

2. *Shéi* "who?, whom?" is a question word. **The word order in questions that use a question word is the same that is used in the answer.** Thus: *Nèi.ge rén shi*

shéi? "Who is that person?" and *Nèi.ge rén shi A* "That person is A" have the same order in Chinese. (Note that the order for questions is not the same in English.)

Since the boy has asked a choice-type question, *Tā shi .bú.shi yí.ge dàxuéshēng?*, the girl replies with a shortened restatement of the terms of the question. The full answer would be *Tā bú.shi dàxuéshēng* (see I.1.9).

3. *Lǎoshī* "teacher" can stand alone or follow a surname as a title. Thus *Wáng Lǎoshī* "Teacher Wáng", *Lǐ Lǎoshī* "Teacher Lǐ", etc.

4. *Lǎo* "old" here means "longstanding" and is not a indication of age.

5. *Zhèi-zhāng zhuō.zi* ("this flat-item-of table") is "determinative + AN + noun". (See note 1(b) above.) The noun suffix *.zi* (*zhuō.zi*, *yǐ.zi*, etc.) originally was *zi* "son", but has now entirely lost its original meaning. Because the suffix is so common, and is always pronounced in the neutral tone, we will always abbreviate *.zi* to *.zi*, omitting the tone mark.

6. *Nǐ.de* "yours". The Modifier + *.de* + Noun group we call a noun phrase or "substantive". In Chinese, if the noun is obvious from context, it can drop out. The remaining modifier + *.de* is still a substantive and performs the grammatical function of a noun. Here *nǐ.de* "yours" stands for *nǐ.de zhuō.zi* "your desk". Other examples:

wǒ.de	mine
lǎoshī .de	the teacher's
shéi.de?	whose?

7. The final particle *.ne* is used in follow-up questions. It conveys the sense of "And what about...?". E.g.: *Nǐ shi dàxuéshēng, tā .ne?* "You are a college student; how about him?"

8. *É?* is an interjection of surprise and interest, like the English "Well, look what we have here!". It is pronounced in a high pitch, close to second tone. The vowel sound, which is slightly different from the *ei* listed in the Table of Finals (blue book p. 12), is close to "*edge*" in English.

9. *Shém.me* "what?" can be used in two ways:

(a) As a pronoun to ask what something is:

Nà.shi shém.me?	What is that?
Zhèi.ge shi shém.me?	What is this one?

(b) As a modifier of a noun, to ask what kind of thing something is:

Nà.shi shém zhuō.zi?	What table is that? (Or: What tables are those?)
Nǐ jiào shém míng.zi?	What is your name? (What name are you called?)

Note: There is no *em* final in the Table of Finals. This spelling represents a contraction of *en* and *me*. When the word *shém.me* is used by itself or at the end of a phrase, it is pronounced in two syllables, *shém.me*. But when it occurs in the middle of a phrase, it is usually shortened to one syllable, *shém*. The same is true of *zěm(.me)* "how", *zèm(.me)* "so, this way", and *nèm(.me)* "so, that way".

Note again, in all four of the above examples, that the word order is different from English word order. (Review Note 2.) Remember to ask your question using the word order of the answer you expect:

Question	Answer
Nà.shi shém.me?	Nà.shi yì-zhī gǒu.
Nǐ jiào shém míng.zì?	Wǒ jiào Zhāng Rúsī.

10. *Duì .bú.duì* "is that right?" or *shì .bú.shi* "is that so?" can be added at the end of statements to make them into questions. Such questions are answered with agreement or disagreement (see I.1.13).

11. Questions made by adding *duì .bú.duì?* or *shì .bú.shi?* to the ends of statements are answered in the same way that *.ma* questions are answered. (Review I.1.13.) Another example of how the answers are different in Chinese and English would be:

Question: Nǐ bù chōu-yān, shì .bú.shi? "You don't smoke, do you?"

Answer

	English	Chinese
(If you do smoke)	"Yes, I do."	Bù, wǒ chōu. "No, I do."
(If you don't smoke)	"No, I don't."	Shì, wǒ bù chōu. "Yes, I don't."

12. *Suírán* "although" is usually paired with *kě.shi*, *dàn.shi*, or *búguò*, all meaning "but". Note that in English "although" and "but" **cannot** be paired in this way.

$$\text{suírán (clause 1)} \begin{Bmatrix} \textit{kě.shi} \\ \textit{dàn.shi} \\ \textit{búguò} \end{Bmatrix} \text{(clause 2)}$$

Example: Suírán nǐ bú.shi gǒu, dàn.shi nǐ hái.shi wǒ.de péng.yǒu.
          (Although you are not a dog, you are still my friend.)

Either the *suírán* or the word meaning "but" (*kě.shi*, *dàn.shi*, *búguò*) can be omitted in this pattern.

Nǐ bú.shi gǒu, kě.shi nǐ hái.shi wǒ.de péng.yǒu.
Suírán nǐ bú.shi gǒu, nǐ hái.shi wǒ.de péng.yǒu.

Both of these forms accord with what is customary in English, but it is important to remember the original form and its difference from the English usage.

Suírán can come either before or after the subject. Both of the following are proper:

1) Suírán nǐ shì wǒ.de péng.yǒu, kě.shi nǐ bú.shi wǒ.de nánpéng.yǒu.

2) Nǐ suírán shi wǒ.de péng.yǒu, kě.shi nǐ bú.shi wǒ.de nánpéng.yǒu.

NOTE: *Suírán*, technically an adverb, is among a small group of adverbs that can come either before or after a subject. We call these "moveable adverbs". Because they are often the first word in a sentence, they are called "sentential adverbs".

13. *Hái.shi* here means "still are". It is not the same as *hái.shi* "or" discussed in I.1.15.

Culture Note 2: Chinese Names for Westerners

Westerners have, in the past, taken Chinese names in one of three ways:

1. Syllable-by-syllable transliteration of sounds, with little or no regard for meaning (except for avoidance of characters with obviously negative meanings). An example would be *Shǐláixīngjí'ěr* for "Schlesinger".

2. Creation of a natural-sounding Chinese name based on the sound of the Western surname. If chosen well, the meanings of such names can be elegant, as well as reflective of a person's character. For example Dwight D. Eisenhower has been rendered *Ài Sēnháo* 艾森豪, where *Ài* is a common Chinese surname, *Sēn* means "dignified", and *háo* "grand, heroic".

3. Choice of a common Chinese surname based on the sound of the Western surname, combined with a Chinese *míng.zi* based on a) its meaning, b) the resemblance of its sound to the Western personal name, and c) the sound of the name (*xìng* plus *míng.zi*) as a

whole.   For example, a name like Bruce Johnson could become *Zhāng Rúsī*, because *Zhāng* is a standard surname and suggests the "John" sound in "Johnson", while *Rúsī* resembles the "ruce" in "Bruce".   Moreover the meanings of *Rú* "Confucian, scholarly" and *sī* "think, contemplate" make a felicitous combination that suggests "he who thinks deeply and correctly".

   Another example of method 3, *Shí Kělěi* for "Claire Smith", is explained in IV.1.1.

   Sometimes an English surname, such as "White", happens to have the same meaning as a common Chinese surname, like *Bái* 白 .   In such cases it is natural to base the Chinese *xìng* on meaning rather than sound.   Other examples are *Shí* for "Stone" and *Jīn* for "Gold".

Exercises

In-class exercises:

1.   Fill in the blanks.   Read all of the sentences aloud using the English in parentheses as a clue.

   A.   Statement and question

   1.   Zhè.shi wǒ.de ... .   (desk)
   2.   Zhèi-zhāng zhuō.zi shi ... .   (mine)
   3.   Zhè shi .bú.shi ... yǐ.zi?   (your)
   4.   Zhèi- ... yǐ.zi shi nǐ.de .ma?   (measure word)

   B.   . *Suírán*   although

   1.   Suírán tā shi lǎoshī, dàn.shi tā hái.shi wǒ.mén.de ... .   (friend)
   2.   Wǒ.mén suírán shi xīn péng.yǒu, kě.shi wǒ.mén hái.shi ... péng.yǒu. (good)
   3.   ... wǒ shi xué.shēng, dàn.shi wǒ shi dàxuéshēng, bú.shi zhōngxuéshēng.
   4.   Suírán tā shi wǒ.de lǎoshī, ... tā yě.shi yí.ge xué.shēng.
   5.   Suírán zhèi-zhī gǒu shi nǐ.de, ... tā shi wǒ.de hǎo péng.yǒu.
   6.   Suírán tā shi yí.ge Měi.guó xué.shēng, ... tā.de péng.yǒu dōu.shi Zhōng.guórén.

2.   Complete sentences without clue and read aloud.

   A.   Zhè.shi yì-zhāng ... .
   B.   Zhè.shi yì-bǎ ... .
   C.   Zhè.shi yì-zhī ... .
   D.   Zhè.shi yí.ge ... .
   E.   Zhèi- ... yǐ.zi shi wǒ.de.
   F.   Zhèi- ... gǒu shi shéi.de?
   G.   Zhè shi .bú.shi nǐ.de ... ?
   H.   Suírán tā shi wǒ.de xīn péng.yǒu, ... tā shi wǒ.de hǎo péng.yǒu.
   I.   Zhè.shi wǒ.de ... , zhèi-zhī ... shi wǒ.de.

3. Change the following statements into V-not-V questions first in closed form, then in open form. Then give the answer.

    Example: Given: Wǒ shi Zhōng.guórén.

              Answer: Nǐ shi .bú.shi Zhōng.guórén?
                       Nǐ shi Zhōng.guórén .bú.shi?
                       Shi, wǒ shi Zhōng.guórén.

    A.   Zhè.shi wǒ.de gǒu.
    B.   Zhèi-*bǎ* yǐ.zi shi wǒ.de.
    C.   Nèi.ge dàxuéshēng shi lǎoshī .de lǎo péng.yǒu.
    D.   Nèi-*bǎ* yǐ.zi shi wǒ.mén.de.
    E.   Nèi.ge dàxuéshēng shi yí.ge hǎo xué.shēng.

4. Read the following questions aloud and answer them.

    A.   Nǐ shi lǎoshī hái.shi xué.shēng?
    B.   Zhèi-zhāng zhuō.zi shi nǐ.de .ma?
    C.   Zhèi-*bǎ* yǐ.zi shi nǐ.de .bú.shi?
    D.   Zhè shi .bú.shi nǐ.de gǒu?
    E.   Nèi-zhī gǒu shi shéi.de?
    F.   Nèi.ge rén shi shéi?
    G.   Nèi-zhāng zhuō.zi shi nǐ.de?
    H.   Nèi-zhāng zhuō.zi gēn nèi-*bǎ* yǐ.zi dōu.shi nǐ.de .ma?
    I.   Xué.shēng dōu.shi péng.yǒu, lǎoshī yě.shi péng.yǒu .ma?
    J.   Tā shi nǐ.de nǚpéng.yǒu, *suǒ*.yǐ nǐ shi tā.de nánpéng.yǒu, duì .bú.duì?
    K.   Suírán tā shi lǎoshī, dàn.shi tā hái.shi péng.yǒu, shi .bú.shi?

5. *Shi ... hái.shi ...* ?   Is A or B?

    Make questions on the model of the following example.

    Example: (Chinese, American)

              Nèi.ge xué.shēng shi Zhōng.guórén hái.shi Měi.guórén?

    A.   (student, teacher)
    B.   (high school student, college student)
    C.   (your desk, his desk)
    D.   (your new friend, your old friend)
    E.   (his dog, the teacher's dog)

6. Therefore

    A.   Tā shi nǐ.de lǎoshī, yě.shi wǒ.de lǎoshī, ... tā shi zá.mén.de lǎoshī.
    B.   Xué.shēng shi péng.yǒu, lǎoshī bú.shi péng.yǒu, tā shi lǎoshī; ... tā bú.shi péng.yǒu.

7. Oral Substitution: The following exercises can be done by two or three students. They should be done orally without looking at the notes.

Example:

      1st student: Zhèi-zhāng zhuō.zi bú.shi wǒ.de.

      2nd student: Zhèi-zhāng zhuō.zi bú.shi nǐ.de, shi shéi.de .ne?

      3rd student or 1st student: Zhèi-zhāng zhuō.zi shi lǎoshī .de.

A.   Zhèi-zhī gǒu bú.shi wǒ.de.
B.   Tā bú.shi wǒ.de nǚpéng.yǒu.
C.   Zhāng Rúsī bú.shi nèi.ge Zhōng.guórén .de péng.yǒu.
D.   Nèi-*bǎ* yǐ.zi bú.shi Dīng Xīn .de.
E.   Nèi.ge dàxuéshēng bú.shi wǒ.mén.de lǎoshī.

Homework:

1.   Mark the whole romanized text with tone signs.

2.   Translate the following sentences into Chinese.

    A.   Dogs are my friends, therefore my friends are dogs.
    B.   Although dogs are your friends, your friends are not dogs.
    C.   Whose teacher is he?
    D.   What is that? Is that an elementary school? No, that is not an elementary school. That is a high school.
    E.   My good friend is a teacher at (of) that college.
    F.   Which student is your boyfriend?

LESSON 3

Vocabulary

yāo.qiú	要求	demand, réquest	wū.zi	屋子	room
tài	太	too, excessively	bútài	不太	not quite
zǎo	早	early; good morning	nèm.me (nèm)	那麼	so, to that extent
huài	壞	bad	zèm.me (zèm)	這麼	so, in this manner
jīn.tiān	今天	today	jiān	間	AN for room
yǒu yìdiǎnr	有一點儿	a bit, a little	jiàoshì	教室	classroom
yǒu	有	have; there is (are)	búcuò	不錯	not wrong; not bad, pretty good
shū.fú	舒服	comfortable	chuāng.hù	窗户	window
bùshū.fú	不舒服	uncomfortable; not feeling well	mén	門	door
jué.de	覺得	to feel; feel that, think that	liàng	亮	bright
			xuéxiào	學校	school
hěn	很	very	fàn	飯	cooked rice, meal, food
lèi	累	tired			
chuáng	牀	bed	zhēn	真	truly; true
ruǎn	軟	soft	zǎofàn	早飯	'early-meal', breakfast
búgòu...	不够	not...enough, insufficient (-ly)...	chī	吃	eat
			bùhǎochī	不好吃	not tasty
yìng	硬	hard	hǎochī	好吃	'good-eat', tasty, delicious
yěxǔ	也許	perhaps			
jiù	舊	old (state)	zhōngfàn	中飯	'middle-meal', lunch
.le	了	particle for new situation	wǎnfàn	晚飯	'late-meal', supper
sùshè	宿舍	dormitory	shuō	説	say

bùhǎo	不好	'not good', bad	Zhōngwén	中文	Chinese
zuó.tiān	昨天	yesterday	kàn	看	look (at)
zhōng.wǔ	中午	noon	duó.me	多麼	how, how?
jī	雞	chicken	.a	啊	particle with many functions (see Grammar Notes)
shēng	生	raw, undercooked			
wǎn.shàng	晚上	evening			
niúròu	牛肉	'cow-meat', beef	wèi	位	AN for people (polite)
ròu	肉	meat	ǎi	矮	short (measured from ground up), low
zǎo.shàng	早上	morning			
jīdàn	雞蛋	(chicken) egg	bí.zi	鼻子	nose
yòu	又	again (emphatic usage)	bùhǎokàn	不好看	ugly, not hand-some
lǎo	老	overcooked, tough (of food)	hǎokàn	好看	good-looking
			yǎn.jīng	眼睛	eye
yǒumíng	有名	'have-name', famous	bié...	別	don't...
duō	多	many	huàidàn	壞蛋	"rotten egg!"
qiúchǎng	球場	ball field or court	mǔ.qīn	母親	mother
			.ei	也	final particle expressing "you know, you see"
shǎo	少	few; less			
xìng.qíng	性情	temperament	Â	嗄	interjection expressing sur-prise
qíguài	奇怪	strange			

Vocabulary Classified by Type

Nouns	fàn	xìng.qíng
yāo.qiú	zǎofàn	Zhōngwén
chuáng	zhōngfàn	bí.zi
sùshè	wǎnfàn	yǎn.jīng
wū.zi	jī	huàidàn
jiàoshì	niúròu	mǔ.qīn
chuāng.hù	ròu	
mén	jīdàn	**Verbs**
xuéxiào	qiúchǎng	yǒu

jué.de
chī
shuō
kàn

duō
shǎo
qíguài
ái
bùhǎokàn
hǎokàn

ANs

jiān
wèi

Adjectives

zǎo
huài
shū.fú
bùshū.fú
lèi
ruǎn
yìng
jiù
búcuò
liàng
bùhǎochī
hǎochī
bùhǎo
shēng
lǎo
yǒumíng

Adverbs

tài
hěn
búgòu
bútài
nèm.me (nèm)
zèm.me (zèm)
zhēn
yòu
duó.me
bié...

Sentential Adverbs
(Moveable Adverbs)

yěxǔ

Time Words

jīn.tiān
zuó.tiān
zhōng.wǔ
wǎn.shàng
zǎo.shàng

Particles

.le
.a
.ei

Interjection

Á

Idiomatic Expressions

yǒu yìdiǎnr

Grammar Notes

1. *Gāo*, like all Chinese adjectives, can function as a verb. (Some grammars call these words "stative verbs".) Thus *yāo.qíu tài gāo* means "the demands are (or were) too high", where the verb is "built into" the adjective *gāo*. (In English such usage is acceptable only in headlines or telegrams, as in "Terrorist Demands Too High, Outcome in Doubt". But in Chinese it is extremely common and entirely correct grammar.)

2. *Zǎo* "early" is short for *nǐ zǎo*, which originally was a compliment "you're so early (in getting up)." But in common speech *zǎo* is just a routine greeting, like English "'Morning!". *Nǐ hǎo .ma?* "How are you?" is also a standard greeting, not necessarily a serious question about the health of the person addressed. (See Culture Note 3, Unit I, Lesson 3.)

3. *Hái* "still" here is like the English words "fairly" or "pretty" as in "fairly good" or "pretty good".

4. **Time Words** are an important class of words that refer to times or time periods. Examples in this lesson are: *jīn.tiān* "today", *zuó.tiān* "yesterday", *zhōng.wǔ* "noon", *wǎn.shàng* "evening", and *zǎo.shàng* "morning". Although nouns, Time Words are frequently used in ways that make them resemble adverbs:

    Wǒ jīn.tiān bùshū.fú.   I'm not feeling well today.
    Wǒ zuó.tiān yě bùshū.fú.   I wasn't feeling well yesterday,
                                                 either.

Like adverbs, Time Words must appear before the verb. But unlike ordinary adverbs, they are "moveable", meaning they can come either before or after the subject. The first sentence above could have been said:

        Jīn.tiān wǒ bùshū.fú.   I'm not feeling well today.

In the second sentence, *zuó.tiān* can move but *yě*, an adverb, cannot:

        Zuó.tiān *wǒ* yě bùshū.fú.   I wasn't feeling well yesterday, either.

5.   *Yǒu yìdiǎnr* (often shortened to *yǒu .diǎnr*) means "a little" or "a bit". It frequently modifies a following adjective:

        yǒu yìdiǎnr bùshū.fú   a little uncomfortable
        yǒu .diǎnr gāo   a bit (too) tall
        yǒu .diǎnr búduì   somewhat incorrect

WARNING: Do not forget *yǒu* in this pattern. IT CANNOT BE OMITTED. English can mislead you, because in English we say "a bit too tall", not "have a bit too tall". It is also possible to be confused by a related Chinese pattern, in which *yìdiǎnr* precedes nouns:

        Wǒ huì shuō yìdiǎnr Zhōngwén.   I can speak a bit of Chinese.

You will avoid mistakes by just remembering this rule: *yìdiǎnr* cannot come before an adjective unless it follows *yǒu*.

    Yǒu (yì).diǎnr + Adjective usually suggests something excessive, beyond what the speaker would desire. Accordingly it is often used with *negative* adjectives. *Yǒu .diǎnr bùshū.fú* is very common; it would be peculiar to say *yǒu .diǎnr shū.fú*.

    The *r* in *yìdiǎnr* is the retroflex ending that you learned in the foundation work. The same word without this ending is pronounced *yìdiǎn*. Both *-r* and the noun suffix *-.zi* were originally "diminutive" suffixes, but by now have lost the implication of "small". Now *-r* simply indicates less formality, or more intimacy.

    The *-r* endings are quite common in northern Mandarin, and especially in the dialect of Běijīng. They are used much less in the standard Mandarin of both the People's Republic of China (PRC) and the Republic of China (ROC), although they are still common with certain words. This textbook introduces examples both with and without *-r* endings, so that students can be broadly prepared to understand native speakers of several kinds. When you learn vocabulary with *-r* endings be sure to learn the standard versions that omit *-r* as well. Here are some examples from the vocabulary you have learned so far:

with -r	*without -r*
yìdiǎnr	yìdiǎn
zhuōr	zhuō.zi
ménr	mén
wūr	wū.zi
jīnr	jīn.tiān

        zuór   zuó.tiān

Note that in the Character Text and Character Workbook we use ╱ʋ, written small, to indicate an -r ending.

6. *Shū.fú* "comfortable". The negative *bùshū.fú* can mean "uncomfortable" or "not feeling well".

7. The word *hěn* has two senses depending on whether it is stressed or not. When it is stressed, it means "very":

        Tā **hěn** lèi.   She is **very** tired.

Most commonly it is unstressed, however, and its unstressed usage requires some explanation. In general, an adjective that directly follows a subject usually **implies comparison** with another specific thing. For example:

        Zhèi-zhāng zhuō.zi dà.   This table is big(ger).
        Wǒ.de yǐ.zi shū.fú.   My chair is (more) comfortable.

These two sentences imply comparison with other, unspecified, tables or chairs. But how then, you might ask, does one simply say, "This table is big" or "My chair is comfortable" **without** implying comparison to something else? The way you do this is to use *hěn* without stressing it. (In this example we will make the lack of stress clear by using the neutral tone dot.)

        Zhèi-zhāng zhuō.zi .hěn dà.   This table is big.
        Wǒ.de yǐ.zi .hěn shū.fú.   My chair is comfortable.

Hence the sentence in the text could mean either "I feel very tired" or simply "I feel tired", depending on whether the *hěn* is stressed.

8. Note that in English we say "not hard enough" but in Chinese *búgòu yìng*, literally "not enough hard". Similarly, *gòu gāo* means "tall enough", *búgòu hǎo* means "not good enough", etc. This happens because the modifier always precedes what it modifies.

9. **New Situation .le.** The particle *.le* can be used at the end of sentences to indicate either (a) that the situation described is new, or (b) that the speaker has made a new discovery of an existing situation. In this sentence, the bed was probably too soft many months before the girl was assigned to it, and thus we have a case of (b). The case would be (a) if the girl's bed should suddenly collapse (*kuǎ* in Chinese) while she is sitting on it. Then she might say:

        .Ai.ya! Chwáng kuǎ .le!   Eeek! The bed's caved in!

When the verb (or adjective) in a sentence is positive, *.le* often conveys the sense of "now" in English.

        Wǒ shi zhōngxuéshēng .le.   (Now) I'm a high school student (I
                                             didn't use to be).

With a negative verb (or adjective), .le often has the sense of "any more" in English.

Wǒ bú.shi zhōngxuéshēng .le.   I'm not a high school student (any
                                         more).
Zhèi-zhāng chwáng bù ruǎn .le.   This bed isn't soft (any more).

10. Tài "excessively, too" and bútài "not very" are used before adjectives: tài gāo "too tall", bútài shū.fú "not very comfortable", etc. They operate like gòu and búgòu (see note 8).

11. Zèm.me and nèm.me can be used before adjectives to indicate "this" or "that" extent:

Zèm.me dà   this big, as big as this
Nèm.me hǎo   that good, as good as that

Zèm.me and nèm.me are often pronounced as a single syllable, in which case we spell them zèm and nèm (see I.2.9):

Zèm xiǎo   this small, as small as this
Nèm yìng   that hard, as hard as that

12. Zá.mén .de zhèi-jiān jiàoshi "our this classroom—this classroom of ours".

13. Búcuò, literally "not wrong", means "not bad" or "pretty good".

14. Fàn is literally "cooked rice", but in ordinary usage also means "staple food" or a "meal". Thus, chī-fàn means simply "eat (a meal)", whether the staple happens to be cooked rice or something else.

15. Hǎo "good" can precede certain verbs to mean "good to ...". For example, hǎochī "good to eat, tasty"; hǎokàn "good-looking, pretty"; bùhǎokàn "bad-looking, ugly".

16. Yòu, which usually means "again" or "moreover", can also be used, as in this example, to emphasize the verb or adjective that follows. The emphasis carries a negative or dissenting tone.

17. Lǎo, originally meaning "old", means "hard" or "overcooked" when referring to boiled eggs, meat, or other foods. Note also that, in Chinese, clauses can be strung together without conjunctions such as "and" in English. In English, such a string of clauses would be called a run-on sentence, but in Chinese it is quite grammatical.

18. Duō and hǎo in this sentence are clear examples of adjectives serving as verbs. (See note 1.)

19. Zhèi.ge rén. When zhèi.ge rén comes immediately after a noun or pronoun referring to a person, it emphasizes a following comment on the person's disposition, habits, or personality.

20. The adjective duō "many, much" can be pronounced in the second tone duó to mean "how much? to what degree?". The "how much" can be a question, as in:

Ni.de wū.zi duó dà?   How big is your room?
Nèi-zhāng zhuō.zi duó gāo?   How high is that table?

or an exclamation, as in:

Wǒ.mén.de lǎoshī duó(.me) hǎo .a!   How good our teacher is!
Ni kàn, nèi.ge nǚ xué.shēng   How pretty that schoolgirl is!
   duó(.me) hǎokàn .a!

The .me in the latter examples can be omitted.

21. .A at the end of this sentence indicates that a strong opinion has been expressed.
Another example:

Jī zhēn hǎochī .a.   The chicken's delicious!

22. Wèi, originally "place", is a polite form for the AN .ge when referring to a
person.

23. **V-shi-V or Adj-shi-Adj Constructions**. Shi can be inserted between verbs or
adjectives to make a concession, which then is usually followed by a "but"
(kě.shi, dàn.shi, etc.). For example:

Niúròu duō shi duō, kě.shi   There's lots of beef, all right,
   bùhǎochī.   but it doesn't taste good.
Sùshè shū.fú shi shū.fú,   The dormitory is comfortable all
   dàn.shi wū.zi búgòu.   right, but doesn't have enough
                                         rooms.

Adverbs can modify the repeated verb or adjective, but only before the **second**
occurrence or before **both** occurrences. Thus:

Niúròu duō shi hěn duō,   There's a very lot of beef, yes,
   kě.shi bùhǎochī.   but it doesn't taste good.
Zhèi-jiān wū.zi shū.fú shi hěn   This room is very comfortable
   shū.fú, kě.shi búgòu liàng.   all right, but not bright enough.

24. .Diǎnr is the short form of yìdiǎnr. (See note 5.)

25. Bié is a contraction of búyào "don't". .Le, here, still has the sense of "any
more" as described in note 9.

Bié shūo .le!   Don't talk (any more)!
Búyào chī .le.   Don't eat it (any more).

26. To call a person bad names in Chinese, you can refer to various kinds of dàn
"egg": huàidàn "rotten egg", bèndàn "stupid egg", etc. Dàn used in this way
always has a bad sense; there is no hǎodàn.

27. Wǒ mǔ.qīn comes from wǒ.de mǔ.qīn "my mother". The .de normally drops out between
a pronoun and words for relatives, parts of the body, and other things for which
one feels a very close affinity. For example, in the previous sentence, tā.de
yǎn.jīng could have been tā yǎn.jīng.

Mŭ.qīn "mother" and *fù.qīn* "father" can be used to refer either to one's own parents or to someone else's: *wŏ fù.qīn*, *tā mŭ.qīn*, etc. Note, however, that they cannot be used for direct address. In direct address of your own parents, use *mā.mā* "Mom" and *bà.bà* "Dad". These can be shortened to *mā* and *bà*.

28. *.Ei* when it appears at the end of the sentence is for emphasis and a tinge of reproach, somewhat like the "you know!" in the English sentence "She's my mother, you know!"

29. *Á?* "hunh?" indicates that the speaker is nonplussed.

Culture Note 3:   Greetings and Partings I

In American English greetings and partings are usually expressed in set phrases. There are a large number of these. Greetings include "Hello", "Good Morning", "Good Afternoon", "Hi", "Howdy", and several others. Parting phrases include "Good-bye", "Bye", "So long", "Take care", "Take it easy", and others.

Chinese does not have nearly so many set phrases for greetings and partings. But Chinese people do, of course, greet and part as much as anyone. How do they do it? Your first rule of thumb should be to avoid over-use of set phrases. For example, some textbooks for Westerners introduce *nǐ hǎo* as an all purpose salutation, equivalent to "hello", "good morning", "good evening", "hi there!", etc. But *nǐ hǎo* is not widely used in this way by Chinese. It is limited to certain set situations—as when a telephone switchboard operator takes an incoming call—but other than that is primarily limited to foreign learners of Chinese. [2]   You should use *nǐ hǎo* sparingly and with caution.

Roughly speaking, greetings in any language can be classified into two categories: 1) Exchanged greetings, in which both parties say the same word or phrases almost simultaneously ("hi!", "hello", "good-bye" in English) and 2) Question-and-answer greetings ("How are you?" — "Fine" in English). In general, exchanged greetings are much more common in English, and question-and-answer greetings more common in Chinese.

Exchanged greetings. The word *zǎo* "early", which is used as a greeting in I.3, originally was a compliment on early rising, and was restricted to early-morning use. By now, however, it has become a standard exchanged greeting like "good morning" in English, and is used in late morning as well. *Zǎo* is the only exchanged greeting that is original to Chinese.

---

[2] Two illustrations are worth citing: 1) In the film *The Great Wall* (1986), which is full of good, natural dialogue in both English and Chinese, two young Chinese men try to start a conversation with two pretty young women by using *nǐ hǎo*. They get the curt response *Shém.me "nǐ hǎo"?! Wŏ.mén yòu bú.shi wài.guó rén!* "What's this '*nǐ hǎo*'?! We're not foreigners, you know!"

2) In the mid-1980s a visiting American professor at a Chinese institute that specializes in teaching Chinese to foreigners made an informal survey of greetings that were used in the morning. The foreign students all exchanged *nǐ hǎo*. The Chinese teachers, when addressing the foreign students, also used *nǐ hǎo*. But when asked how they address one another, the Chinese teachers said that they do not use the phrase.

Another way to exchange greetings is to say the name of the person addressed, adding titles where appropriate. For example, after summer vacation a dialogue might begin this way:

Wú lǎoshī.   Teacher Wu.

Zhāng Rúsī, (nǐ) huí-lái .l'a.   Zhāng Rúsī, you're back.

Question-and-answer greetings. As with the English "How are you?" and its typical answer "Fine", Chinese question-and-answer greetings are often formulaic and should not be regarded as serious questions and answers. The questions *Hǎo .ma?*, *Nǐ hǎo .ma?*, and *Nín hǎo .ma?* have become formulaic greetings similar to "How are you?" in English. (There is one important difference: The Chinese questions are used only when you have not seen someone for some time—at least several days. They are generally not used with people one meets daily.)

Standard answers to *Nǐ* (or *nín*) *hǎo .ma?* are:

> (*Wǒ*) *hěn* hǎo.
> (Wǒ) hái hǎo.
> (Wǒ) hái búcuò.

Any of these answers is often followed immediately by *nǐ .ne?* or *nín .ne?* ("And you?").

Another very common greeting-question is *Zěmyàng?* "What's up, what's new?". You can take this question as an equivalent of *Hǎo .ma?* and give one of the three answers listed above, or you can take it as a broader invitation to begin talking about whatever has been occupying you recently.

While question-and-answer greetings in English are limited to "How are you?", "How's it going?", and a few others, in Chinese the forms are much more numerous and varied. What the various forms all have in common is a) simplicity and b) that they do not call for conscientious answers. Westerners who fail to realize that such questions are merely greetings can sometimes be perplexed by them. For example one very common greeting-question, used close to meal time, is:

Chī.le fàn .méi.yǒu?   Have you eaten?

Normally the person who asks you this question is not really concerned about whether you have eaten or not. Your answer can be *chī.le* or *chī-guò.le* "yes, I have", whether you have eaten or not. (You might also reply *hái méi chī* "I haven't yet", but don't expect this to result in an invitation to lunch. It will normally be taken as a mere greeting-response.)

Exercises

In-class exercises:

1. Fill in the blanks. Read all of the sentences aloud.

    A. Sentences using adjectives as main predicates

        1. Zhèi.ge xuéxiào *hěn* hǎo, *hěn* ... . (famous)
        2. Zhèi-zhāng chuáng hěn dà, .hěn ... . (comfortable)
        3. Tā.de yǎn.jīng hěn dà, *hěn* ... . (good-looking)
        4. Nèi.ge rén .de bí.zi hěn gāo, kě.shi yǎn.jīng ... . (too small)
        5. Zhèi-jiān wū.zi .de chuāng.hù hěn ... . (bright)
        6. Wǒ.mén sùshè .de fàn bútài ... . (tasty, delicious)
        7. Tā.de mǔ.qīn *hěn* ... . (short)
        8. Zhèi.ge jīdàn tài ... . (overcooked)
        9. Xué.shēng tài duō, jiàoshì ... . (not big enough)
        10. Tā.de nei-zhī dàgǒu .hěn ... . (strange)
        11. Nǐ.de chuáng gòu .bú.gòu ... . (hard, firm)
        12. Jīn.tiān wǎnfàn .de niúròu tài ... . (rare, undercooked)

    B. *Yǒu yidiǎnr* Adjective a bit Adjective

        1. Wǒ jīn.tiān ... bùshū.fú.
        2. 'Zhèi.ge rén .de xìng.qíng ... qíguài.
        3. Nèi.ge lǎoshī .de bí.zi ... ǎi.
        4. Jīn.tiān zhōng.wǔ .de niúròu ... yìng.

    C. *Tài* too, excessive

        1. Zhèi-jiān wū.zi .de chuāng.hù ... xiǎo .le.
        2. Tā.de bí.zi ... dà, *suǒ*.yi bùhǎokàn.
        3. Xué.shēng tài ... , lǎoshī tài ... . (many; few)
        4. Wǒ.de chuáng tài ... .le, *suǒ*.yi .hěn ... . (old, worn out; uncomfortable)
        5. Nèi.ge rén .de xìng.qíng tài ... , ... tā.de péng.yǒu *hěn* shǎo. (strange; therefore)

    D. A *shi* A, kě.*shi* ... It's A, to be sure, but ...

        1. Zhè wū.zi ... shi ... , kě.shi búgòu liàng. (good)
        2. Zhèi-wèi ... hǎo shi hǎo, kě.shi tā yǒu yì*diǎnr* ǎi. (teacher)
        3. Zhèi.ge xuéxiào ... shi ... , kě.shi xué.shēng bútài duō. (famous)
        4. Jīn.tiān .de fàn ... shi ... , kě.shi tài shǎo .le. (delicious)
        5. Tā.de gǒu ... shi hěn ... , kě.shi bùhǎokàn. (big)
        6. Niúròu hǎochī shi ... , kě.shi .hěn duō. (not tasty)
        7. Wǒ.de wū.zi dà shi ... , kě.shi .hěn shū.fú. (not big)

    E. Complete the following sentences.

        1. Zuó.tiān zǎofàn .de jīdàn lǎo shi lǎo ....
        2. Nèi-wèi lǎoshī .de yǎn.jīng dà shi dà ....
        3. Chuáng xīn shi búgòu xīn ....

F.　*Zhēn*　truly, really

    1.　Jīn.tiān wǒ zhēn ... .　(tired)
    2.　Ni zhēn.shi .ge ... .　(rotten egg)
    3.　Zhèi.ge ... zhēn hǎo.　(school)
    4.　Nèi.ge rén .de xìng.qíng zhēn ... .　(strange)
    5.　Ni zhēn.shi wǒ.de hǎo ... .　(friend)

G.　*Suírán ... kě.shi ...*　Although ...

    1.　Zhèi-zhāng chuáng ... búgòu yìng, kě.shi hái .hěn shū.fú.　(although)
    2.　Zhèi-jiān wū.zi suírán *hěn* xiǎo, kě.shi chuāng.hù .hěn dà, *suǒ*.yi .hěn ... .　(bright)
    3.　Zhōng.guó-huà (spoken Chinese) suírán .hěn nán shuō (hard to speak), kě.shi Zhōng.guó fàn .hěn ... .　(tasty)
    4.　Suírán zuó.tiān *wǒ* .hěn lèi, kě.shi jīn.tiān wǒ ... *hěn* hǎo, .hěn shū.fú.　(feel)
    5.　Suírán wǒ.de ... .hěn dà, kě.shi tài jiù .le.　(desk, table)

H.　*Bugòu*　Adjective　Not Adjective enough

    1.　Zhèi-zhāng chuáng búgòu ... .　(firm, hard)
    2.　Zhèi.ge xuéxiào ... yǒumíng.　(not enough)
    3.　Zhèi.ge ... búgòu dà.　(ball field)
    4.　Zhèi.ge lǎoshī .de ... búgòu gāo.　(demand)

Homework:

1.　Mark the whole romanized text with tone signs.

2.　Translate the following sentences into Chinese.

    A.　You may say the food is bad, but I think it is all right.
    B.　I think you are asking too much. This is a good school, and it is famous, too.
    C.　There are many students, to be sure, but there are too few teachers.
    D.　Stop it! What a rotten egg you are! She is my mother, you know!
    E.　This ball field is a little small.
    F.　You are too demanding. (Your demands are too high.)
    G.　This bed is comfortable all right, but it's too old (worn out).
    H.　The beef we had tonight was really delicious.
    I.　Although he is very famous, he is not a good teacher.
    J.　There's not enough light from this window. (This window is not bright enough.)
    K.　I do not have enough Chinese friends. (My Chinese friends are not numerous enough.)

Classroom/Homework exercises:

1.　Comment on the truth of the following statements. Don't worry about the "right" answer. Just have fun. If true, say *Dui.le*, or *Shi.de* and repeat the given sentence. If false, say Bù, *Bú.shi*, or *Búduì* (irrespective of whether the false statement is in the affirmative or negative form), and give the true statement by

making the necessary changes. Use the proper pronouns. Example: Nǐ shi rén.
Duì.le, wǒ shi rén. Zhāng Rúsī shi Zhōng.guórén. Bú.shi, tā shi Měi.guórén.

A.   Zhāng Rúsī *hěn* ǎi.
B.   Dīng Xīn .de bí.zi .hěn gāo.
C.   Yǎn.jīng dà .de rén *hěn* hǎokàn.
D.   Zhèi.ge wū.zi méi.yǒu chuāng.hù *suǒ*.yǐ .hěn liàng.
E.   Bùhǎokàn .de rén shi huàidàn.
F.   Xuéxiào .de fàn *hěn* hǎochī.
G.   Xìng.qíng qíguài .de rén méi.yǒu péng.yǒu.
H.   Zá.mén .de lǎoshī dōu bù chī niúròu.
I.   Zhōngwén lǎoshī .de yāo.qiú tài gāo .le.

LESSON 4

Vocabulary

qǐng	請	to request; please		zhǐ	只	only
zuò	坐	sit		xiě	寫	write
kè	課	class		Zhōng.guó-zì	中國字	Chinese characters
xiànzài	現在	now		zì	字	character, word
méi.yǒu (méi)	沒有	have not; there is (are) not		zhēn.de	真的	really
				xìn	信	believe
xià.wǔ	下午	afternoon		.Oh	哦	"Oh, I see"
jǐ	幾	how many?		èr	二	two
táng	堂	AN for classes		sān	三	three
liǎng	兩	two (used with AN)		shàng	上	above
wèishém (wèishém.me)	為甚麽	why?		zěm.me (zěm)	怎麽	how?
yīn.wèi	因為	because		xiā	蝦	shrimp
Zhōng.guórén	中國人	Chinese		xià	下	below
yào	要	to want, to require, to need		.ai.ya	哎呀	interjection of surprise or consternation
xué	學	to study				
Yīngwén	英文	English		jiù	就	then; immediately; only (unrelated homonym of jiù "old")
xǐ.huān	喜歡	to like				
tiān	天	day		è	餓	hungry
měi	每	every		chī-fàn	吃飯	eat (meal) (V-O used as intransitive)
huì	會	know how to, can, know (as a language)				
				.ba	吧	particle of suggestion
huà	話	speech				

Vocabulary Classified by Type

Nouns
kè
Zhōng.guórén
Yīngwén
tiān
huà
Zhōng.guó-zì
zì
xiā

Verbs
zuò
méi.yǒu (méi)
xué
xǐ.huān
xiě
xìn
qǐng

Auxiliary Verbs
yào

hui

Verb-Object Compounds
chī-fàn

ANs
táng

Adjectives
è

Adverbs
zhǐ
jiù
zhēn.de
zěm.me (zěm)

Sentential Adverbs
(Moveable Adverbs)
wèishém (wèishém.me)

Conjunctions
yīn.wèi

Time Words
xiànzài
xià.wǔ

Particles
.ba

Interjections
.Oh
.ai.ya

Determinatives
jǐ
liǎng
èr
sān
měi

Grammar Notes

1. *Zhōngwén-kè* "Chinese class". (See Culture Note 15, Unit V, Lesson 3.)

2. When *qǐng* "invite, request" comes directly before another verb, it is similar to "please" in English; *qǐng zuò* "please have a seat".

3. *Yǒu* meaning "have" or "there is (are)" does not use *bù* for the negative. It uses *méi*. For example:

    Wǒ méi.yǒu kè.   I have no classes.
    Xuéxiào méi.yǒu sùshè.   The school has no dormitories.

    The *yǒu* can drop out in such sentences if a noun follows:

    Wǒ méi kè.   I have no classes.
    Xuéxiào méi sùshè.   The school has no dormitories.

    But note that *yǒu* must be used if there is no following noun:

    Wǒ méi.yǒu. (NOT: Wǒ méi.)   I have none.

    Like other V-not-V questions, *yǒu méi.yǒu* can be open or closed:

    Nǐ yǒu méi.yǒu kè? (closed)   Do you have classes?
    Nǐ yǒu kè .méi.yǒu? (open)

Note that both syllables of *.méi.yǒu* are in the neutral tone when the open form is used.

WARNING: The colloquial English expression "You have my book", when it means "my book is at your place", does not have a Chinese equivalent. For this location sense never say *"Nǐ yǒu wǒ.de shū"*. Say *"Wǒ.de shū zài nǐ.nàr"*.

4. *Jǐ* "how many?" functions grammatically like a number in the pattern No. + AN + Noun: *jǐ-táng kè?* "how many classes?", *liǎng-táng kè* "two classes", etc. *Táng* is the AN for classes.

5. Chinese has two words for "two", *liǎng* and *èr*. *Èr* is used:

(a) Whenever there is no AN, as in simple counting or in reciting or reading off digits (when giving a telephone number, for example).

(b) With or without an AN, as the last part of any higher number that ends in two: *shí'èr* "twelve", *shí'èr-táng kè* "twelve classes", *sì.shí'èr.ge rén* "forty-two people", etc.

(c) With or without an AN, whenever the ordinal prefix *dì* is used to make an ordinal number: *dì'èr* "second", *dì.èr.ge rén* "the second person", *dìshí'èr kè* "lesson twelve", *dì'èr.shísān* "twenty-third", etc.

Liǎng is used:

(d) Every time an AN is used, except as noted above in (b) and (c): *liǎng.ge rén*, *liǎng-bǎ yǐ.zi*, etc.

Liǎng and *èr* can both be used:

(e) In higher numbers before *bǎi* "hundred", *qiān* "thousand", and *wàn* "ten thousand": *èr-bǎi* or *liǎng-bǎi* "two hundred", *èr-qiān* "two thousand", *liǎng-wàn* "twenty thousand", etc.

6. Minor Sentences. Note that in sentences like *Shì shém kè?* "What classes are they?" or *Shì wǒ* "It is I", no subject ("it" or "they") is required in Chinese. These "minor sentences" are perfectly common and correct. Do not try to "supply" subjects for such sentences, as this will simply lead you into mistakes.

7. *Wèishém(.me)*, literally "for what reason?", means "why?". Note that it often **follows** the subject (*nǐ* in this case), which the English "why" cannot do.

    .Ne at the end of this sentence softens it and makes it more polite. For a more aggressive or indignant question, omit *.ne*.

8. *Yīn.wèi* "because" frequently occurs in conjunction with *suǒ.yǐ* "therefore" in the construction:

$$S + yīn.wèi + V_1, \ suǒ.yǐ + V_2$$

Wǒ yīn.wèi huì shuō Zhōng.guó-huà, *suǒ*.yǐ bù xué Zhōngwén.	Because I can speak Chinese, I don't study Chinese.

In this usage *yīn.wèi* can appear either before or after the subject. However, when two different subjects are used, *yīn.wèi* and *suǒ.yǐ* are placed before each of the subjects and the pattern becomes:

$$Y\bar{\imath}n.w\grave{e}i + S_1 + V_1, \quad su\ocaron.y\icaron + S_2 + V_2$$

Yīn.wèi chuāng.hù .hěn dà,
    suǒ.yǐ jiàoshì .hěn liàng.

Because the windows are large, the
    classroom is bright.

In both of the above constructions, either *yīn.wèi* or *suǒ.yǐ* can be omitted.

9. *Huì* is an auxiliary verb meaning "can" in the sense of "know how to". (An "auxiliary verb" is one that precedes another verb and "helps" it.) *Huì* can also be a main verb if one is speaking about knowledge of a language:

Nǐ huì .bú.huì Zhōngwén?   Do you know Chinese?

10. *Zhōng.guó-huà*. *Huà* "speech, words", when added after the name of a country or place, means "language, dialect". Thus:

Zhōng.guó-huà	(spoken) Chinese
Shànghǎi-huà	Shanghai dialect
Guǎngdōng-huà	Cantonese

Wén "language" is a broader term. *Zhōngwén* "Chinese" and *Yīngwén* "English" include both the spoken and written languages.

11. *Yào* can mean either (a) "want" as in:

Wǒ yào chī jī.   I want to eat chicken.

or (b) "need, have to", as in:

Wǒ zěm hái yào xué
    Zhōngwén .ne?

Why would I (still) need to
    study Chinese?

It can be an auxiliary verb, as in the two examples above, or a main verb, as in:

Tā yào yì-*bǎ* yǐ.zi.   She wants a chair.

12. An *x* indicates that the previous syllable is repeated. *Tiān* meaning "sky, heaven", and also "day", is a quasi-AN, i.e., a noun that follows numerals and determinatives (*zhèi*, *nèi*, etc.) directly. Another quasi-AN that you have learned is *kè* "lesson". (Remember that "Lesson 1" is *dìyī kè*, not *dìyí.ge kè*.) Among time words, *tiān* "day" and *nián* "year" are quasi-ANs, but *lǐbài* and *xīngqī*, both meaning "week", and *yuè* "month" require the AN .ge. Thus *sān-nián* "three years" and *wǔ-tiān* "five days"; but *sì.ge yuè* "four months" and *yí.ge lǐbài* "one week".

ANs can be doubled to mean "each or every (of the following noun)":

gègèr rén	each person
zhāngx zhǐ	every piece of paper

Tiān, because it is a quasi-AN, does not need to be followed by a noun in this usage. *Tiāntiān* can also serve as an adverb:

> Wǒ tiānx xué Zhōngwén.   I study Chinese every day.

13. *Měi* "each, every" is a determinative like *zhèi* and *nèi* (see 1.2.1): *Měi-tiān* "every day", *měi.ge rén* "each person", etc.

14. The noun or nouns to which *dōu* refers must be plural. Although "each" and "every" in English are considered singular, *měi-tiān* and *měi.ge rén* in Chinese are considered plural. (If every person has done something, then many people have done it.)

15. There is an "if" or "since" implied at the beginning of this clause. Chinese conditional sentences frequently omit words like "if" and "then" when the context makes them clear:

> Nǐ bù chī, *wǒ* yě bù chī.   (If) you don't eat it, (then) I won't
> either.
>
> Tā bú.shi nǐ.de péng.yǒu, shéi   If he isn't your friend, then who
> shi nǐ.de péng.yòu .ne?   is?

16. *Zhǐ* "only" is an adverb and therefore must always precede verbs, including auxiliary verbs. It cannot appear in different parts of the sentence as the English word "only" can. (See I.1.10.)

17. In their calligraphy homework assignments, Chinese school children are often asked to copy, using a writing brush, a certain number of "large characters" (*dà zì*) and a certain number of "small characters" (*xiǎo zì*). The boy in this dialogue, whether purposely or not, is using the same phrases to mean "the character *dà*" and "the character *xiǎo*". Actually, if his pronunciation of neutral tones were perfect, there would be no ambiguity: "large characters" is pronounced *dà zì*, with a slightly greater emphasis on the *zì*. "The character *dà*" is pronounced *dà .zì*, with the stress on *dà*. The same distinction holds for "small characters" *xiǎo zì* and "the character *xiǎo*" *xiǎo .zì*. (See Culture Note 5, Unit I, Lesson 5.)

18. *Dōu* "in all cases" is an adverb and therefore must precede the verb. The "cases" to which it refers must, in turn, appear **before** the word *dōu*. If these "cases" are subjects, there is no problem, because subjects usually appear before the verb. Thus:

> Nǐ.de Zhōngwén, tā.de Zhōngwén,   Your Chinese and her Chinese are
>   dōu *hěn* hǎo.   both fine.
> Lǎoshī gēn wǒ dōu bútài   Neither the teacher nor I are very
>   xǐ.huān nǐ.de gǒu.   fond of your dog.

But when the "cases" referred to by *dōu* are objects, these objects must be moved from their normal position following the verb to a position in front of both the verb and *dōu*. In this case, the S + V + O changes to O(plural) + S + *dōu* + V. Thus:

> Wǒ huì xiě dà zì.   I can write big characters.
> Wǒ huì *xiě* xiǎo zì.   I can write small characters.

But:

Dà zì, xiǎo zì, wǒ dōu   I can write both big and small
   huì xiě.   characters.
Lǎoshī .de gǒu, nǐ.de gǒu,   I am not very fond of either the
   wǒ dōu bútài xǐ.huān.   teacher's dog or yours.

Sometimes the order of such sentences will be S + O(plural) + *dōu* + V, such as in
the sentence at Note 8 in the next lesson:

Wǒ hóngchá lǜchá dōu bù hē.   I drink neither black tea nor green
                                     tea.

19.   *Hái .yǒu* "and also" comes from *hái* "further" and *yǒu* "there is (are)".

20.   Here the boy incorrectly uses the first tone *xiā* "shrimp" when he clearly means
       the fourth tone *xià* "below".

21.   *Zěm(.me)* means "how?", as in:

Nǐ zěm xiě?   How do you write it?

But it can also mean "how come?" or "why?", as in:

Lǎoshī zěm bù chī-fàn .ne?   Why aren't you eating?
                                      (if addressing the teacher)
                                              or
                                   Why isn't the teacher eating?
                                      (if addressing someone else)

.*Ne*, although not required, often accompanies *zěm.me* at the end of the
sentence. Like *zèm.me* and *nèm.me*, *zěm.me* can be shortened to a single syllable,
zěm. (See I.2.9.)

22.   *Yì (yí)* and *jiù* are used in sentences that have two clauses in the form:

              clause 1   clause 2

$$S_1 + yì\ (yí) + V_1 \qquad S_2 + jiù + V_2$$

to convey the sense of "as soon as" or "whenever". For example:

Nǐ yì shuō xiā, wǒ jiù è .le.   As soon as you mention shrimp I get
                                      hungry.

Note that the .*le* indicates a new situation. WARNING: *yì (yí)* and *jiù* are adverbs
and therefore **must be followed by verbs**. In the previous sentence, you cannot
put *yì* before *nǐ* or *jiù* before *wǒ*.

When the two clauses have the same subject, S_2 is normally omitted to give the
form:

$$S + yì\ (yí) + V_1 + jiù + V_2$$

Tā yì chī jī jiù tù (vomit).   The moment he eats chicken, he
                                      throws up.

23.   *Hǎo* as an interjection means "okay".

24.   **V-O Compounds**. Certain verbs are commonly paired with certain nouns to form
       " verb-object compounds". *Chī-fàn* "eat rice", *shuō-huà* "speak words", and *xiě-zi*
       "write characters" are important examples. *Chī-fàn* should be translated not as
       "eat rice", but simply as "eat". Similarly, other verb-object compounds are to be
       translated as **intransitive verbs**. (In a sense the objects are "dummy" objects.)
       For example:

                   Wǒ.mén tiānx chī-fàn.   We eat every day.
                   Tā xi.huān shuō-huà.   He likes to talk.
                   Tā.mén dōu huì xiě-zi.   They all know how to write.

       Because V-O compounds are intransitive, they cannot take an object. (To say "I
       speak English", you cannot say *wǒ shuō-huà Yīngwén*.) Then what do you do when you
       have an object? You simply remove the "dummy" object and put in the object you
       want:

                   Wǒ shuō-huà.
                        ↓
                   Yīngwén   =   Wǒ shuō Yīngwén.

       In other words, verbs like *shuō*, *chī*, and *xiě* are **transitive** when they appear
       without their "dummy" objects. When they appear with no objects at all, they
       still have a transitive sense, and therefore to translate them into English you
       often have to supply the word "it". For example:

                   Nǐ chī .bù.chī? Wǒ chī.   Do you eat (it)? Yes, I do.
                   Qǐng nǐ xiě.   Please write it.

25.   *.Ba* is a particle used at the ends of sentences. After suggestions, it means
       "let's..." or "how about...?":

                   Chī-fàn .ba!   Let's eat!
                   Jīdàn bùhǎochī, chī niúròu .ba?   The eggs taste awful—how about
                                                     having beef?

       After statements of fact, *.ba* is like the English "I suppose"—indicating that the
       speaker believes the statement is true, but is not quite sure:

                   Xuéxiào yǒu sùshè .ba?   The school has dormitories, I
                                                     suppose?

                   Tā bú.shi Zhōng.guórén .ba?   She's not Chinese, is she?

Culture Note 4:   Greetings and Partings II

If you are out and about, another standard greeting-question is:

(Nǐ) shàng nǎr qù?	Where are you going?

To which the answer can be:

(Wǒ) shàng [any Place Word].	To the [Place Word]. (See I.5.23.)
(Wǒ) huí [jiā, sùshè, etc.]	Returning [home, to the dorm, etc.]

Frequently the person who initiates a greeting observes what the other person is doing and puts his question in the form of a presumption. For example:

Huí sùshè .a?	Returning to the dorm?
Shàng túshūguǎn .a?	Going to the library?

It may be perfectly obvious that you are going back to the dorm, or are off to the library, and hence these questions do not actually call for genuine answers. But as greetings they should be reciprocated, and the correct way to reciprocate is simply with È or .Ng "Yeah, yup", or with somewhat fuller responses like:

È, huí sùshè.	Yeah, back to the dorm.
.Ng, shàng túshūguǎn.	Yup, off to the library.

Greeting-questions with obvious answers are not limited to verbs of motion (shàng, huí, etc.). They can also comment on what someone is doing, or about to do, while staying in one place. For example, if friends meet at a newsstand the greetings might be:

Mǎi bào .a?	Buying a paper?
È, mǎi bào.	Yup, buying a paper.

Or on a railway platform:

Děng huǒchē .ia?	Waiting for a train?
.Ng, nǐ .ne?	Yeah, you?

In all such greetings, both question and answer should be spoken in a casual and unstressed manner. The subjects of both question and answer (nǐ and wǒ) are usually omitted. Practice the greetings without these subjects.

WARNING: As you practice these greeting-questions with obvious answers, remember that the questions are always very simple and general. Do not be too specific. For example if you see a friend nodding off, don't greet him with Dǎdǔnr .a? ("Nodding off?"). Or if you meet a friend in a restaurant, and notice that he is eating beef noodles, you can say Chī wǔfàn? ("Having lunch?") or perhaps Chī miàn? (Having noodles?"), but not Chī *niúròu miàn .a?* ("Having beef noodles?"). When your questions are this specific they become genuine inquiries rather than mere greetings.

Partings. In place of the various English parting-expressions such as "Good-bye", "So long", "Take it easy", etc., the overwhelmingly most common phrase in Chinese is *Zàijiàn* (lit., "see [you] again"). Traditionally it was considered abrupt to say simply *zàijiàn*; it was better to soften the expression by adding *.a* (*zàijiàn .a*) or by repeating both syllables (*zàijiàn .zài.jiàn*). But in recent decades, just plain *zàijiàn* has become quite acceptable.

Other common parting-expressions are of the form: "[certain time] *jiàn*":

Míng.tiān jiàn.	See you tomorrow.
Děng .huǐr jiàn.	See you in a moment.
Dāi .huǐr jiàn.	" " " " "
Huí-tóu jiàn.	See you soon.

American parting expressions of the form "Have a nice _____" have no equivalents in Chinese. It is better not to try to translate these expressions. Just use *Zàijiàn .vx*.

The English "Good night" also has no standard equivalent. Traditionally Chinese did not have a set phrase for use before retiring, although people often did say *Wǒ shuì .le* "I'm (preceding you in) going to bed." In recent years in Taiwan, the phrase *wǎn ān* ("evening peace") has appeared as an equivalent of "good evening". But *wǎn ān*, like *ni hǎo*, has the flavor of being a translation of a Western term, and is not widely used in daily-life Chinese.

Exercises

In-class exercises:

1.   Fill in the blanks. Read all of the sentences aloud.

   A.   *Yǒu* to have

      1.   Ni jīn.tiān hái.yǒu ... .méi.yǒu? (class)
      2.   *Wǒ* yǒu *yí*.ge ... , xìng Dīng. (good friend)
      3.   Wǒ ... méi.yǒu kè .le. (today)

   B.   *Huì* to know how to

      1.   Ni huì shuō ... .bú.huì? (spoken Chinese)
      2.   Wǒ huì shuō Zhōng.guó-huà, yě huì xiě ... .   (Chinese characters)
      3.   Ni huì ... jǐ.ge Zhōng.guó-zì .a? (write)
      4.   Wǒ.de péng.yǒu huì xiě ... Zhōng.guó-zì, *wǒ* zhi huì xiě yī, èr, sān, hái.yǒu shàng, hái.yǒu xià. (a lot)
      5.   Ni ... huì .bú.huì shuō Zhōng.guó-huà? (mother)

6.   ... , kě.shi tā.de Zhōng.guó-huà bútài hǎo.   ("Yes" in answer to the
       preceding question)

C.   *Xǐ.huān* to like, to like to

       1.   *Wǒ* xǐ.huān ... . (English)
       2.   *Wǒ* xǐ.huān ... Zhōngwén. (study)
       3.   *Wǒ* xǐ.huān ... . (Chinese food)
       4.   *Wǒ* xǐ.huān ... jī. (eat)
       5.   *Wǒ* xǐ.huān ... . (this classroom)
       6.   Wǒ bù xǐ.huān ... . (that dormitory)
       7.   Wǒ bù xǐ.huān ... . (write Chinese characters)

D.   *Chī* to eat

       1.   Jīn.tiān zǎo.shàng wǒ.mén chī ... . (eggs)
       2.   Tā *hěn* xǐ.huān chī ... . (beef)
       3.   ... dōu xǐ.huān chī Zhōng.guó-fàn. (Americans)

2.   Read the following questions aloud and answer them.

A.   Jīn.tiān *nǐ yǒu* jǐ-táng kè? Yǒu méi.yǒu Zhōngwén-kè?
B.   Nǐ xiànzài huì *xiě* jǐ.ge Zhōng.guó-zì?
C.   *Nǐ* xǐ.huān shém kè? Zhōngwén-kè hái.shi Yīngwén-kè? Wèishém.me?
D.   Wèishém xué.shēng dōu bù xǐ.huān chī xuéxiào .de fàn?

Homework:

1.   Mark the whole romanized text using short-form tone signs: ‾ ⁄ ∨ ⌐ ＼   and · .

2.   Translate the following sentences into Chinese.

A.   Can you speak English?
B.   He doesn't eat supper every day.
C.   Really? I don't believe it.
D.   I have three classes every day.
E.   Does that famous high school have a big playing field?
F.   I can write only the two characters "*měi.guó*".
G.   How do you write the character "*guó*"? (How is the character "*guó*" written?)
H.   As soon as he eats the school food, he (then) feels very uncomfortable.
I.   As soon as I look at her eyes, she says that I am a rotten egg.
J.   That American student is truly strange. As soon as he speaks Chinese, he
      wants to eat shrimp.

LESSON 5

Vocabulary

chī-kuī	吃虧	'eat loss', be on the losing end	....sǐ.le	死了	extremely...
			qián	錢	money
xiān	先	first, in advance	qǐng	請	to invite, to treat
hē	喝	to drink	jiā	家	AN for stores, restaurants, etc.
shém.me (shém)	甚麼	something (indefinite)			
			fànguǎnr	飯館儿	restaurant
qìshuǐ	汽水	'bubbling water', soda	lóngxiā	龍蝦	'dragon-shrimp', lobster
(qìshuǐr)	汽水儿				
chá	茶	tea	...jí.le	...極了	extremely...
qīng	清	clear	xiǎng	想	would like to (basic meaning: to think)
qīngchá	清茶	green tea			
jiù.shi	就是	be just the same thing as, simply is	nà	那	in that case, then
			píbāo	皮包	'leather-bag', wallet, purse
lǜ	綠	green			
duōbàr	多半儿	for the most part, the majority	shàng PW qù	上 去	go to... (a place)
			běnlái	本來	originally
hěn shǎo	很少	'very few', seldom	zài	在	to be in (at, or on)
hóng	紅	red			
hóngchá	紅茶	black tea	zhèr	這儿	here
			nàr	那儿	there
dù.zi	肚子	stomach; abdomen	dōng.xī	東西	thing (object)
huì	會	will likely	dōng	東	east
Ê	世	"by the way"	xī	西	west
sǐ	死	die			

bùzhīdào	不知道	don't know (whether)	jiǔ	九	nine	
nǎr	哪儿	where	shí	十	ten	
nǎ.li	哪裏	where	kuài	塊	AN for money or things that come in lumps or pieces	
sì	四	four				
wǔ	五	five	néng	能	can, be able to	
liù	六	six	bié.de	別的	other	
qī	七	seven	xiè	謝	to thank	
bā	八	eight	xiè.x	謝謝	"thank you"	

Vocabulary Classified by Type

Nouns
qìshuǐ (qìshuǐr)
chá
qīngchá
hóngchá
dù.zi
qián
fànguǎnr
lóngxiā
píbāo
dōng.xi

Verbs
hē
sǐ
qīng
zài
bùzhīdào
xiè

Auxiliary Verbs
xiǎng
néng

Verb-Objects (V-Os)
chī-kuī

ANs
jiā

Adjectives
qīng
lǜ
hóng
dōng
xī

Adverbs
xiān
duōbàr
hěn shǎo

Sentential Adverbs
běnlái

Place Words
zhèr

nàr
nǎr
nǎ.li

Complements
....sǐ.le
...jí.le

Interjections
Ē̄

Numerals
sì
wǔ
liù
qī
bā
jiǔ
shí

Grammar Notes

1. *Chī-kuī*, literally "eat loss", means "to suffer a. loss", "to be wronged", "to be at a disadvantage", etc.

2. *Shém.me* "what?" here means "something". Other interrogatives can also change in this way. For example, *jǐ* "how many?" can mean "a few".

3. *Jiù.shi* can link two terms to say that they are the very same. A *jiù.shi* B means "A is (the very same as) B".

4. The usual word in Chinese for "green tea" is *qīngchá*. ("Green", by the way, refers to the color of the brewed tea, not the tea leaves.) *Lùchá* in this sentence simply explains what *qīngchá* is. In the next sentence, *lùchá* is used in contrast to *hóngchá* ("red tea") to mean "all tea that is not *hóngchá*".

5. *Duōbàr* "more (than) half--for the most part" and *hěn shǎo* "very few (times)--seldom" are here acting as adverbs telling the extent of drinking (*hē*).

6. *Hóngchá* "red tea" is actually what in English is called "black tea".

7. *Wǒm* is the shortened spelling of *wǒ.mén* when used before labial initials (b, p, m, f). *Nǐ.mén*, *tā.mén*, and *zá.mén* can similarly be shortened to *nǐm*, *tām*, and *zám*.

8. On *dōu*, see I.4.18.

9. *Jiù* here means the same as *zhǐ* "only".

10. *Huì* here means "will likely".

11. *Ē̄* (pronounced like "edge" in English with a half-low pitch) is a common interjection for calling attention, functioning like "by the way" in English. With different pitches, this interjection also expresses surprise, agreement, approval, or agreement and approval with some excitement. In this text the three usages of this interjection are expressed in the following ways:

    (1)   *Ē̄*: calling attention (I.5, III.3)

    (2)   *É?*: surprise (I.2, IV.4)

    (3)   *É*: (pronunciation similar to *É?*, but shorter) agreement or approval with excitement (III.1, VIII.2)

    The tone marks added to interjections such as *Ē̄* or *É* indicate approximate intonations, not standard tones. For exact pronunciation, listen carefully to your teacher and/or the audio tapes.

    NOTE: In the Chinese character text, this interjection is represented by the phonetic symbol 廿 . (See p. 131 of Character Workbook.)

12. **Resultative Complements.** In English we occasionally put an adjective after a verb to tell the result or effect of the verb, such as in: "I was scared silly", "she was tickled pink", etc. In Chinese the same kind of usage is extremely

common, and basic to many grammatical patterns. The verb or adjective that follows a main verb and tells its result, effect, or extent is called a resultative complement. Here, *è* is the main verb and *sǐ* the resultative complement. "I am hungry (to the point of) dying." (Cf. "I'm starving" in English.)

13. This is a new situation *.le*. The speaker has just realized that she is extremely hungry.

14. *Qǐng* here is the main verb and means "invite", implying that the speaker will pay the bill.

   Wǒ qǐng .nǐ.   I'll treat.
   Wǒ qǐng .nǐ kàn diànyǐngr.   I invite you to a movie.
   Wǒ qǐng .tā.mén chī wǎnfàn.   I invited them for dinner.

15. When pronouns are used as the direct objects of verbs, they are pronounced in the neutral tone.

16. *Jīa* "home" is usually a noun, but here it is an AN for *fànguǎnr*.

17. *Xiǎng* "think, think about, wish to" has different senses depending on how it is used:

   (a) Before a whole clause (subject + predicate), *xiǎng* means "think that":

      Wǒ xiǎng tā jīn.tiān búhuì lái.   I don't think that he will come
                                            today.

   NOTE: *Xiǎng* in this sense can never be negated using *bù* (or *bú*). Although in English it is natural to say one "doesn't think" something is the case, in Chinese, for the same thought, you have to say one "does think" something is *not* the case.

   (b) Before another verb (as an auxiliary verb), *xiǎng* means "would like to":

      Nǐ xiǎng .bù.xiǎng chī lóngxiā?   Would you like to eat lobster?
      Wǒ bù xiǎng kàn-bào.   I don't feel like reading the paper.

   This use of *xiǎng* is very similar to *yào* "want to", except that *xiǎng* is softer, closer to "would like to" than "want".

   (c) Before certain nouns, *xiǎng* can mean "think of, think about". It is often nostalgic, somewhat like "miss" in English.

      Tā tiānx xiǎng tā.de nǔ-péng.yǒu.   He thinks of his girlfriend every day.
      Wǒ xiǎng jīa.   I miss home.

18. *Nà* here means "in that case". In this meaning, it must come at the beginning of a sentence.

19. *Jiù* here means "then". It accompanies the *nà*, but is not required every time *nà* is used.

20. *...-jí.le* is an adjectival suffix meaning "extremely...":

```
hǎo-jí.le                      extremely good
yìng-jí.le                     extremely hard
shū.fú-jí.le                   extremely comfortable
```

Note other uses on a case-by-case basis. *Jí.le* is not used with every adjective.

21. *Yào* "want, need" (see I.4.11) can also mean "order" as in ordering food in a restaurant.

22. **Place Words (PW).** Place words are a special group of nouns that are called for in certain grammatical patterns. There are three types of place words:

1. *Nǎr* or *nǎ.li* "what place?", *zhèr* or *zhè.li* "this place", and *nàr* or *nà.li* "that place". You will encounter other examples in later lessons.

2. Some of the place words of type 1 are called **localizers**. A localizer can combine with another noun or pronoun to make a Place Word. *Zhèr* and *nàr* are both localizers, used to identify places "near to" the speaker and "at a distance from" the speaker, respectively. For example:

```
wǒ.zhèr                   "I-locality"—where I am, here by me
zhuō.zi.nàr               "desk-locality"—there by (or near)
                          the desk
```

Localizers are normally pronounced in the neutral tone.

3. All geographical place names (*Zhōng.guó*, *Měi.guó*, *Běijīng*, *Shàng.hǎi*, *Niǔyuē*, etc.) are Place Words. Although sometimes used with localizers, they are Place Words automatically, with or without localizers.

23. *Shàng* "up, go up, up to" and *dào* "arrive" are used in the pattern:

$$\text{Subj.} + \begin{Bmatrix} sh\grave{a}ng \\ d\grave{a}o \end{Bmatrix} + \text{Place Word} + \begin{Bmatrix} l\acute{a}i \\ q\grave{u} \end{Bmatrix}$$

to mean "come to a place" (if *lái* is used) or "go to a place" (if *qù* is used). For example:

```
Wǒ.de píbāo shàng nǎr .qù .le?        Where has my wallet gone?
Bié dào zhèr lái, .hǎo.bù.hǎo?        Don't come here, okay?
Lǎoshī dào Guǎngzhōu .qù .le.         The teacher has gone to Canton.
```

24. Although *zài* "be in, at, on" superficially resembles English prepositions, it is important to remember that *zài* is a **verb**. Moreover, it is a verb that *requires that a Place Word follow*. In the present sentence, the Place Word is *zhèr*.

Although "[Noun] *zài zhèr*" is normally translated "[Noun] is here", note that the correspondence is not word-for-word. The two phrases correspond as follows:

```
            zài                      zhèr
        ┌────────┐              ┌──────────────┐
        is   in                 this   place
        └──────────────────────────────┘
        is                    here
```

The same principle applies to *zài nàr* "is in that place" and *zài nǎr?* "is in what place?". Provided you have understood this principle, there is no harm in thinking, for general purposes, of *zhèr* as "here", *nàr* as "there", and *nǎr?* as "where?".

25. The standard AN for *dōng.xī* is *jiàn*. Here the speaker's use of the general AN *.ge* is appropriate because of her obvious uncertainty about what the thing is. She is willing to be a bit vague.

   Nàr yǒu yí.ge dōng.xī ("something is over there") is an example of another important pattern that uses Place Words:

$$\text{Place Word} + \begin{Bmatrix} y\check{o}u \\ m\acute{e}i.y\check{o}u \end{Bmatrix} + \text{Noun}$$

In Note I.1.8 we said that Chinese nouns do not require articles such as "the" and "a" in English. However, the distinction between "definite" and "indefinite" reference that these words often convey in English is sometimes conveyed in other ways in Chinese. For example, the "PW *yǒu* N" pattern is used for *indefinite* reference to the noun:

Zhuō.zi.nàr yǒu shū.	A book is (or some books are) there by the desk.
Wǒ.zhèr méi.yǒu qīngchá.	I have no green tea here.

The nouns referred to here are not *definite* books or tea, and therefore words like "a" or "some" in English are used to translate them. To refer definitely to "the" books or tea, you can use the pattern from note 24 above:

$$\text{Noun} + \begin{Bmatrix} z\grave{a}i \\ b\acute{u} \ z\grave{a}i \end{Bmatrix} + \text{Place Word}$$

Shū zài zhuō.zi.nàr.	The book is (or the books are) there by the desk.
Qīngchá bú zài wǒ.zhèr.	I don't have the green tea here. (Or: The green tea is not here with me.)

26. *Bùzhīdào* "don't know", when used without a subject and followed by a question (either a V-not-V question or one using a question word), means "I wonder whether (or if, or where, etc.)...". For example:

Bùzhīdào shi .bú.shi nǐ.de píbāo.	I wonder if it's your wallet.
Bùzhīdào lǎoshī zài nǎr.	I wonder where the teacher is.

In this usage *bùzhīdào* is underarticulated, to sound something like *bù'r'dào*.

27. *Nǎr* and *nǎ.li* are equivalent except that one uses the -r ending and one does not (see I.3.5). *Nǎ.li* is preferred to *nǎr* in some formal contexts. But often, as here, either term can be used equally well.

28. This sentence exemplifies the "Noun *zài* Place Word" pattern as explained in note 24, except that the noun and *zài* are understood. The full sentence would be: *Dōng.xī zài nèi-bǎ yǐ.zi .nàr.*

29.   **Numbers.**   The numbers from 1 to 100 are:

1 *yī*	11 *shíyī*	21 *èr.shíyī*	...	91 *jiǔ.shíyī*
2 *èr*	12 *shí'èr*	22 *èr.shí'èr*	...	92 *jiǔ.shí'èr*
3 *sān*	13 *shísān*	23 *èr.shísān*	...	93 *jiǔ.shísān*
4 *sì*	14 *shísì*	24 *èr.shísì*	...	94 *jiǔ.shísì*
5 *wǔ*	15 *shíwǔ*	25 *èr.shíwǔ*	...	95 *jiǔ.shíwǔ*
6 *liù*	16 *shíliù*	26 *èr.shíliù*	...	96 *jiǔ.shíliù*
7 *qī*	17 *shíqī*	27 *èr.shíqī*	...	97 *jiǔ.shíqī*
8 *bā*	18 *shíbā*	28 *èr.shíbā*	...	98 *jiǔ.shíbā*
9 *jiǔ*	19 *shíjiǔ*	29 *èr.shíjiǔ*	...	99 *jiǔ.shíjiǔ*
10 *shí*	20 *èrshí*	30 *sānshí*	...	100 *yìbǎi*

When *èrshí, sānshí,* etc. are followed by an AN, *shí* is in the neutral tone. Thus: *èr.shí.ge rén* "twenty people" and *sān.shí-zhāng zhǐ* "thirty sheets of paper".

30.   *Kuài* is the AN for things that come in lumps, such as rocks, coal, and money (originally lumps of silver, gold, etc.). Thus *yí-kuài qián* means "one dollar (or other unit of currency)". *Kuài* is also the AN for *hēibǎn* "blackboard", originally made from a big lump of slate.

31.   *Néng* "can, be able to" is an auxiliary verb. It is similar in both meaning and usage to *huì* "can, know how to, will likely" (see I.4.9 and I.5.10). Yet the senses of the two words are different. Use *huì*:

(a)   For "can" in the sense of "know how to":

Tā búhuì xiě Zhōngwén.   She cannot write Chinese (doesn't know how to).

(b)   For predictions ("will" or "will likely"):

Tā huì lái.   He will come (I say).

Use néng:

(a)   For "can" in the sense of "have the physical ability to":

Tā bùnéng xiě Zhōngwén.   She cannot write Chinese (perhaps has hurt her hand).

Tā bùnéng chī lóngxiā.   She cannot eat lobster (due to a physical reason, such as an allergy).

(b)   For "can" in the sense of "have the opportunity to" (because nothing prevents it):

Tā néng lái.   He can come (nothing bars his way).

32.   This *.le* indicates a new situation.

33. *Bié*, the same character that means "don't" (I.3.25), also means "other". *Bié.rén*
     "other people"; *bié.de* "other (things), something else".

34. In note 15 we said that pronouns used as direct objects are pronounced in the
     neutral tone. This is always the case *except* when a pronoun needs, because of the
     meaning of a sentence, to be stressed. (When stressed, *any* word regains its
     regular full tone.) For example:

     Wǒ qǐng .ni chī-fàn.   I invite you to eat.
     Wǒ qǐng **nǐ** *chī-fàn, bù*   I am inviting **you** to eat, not **him**.
        qǐng **tā**.

35. *Xiè* "thank" is a bound word, meaning that it cannot appear alone. For "thank
     you", use the duplicated *xiè.x*.

36. *Chī dōng.xi* "eat something". *Dōng.xi* "thing" is used for concrete objects. For
     the abstract sense of "thing", use *shì* or *shì.qíng*:

     Wǒ jīn.tiān yǒu hěn duō shì.qíng.   I have a lot of things (to do) today.

Culture Note 5: "Big Characters, Little Characters", Chinese Calligraphy

Handwriting as an art—which is called "calligraphy"—has existed for centuries in
both Eastern and Western tradition. But its cultural importance has been much greater
in China than in Western countries. And while Western calligraphy has almost died out
in the twentieth century, in China it remains a major art form.

Chinese calligraphy is closely related to Chinese painting: both use brush and ink,
employ similar techniques of stroke, and are hung as art work. Painting and calligraphy
are often combined in the same work. They are regarded, fundamentally, as two branches
of the same art. (*Xiě* "to write" cán also mean "to paint": *xiě-shēng* "paint (from)
life"; *xiě-yi* "write (freely) one's idea—freehand brush work"; etc.) In fact, between
painting and calligraphy, calligraphy traditionally was considered the "higher" art
form. Although painting might include some colors other than black, the colors were
considered incidental to the standard black ink in which the pure art of both
calligraphy and painting was created.

The traditional high regard for calligraphy was based on aesthetic, moral, and
spiritual values that went far beyond the content of what was written. Superior
calligraphy was admired for the spirit, fluency and life of its form alone. Even barely
literate people could join in this admiration.

One's handwriting was taken, moreover, to reveal one's moral character and
cultivation. Scholars in imperial China who wished to become officials by passing the
civil service examinations had to show excellent handwriting in order to be successful.
No essay, however brilliant in content, could pass if written in an awkward hand.
Although the spiritual and moral importance of calligraphy has declined in the twentieth
century, even today people with good handwriting tend to be respected for it, and people
whose handwriting is not so good tend to feel apologetic. Good-looking characters are a
definite asset in finding a job as an office worker.

In the PRC, the calligraphy of political leaders is used to adorn mastheads of newspapers, covers of books and magazines, and gates to universities, museums, government buildings, and other public places. These appearances of calligraphy are important signs of political patronage and power. They also change from time to time as individual leaders rise and fall.

The great significance of calligraphy in traditional China made it, naturally, a very important subject for instruction of the young. Traditionally, school children were assigned to copy a certain number of characters every day—first by tracing models, then by imitating them. (For an example of a model, see blue book, pp. 48-49.) Small children, under about ten years of age, would do 10 or 20 "big characters" each day. Over age ten, they would do an additional 50 or more "small characters" each day. In copying the characters, they were carefully watched by elders, not only for the actual results, but for proper posture, technique, and concentration.

In recent decades this strict training has declined. During the Cultural Revolution character-copying, as well as calligraphy as art, was consciously repudiated as "feudal" in the PRC. But beginning in the late 1970s, primary schools in the PRC again began to require the copying of characters as daily homework assignments. In Taiwan and overseas Chinese communities the copying of characters has continuously been honored, even if it has not been practiced with the rigor of earlier times.

The modern use of pencils and ballpoint pens has changed the nature of character-writing (traditionally done only with a brush), and thus has inevitably caused a decline in the importance of good handwriting and in calligraphy as an art. The advent of Chinese computer software programs will likely accelerate this decline.

What does all this mean for the beginning Western student? It is unreasonable to demand of yourself to make up for years of the "basic training" that Chinese primary school graduates traditionally had. You cannot expect to write beautiful characters overnight. But you should be aware, at least, of the larger world into which you are venturing when you begin to write Chinese characters. You should realize why it is important to begin properly: observe correct stroke order, try to keep your vertical lines vertical and your horizontal lines horizontal, and apportion your characters, as much as possible, into nicely-balanced square shapes. If and when you gain basic mastery of the fundamentals (normally after at least three or four years), you may wish to try calligraphic art yourself, bearing in mind its very rich tradition.

Exercises

In-class exercises:

1.   Counting:

   A.   Count in Chinese from 1 to 100.
   B.   Count in Chinese from 1 to 100 by five: yì-wǔ, yì-shí, shíwǔ, èrshí, èr.shíwǔ, ... yìbǎi.
   C.   Count in Chinese from 1 to 99 by two: yī, sān, wǔ, qī, jiǔ, ... jiǔ.shíjiǔ.
   D.   Count in Chinese from 2 to 100 by two: èr, sì, liù, bā, shí, ... yìbǎi.
   E.   Count from one to forty using the AN bǎ. Be careful to make the necessary changes for tone sandhi.

F.   Count from dìyī dānyuán dìyī kè (Unit One, Lesson One), dì'èr dānyuán dì'èr kè ... to dì'èrshí dānyuán dì'èr.shí kè.

2.   Fill in the blanks. Read all of the sentences aloud.

A.   *Yǒu* to have

1.   *Wǒ* yǒu hóngchá, *yě* yǒu ... , nǐ yào hē shém.me? (green tea)
2.   Nǐ kàn, nàr yǒu yí.ge dōng.xī, bùzhīdào shi .bú.shi nǐ.de ... . (wallet)
3.   *Wǒ* yǒu ... , *wǒ qǐng* .nǐ chī-fàn .ba. (money)

B.   *Zài* to be at, in, on

1.   Píbāo ... zài zhèr, xiànzài bú zài .le. (originally)
2.   ... ? Zài nǎr? (where)
3.   Nàr, zài nèi-*bǎ* ... .nàr. (chair)
4.   Chá zài nǎr? Zài ... .nàr. (table)
5.   ... zài nǎr? Zài tā.nàr. (money)
6.   Píbāo zài nǎr? Píbāo bú zài .le. Běnlái *wǒ* yǒu .ge píbāo, ... wǒ méi.yǒu píbāo .le. (now)

C.   *Běnlái* originally

1.   Wǒ.de píbāo běnlái zài zhèr, ... bú zài .le. (now)
2.   *Wǒ* běnlái xǐ.huān hē qìshuǐ, xiànzài méi.yǒu qìshuǐ, jiù hē ... .ba. (tea)
3.   *Wǒ* běnlái ... *qǐng* .nǐ chī lóngxiā, xiànzài qián ... , jiù *qǐng* .nǐ chī bié.de .ba. (want; not enough)
4.   *Wǒ* běnlái .hěn ... , xiànzài bú ... .le. (hungry)
5.   *Wǒ* běnlái xiǎng shàng ... qù chī-fàn, xiànzài píbāo bú zài .le, méi.yǒu qián, *suǒ*.yǐ bú qù .le. (restaurant)

D.   *Qǐng* please; to request, to treat

1.   Qǐng ... , qǐng ... . (sit)
2.   Qǐng ... . (drink a little tea)
3.   *Qǐng* .nǐ ... shuō .le. (don't)
4.   *Wǒ qǐng* .nǐ shàng fànguǎnr .qù chī ... , .hǎo .bù.hǎo? (lobster)

3.   Verb-object construction: Use the verb with the objects suggested by the clues. Then use each verb-object to make a sentence.

A.   chī-fàn, chī zǎofàn (lunch, supper, Chinese food, American food, chicken, beef, eggs, lobster, "a loss")
B.   xiě-zì (big characters, small characters, Chinese characters)
C.   hē-chá (black tea, green tea, Chinese tea, soda)

Homework:

1.   Mark the whole romanized text with short form tone signs.

2.   Translate the following sentences into Chinese.
     A.   You write it first.
     B.   Would you like something to drink first?
     C.   I probably don't have enough money (my money may be not enough). So, I
          can't go to that restaurant to have supper.
     D.   She has only a green purse. She doesn't have a red purse.
     E.   Chinese mostly drink green tea, (they) rarely drink black tea.
     F.   This restaurant's lobster is very famous. How about having that?
     G.   Nobody likes to suffer a loss (everyone, i.e., *rénrén*, does not like to
          suffer a loss).
     H.   Oh, where is my wallet? My wallet used to be here, but now it's not.
     I.   My belly (stomach) is too big. I can't eat eggs.

Classroom/Homework exercises:

1.   Oral Substitution

     Example: A: Nǐ wèishém bù chī lóngxiā?

                B: Wǒ méi.yǒu qián.

                A: .Oh, yīn.wèi nǐ méi.yǒu qián, *suǒ*.yǐ nǐ bù chī lóngxiā .a.

     A.   Nǐ wèishém yào xué Zhōngwén?
     B.   Nǐ wèishém xiànzài chī-fàn?
     C.   Nǐ wèishém bù hē hóngchá?
     D.   Nǐ wèishém qǐng tā chī wǎnfàn, bù *chǐng* wǒ?
     E.   Nǐ wèishém shuō tā shi huàidàn?

UNIT II

LESSON 1

Vocabulary

pǎo-bù	跑步	'run-step', jog		huò.zhě	或者	or
jìn	進	enter		xíng	行	be fine, will do
máng	忙	busy		liǎng-yàngr	兩樣兒	both kinds
kòngr	空兒	unoccupied time or space, leisure		yàng	樣	kind
				yào.shi	要是	if
yǒu kòngr	有空兒	have free time		cháyè	茶葉	tea leaves
shì	事	matters, things (business affairs)		shí.hòur	時候兒	time
				fá.zi	法子	method
				pào-chá	泡茶	steep tea
méi-shì	沒事	'have no business', have free time; doesn't matter		guàn	慣	accustomed
(méi-shèr)	沒事兒			dāngrán	當然	of course
tán	談	to talk, to chat		zhù	住	to live
rè	熱	hot		.le	了	particle for completed action
liáng	涼	cool		nián	年	year (see Grammar Notes)
kāfēi	咖啡	coffee				

Vocabulary Classified by Type

Nouns				
	nián			tán
kòngr				zhù
shì		**ANs**		
kāfēi	yàng			**Adjectives**
cháyè				máng
shí.hòur		**Verbs**		rè
fá.zi	jìn			liáng

xíng   **Conjunctions**   **V-Os**
                                        huò.zhě   pǎo-bù
    Sentential Adverbs   yào.shi   yǒu kòngr
    (Moveable Adverbs)   méi-shì (méi-shèr)
dāngrán   **Particles**   pào-chá
                                        .le

Grammar Notes

1.   *Pǎo-bù* "run-step—jog or run (as exercise)".

2.   Here *.a* softens the question. *Shéi?* by itself would seem abrupt or impatient. Similarly, *tā shi shéi .a?* is softer than *tā shi shéi?*.

3.   *Shi wǒ* is a minor sentence. See I.4.6.

4.   *Kōng* is an adjective meaning "empty"; in the fourth tone *kòng*, it means "unoccupied, vacant" or, as a noun, "empty space" or "spare time". Thus *yǒu kòng* (or *yǒu kòngr*) means "have free time" or "be at leisure". The same meaning is expressed by *méi-shì* (or *méi-shèr*), literally "have nothing (to do)".

5.   In English, imperative sentences normally do not use subjects, as in "Look!", "Please have a seat", etc. But in Chinese, subjects are often added, as in *Nǐ kàn!*, *Nǐ qǐng zuò*, etc.

6.   In identifying times and places in Chinese, always start with the largest unit and move successively to the smallest. (The order is normally the opposite in English. Note also that "this afternoon" cannot be translated using *zhè* or *zhèi*; you must say *jīn.tiān xià.wǔ.*) Other examples:

        zuó.tiān zhōng.wǔ   yesterday noon
        Zhōng.guó Guǎngzhōu   Canton, China

7.   *Shém* is used here in an indefinite sense to mean "much" or "any" (see I.5.2). *Wǒ méi shém shì* implies that the speaker does, in fact, have a few things to do, but that they aren't very important.

8.   *Gēn* (originally "follow") is used here as a **First Position Verb (FPV)**. FPVs are always a) followed by an object and b) next followed by a main verb. For example:

        gēn .nǐ tán   chat with you
        gēn .tā wánr   play with him
        dào Zhōng.guó .qù   go to China

9.   *Tán.x* is short for *tán .yì.tán*, which is in the form V + *.yì* (*.yí*) + V and literally means "chat a chat". Many Chinese verbs can be used this way, where the first V functions as a verb and the second as a temporary AN. The effect is livelier and less formal than when the verb is used alone.

10. Both *rè .de* and *liáng .de* in this sentence are substantives. (The noun "beverage" is understood.)

"Cool" in English usually can be translated as *liáng*, while "cold" in English is *léng*. An exception is that, in Běijīng Mandarin, "cold water" for drinking is *liángshuǐ*.

11. *Kāfēi* "coffee" is a word borrowed from Western languages. Most foreign things introduced into China have Chinese names based on their meanings. For example: *fēijī* "flying-machine—airplane" and *diànbào* "electric-message—telegram". But a few words, such as *kāfēi*, are made by imitating foreign sounds.

12. *Huò.zhě* (or *.huò.zhě*, *.huò.shi*, *.hè.shi*) means "or". But review I.1.15 on the two meanings of "or" in English. *Hái.shi* and *huò.zhě* are used in Chinese for these two different meanings. Bear in mind two rules of thumb about *hái.shi*:

(a)   it asks the listener to choose between alternatives;

(b)   it makes sentences into questions.

And two rules about *huò.zhě*:

(a)   it accepts either alternative, and does not ask that a choice be made;

(b)   it does not make sentences into questions. (If the sentence it appears in happens to be a question, something else has made it so.)

In English, the distinction between *hái.shi* and *huò.zhě* is normally conveyed by intonation. "Would you like coffee or (*huò.zhě*) tea?" is pronounced with a rising intonation on "tea"; "Would you like coffee or (*hái.shi*) tea?" with a falling intonation on "tea".

13. *Xíng*, originally meaning "move, go", here is similar to the English "will do, will be fine". The phrase *xíng .bù.xíng?* (or *.xíng .bù.xíng?*) commonly follows a suggestion or proposal to mean "will that work?" or "would that be all right?". Thus:

Xiān hē chá, xíng .bù.xíng?	Would it be all right to have tea first?
Wǎn.shàng chī niúròu, .xíng .bù.xíng?	Could we have beef for dinner?

14. *Liǎng-yàngr* "two kinds". When *liǎng-yàngr* and *dōu* are combined the expression means "both kinds".

15. *Yào.shi* "if". Note these important differences between *yào.shi* in Chinese and "if" in English:

(a)   As explained in I.4.15, "if" can often be understood in a Chinese sentence, in which case *yào.shi* will not appear at all:

Nǐ qù, wǒ yě qù.	If you go, I'll go too.

(b)   In English, "if" has to come before the subject; but in Chinese, *yào.shi* can come either before or after:

Nǐ yào.shi yǒu kè...   If you have a class...
Yào.shi *nǐ* yǒu kè...

(c)   The word "if" is often used in English as an equivalent for "whether" in sentences like "I don't know whether (or if) it will rain." WARNING: In Chinese, *yào.shi* can **never** be used for "if" in this sense. See the next note for how to express this other meaning of "if".

16.   The way to say "whether" or "if" in sentences such as "I don't know whether (if) you like green tea" is to follow the "I don't know" (or similar phrase) with a **choice-type question**, as is the case here in the text. Some other examples:

Tā bùzhīdào xuéxiào yǒu   He didn't know whether the school had
   méi.yǒu sùshè.   dormitories.
Bùzhīdào nǐ yǒu kòngr .méi.yǒu.   I wonder if you have some time.

WARNING: Do not use *yào.shi* for this sense of "if". To say "I don't know if you like lobster," you must say *Wǒ bùzhīdào nǐ xǐ.huān .bù.xǐ.huān lóngxiā*. Never start such a sentence *Wǒ bùzhīdào yào.shi...*

17.   ... .de shí.hòur "at the time of ..." is a very common phrase that can usually be translated "when ..." or "while ...".

18.   Potential Complements. First see I.5.12 on Resultative Complements. When *.de* is inserted between a verb and its complement, the sense is that the attempt to perform the action of the verb **can** attain the result expressed by the complement.

For example, *tīng* "listen" as a verb and *doong* "understand" as a resultative complement can make sentences like:

Wǒ tīng-dǒng.le.   I have listened and (as a result have)
                                         understood.

Using *.de* to make a potential complement, the sentence becomes:

Wǒ tīng.de-dǒng.   I can understand (from listening).

A negative potential complement uses *.bù* (or *.bú*) instead of *.de*:

Wǒ tīng.bù-dǒng.   I can't understand (from listening).
Tā tīng.bù-*dǒng* lǎoshī .de huà.   She can't understand what the teacher
                                         says.

In the example in the text, *hē* "drink" is the verb and *guàn* "accustom" is the complement. *Hē.de-guàn* thus means "can accustom (oneself) to drinking".

19.   *Zài* is a verb meaning "be in or at" and can be used as a main verb. Therefore the sentence in the text actually could stop after *Zhōng.guó*:

Wǒ zài Zhōng.guó.   I am in China.

Here, however, *zài* acts as a first position verb (FPV) like *gēn* (Note 8). It precedes the main verb *zhù*. In a similar sentence to the one in the text, one could say:

Wǒ zài Měi.guó xué Zhōngwén.   I am studying Chinese in America.

20.   **Completed Action .le.** The use of *.le* as described in I.3.9 can be called, for short, "the new situation *.le*". The second major usage of *.le* can be called the "completed action *.le*", which is what is used here in the text.

The completed action *.le* is a verb suffix. It indicates that a specific instance of the verb had been, has been, or will have been completed. **It is by no means equivalent to the past tense in English.** It has many uses that are not in the past, and the English past tense has, in turn, many uses that have nothing to do with it. The best way to master it is to study its uses as they arise one by one.

Here, the *.le* comes after the main verb *zhù* and is followed by a time expression, *liǎng-nián*, telling the duration of this instance of the verb's occurrence. The pattern is:

S + V.*le* + Time Expression

Tā xiě.le sān-tiān.   She wrote for three days.

Be on the alert for other uses of the completed action *.le* as you progress. Note one big difference between the completed action *.le* and the new situation *.le*. The completed action *.le*, since it is a verb suffix, always follows the verb immediately, whereas the new situation *.le* can follow anything, but it must be at the very end of the sentence (or clause).

21.   If you remember that *dōu* is not the same as English "all", but is an adverb meaning "in all cases" (see I.1.18), its meaning in this sentence will be clear.

22.   *Zèm(.me)* and *nèm(.me)* before adjectives indicate "this" or "that" extent, as explained in I.3.11. Before verbs, they mean "in this way" or "in that way". Thus:

Wǒ zèm hē.   This is the way I drink (or drank) it.
Tā xǐ.huān nèm xiě, kě.shi   He likes to write it that way, but
   wǒ xǐ.huān zèm xiě.   I like to write it this way.

23.   In *(Wǒ) dōu.shi zèm hē .de*, a *shi....de* construction emphasizes the verb (plus modifiers) that appears between the *shi* and *.de*. Both *Wǒ dōu zèm he* and *Wǒ dōu.shi zèm hē .de* mean "I always drink it this way", but the latter is more emphatic.

Tā bù hē kāfēi "He doesn't drink coffee" is a plain statement. You could add *shi....de* for emphasis in a case where, for example, you are discussing with your roommate what to offer to a visitor who never drinks coffee. You might warn of the necessity to make tea, not coffee, because *tā shi bù hē kāfēi .de* "he *doesn't drink* coffee."

Culture Note 6: How to Address and Refer to People I

Addressing people you know well. For good friends you should use *míng.zi* only, without *xìng*. For example *Zhāng Rúsī* would be called *Rúsī*. An exception to this rule are friends whose *míng.zi* consist of only one character. For them you use the *xìng*, too. *Dīng Xīn*, for example, would be called *Dīng Xīn*, not just *Xīn*.

Chinese normally address classmates, including former classmates, using both *xìng* and *míng.zì*. For example: *Zhāng Rúsī*.

To address your teachers, use the *xìng* plus *lǎoshī* ("teacher"): *Dīng lǎoshī*, *Zhāng lǎoshī*, etc. If the teacher is a professor, you can use the *xìng* plus *jiào.shòu* ("professor"): *Zhāng jiào.shòu*, *Lǐ jiào.shòu*, etc. NEVER address your teacher using *xìng* plus *míng.zì*. This is extremely impolite; it suggests that you regard your teacher as a classmate.

Use of lǎo and xiǎo. *Lǎo* ("old") and *xiǎo* ("young, little") can be used before a *xìng* to address familiar people in a friendly, informal manner: *Lǎo Zhāng* ("Old Zhang"), *Xiǎo Dīng* ("Little Ding"), etc. The same terms can be used to refer to a third person who may or may not be present at the conversation. Although used everywhere, *lǎo* and *xiǎo* are especially common in the PRC. Western students in China are often addressed with *xiǎo*.

The question of when to use *lǎo* and when to use *xiǎo* depends primarily upon the age of the person referred to. Generally, people over 35 are unlikely to be called *xiǎo*, although they still may be if they are comparatively short, or if their friends are in the habit of calling them *xiǎo* from earlier years. (It can happen that the same person, of roughly middle age, will be called *xiǎo* by older acquaintances and *lǎo* by newer or younger ones.) Women tend to be called *xiǎo* to a somewhat more advanced age than men.

Exercises

In-class exercises:

1.   Fill in the blanks and read aloud.

    A.   V-not-V

        1.   Nǐ ... .bù ... ? (busy)
        2.   Zhèi.ge chá ... .bú ... ? (hot)
        3.   Wǒ.de fá.zi ... .bù ... ? (good)
        4.   Nǐ jīn.tiān ... .bú ... ? (tired)
        5.   Tā shuō .de huà ... .bú ... ? (right)

    B.   *yǒu 0 .méi.yǒu?*

        1.   Nǐ jīn.tiān yǒu ... .méi.yǒu? (free time)
        2.   Wǒ .de píbāo shàng nǎr .qù .le? *Nǐ* yǒu ... .méi.yǒu? (money)
        3.   Nǐ jīn.tiān xià.wǔ yǒu ... .méi.yǒu? (Chinese class)
        4.   Nǐ.zhèr yǒu ... .méi.yǒu? (coffee)
        5.   Tā yǒu ... .méi.yǒu? (girl friend)

C.   V .de C, V .bù (.bú) C

1.   Hē qīngchá nǐ hē.de-... .hē.bú... ? (accustomed)
2.   Yòng liángshuǐ pào-chá ... .de-hǎo ... .bù.hǎo? (steep)
3.   Zhōng.guó-fàn nǐ chī.de-... .chī.bú... ? (accustomed)
4.   Zhōng.guó-zì *nǐ* xiě.de-... .xiě.bù... ? (well)

D.   *Yào*.shi ... *nà* ... *jiù* ...

1.   Nǐ yào.shi méi.yǒu kāfēi, nà wǒ jiù hē ... .ba. (tea)
2.   Yào.shi *nǐ* yǒu kòngr, nà wǒ.mén ... tán .yì.tán .ba.
3.   Yào.shi nǐ xiànzài méi.yǒu ... shì, zá.mén shuō Zhōng.guó-huà, .hǎo .bù.hǎo? (other)
4.   Yào.shi nǐ hē qīngchá hē.bú-guàn, nà jiù hē ... .ba. (coffee)
5.   Yào.shi nǐ ... huì shuō Zhōng.guó-huà, zá.mén jiù dào Zhōng.guó ... qù chī Zhōng.guó-fàn .ba. (really; restaurant)

2.   Complete the following sentences.

A.   Nǐ pào-chá .de fá.zi ... . (incorrect)
B.   Tā.de bí.zi tài ǎi, bù ... . (pretty, good-looking)
C.   Tā shuō .de Zhōng.guó-huà hěn ... . (pleasant to hear)
D.   Zuó.tiān wǎn.shàng .de jīròu tài ... .le, zhēn bùhǎochī. (hard)
E.   ... shuō ... dà bùhǎokàn? (Who; eyes)

Homework:

1.   Translate the following sentences into Chinese.

A.   Which do you prefer, chicken or beef?
B.   Chicken or beef are both fine. I like both.
C.   Which is more tasty, black tea or green tea?
D.   I find both black tea and green tea taste great.
E.   Then how about coffee. Is coffee also tasty?
F.   Sure it is, but if I drink coffee I feel uncomfortable.
G.   If that's the case, then don't drink coffee anymore.
H.   When I lived in China, I jogged every morning. Now I am too busy, and do not have free time to jog anymore.
I.   I don't know if he likes to eat lobster.
J.   I don't know if I have enough money (if my money is enough).
K.   I don't know if dogs are my friends.
L.   I don't know if he has classes this afternoon.
M.   He lived in China for two years.
N.   I drank a lot of soda at lunch today.
O.   When I was in China, I spoke Chinese everyday.

Classroom/Homework exercises:

1.   Dialogues to be extended

A.   Zǎo, nǐ shàng nǎr .qù?
B.   Wǒ shàng xuéxiào .qù.

A.   (A points at C) Zhèi-wèi shi ... ?
B.   (B śays) Zhèi-wèi shi wǒ.de xīn péng.yǒu Zhāng Rúsī.
(Use your own imagination and the Chinese that you have learned to continue this
dialogue.)

2.   Comment on the truth of the following statements. (For format, see I.3 C/H Ex.1.)

A.   Zhōng.guórén duōbàr hē hóngchá.
B.   Zhōng.guórén pào-chá .de fá.zi hěn qíguài.
C.   Měi.guórén xǐ.huān hē liáng .de kāfēi.
D.   Hěn máng .de shí.hòur nǐ dāngrán méi.yǒu kòngr.
E.   Hē tài duō qìshuǐ dù.zi huì bùshū.fú.
F.   Méi.yǒu qián .de rén bùnéng qǐng rén chī-fàn.
G.   Wǒ.mén měi-tiān dōu yǒu Zhōngwén-kè.
H.   Wǒ.mén xuéxiào .de qiúchǎng hěn xiǎo.
I.   Suírán chuáng tài ruǎn kě.shi hěn shū.fú.

LESSON 2

Vocabulary

.mm	嗯	interjection indicating approval or appreciation	yòng	用	to use
			dāo-chā	刀叉	knife and fork
			zěm.me?	怎麼	how come?
Lǐ	李	common surname	dāo.zi	刀子	knife
lái	來	come	chā.zi	叉子	fork
yǐ.jīng	已經	already	shuǐ	水	water
yuè	月	month	ná	拿	to hold
guò	過	pass (the days), lead (a life)	jiāo	教	to teach
			yòu	右	right
jiàn	件	AN for things	zuǒ	左	left
shì.qíng	事情	matters, things (business, affairs)	zèmyàngr (zèmyàng)	這麼樣ㄦ 這麼樣	in this way
búdà	不大	not very	qiē	切	to cut
xíguàn	習慣	be accustomed to	wán	完	to finish
shuǐpíng	水平	level	fàng.xià	放下	put down
shàng-kè	上課	hold class, attend class	zài	再	again
kuài	快	fast	róng.yì	容易	easy
shuō-huà	說話	to talk, to speak	duì (nǐ)	對你	for (you)
yǒu shí.hòur	有時候ㄦ	sometimes	.kě	可	emphatic adverb
yǐwéi	以為	think (mistakenly)	nán	難	difficult
tīng	聽	to listen (to)	nào-xiào.huà	鬧笑話	'stir up a joke', make a fool of oneself
tīng-dǒng	聽懂	understand from listening	.guò	過	verb suffix, did or have...before
qíshí	其實	actually			

cì	次	a time, AN for verbs	.dào	到	to, into
tiào	跳	to jump	pángbiānr	旁邊ㄦ	side
diào	掉	to fall	bēi.zi	杯子	cup
			.lǐ	裏	inside

Vocabulary Classified by Type

Nouns
yuè
shì.qíng
shuǐpíng
dāo
chā
shuǐ
bēi.zi

Verbs
lái
guò
xíguàn
yǐwéi
tīng
yòng
ná
jiāo
qiē
wán
tiào
diào

First Position Verbs
duì

Adjectives
kuài
yòu
zuǒ
róng.yì
nán

Adverbs
yǐ.jīng
búdà
zěm.me
zèmyàngr (zèmyàng)
zài
.kě

Sentential Adverbs
(Moveable Adverbs)
qíshí

ANs
jiàn

ANs for Verbs
cì

V-Os
shàng-kè
shuō-huà
nào-xiào.huà

Verb-Complements (V-Cs)
tīng.dǒng
diào.dào
fàng.xià

Interjections
.mm

Localizers
pángbiānr
.lǐ

Idiomatic Expressions
yǒu shí.hòur

Grammar Notes

1. .Mm in a prolonged, falling intonation, indicates comfort and approval.

2. Review I.2.1 (d): zhè can occur directly before a noun without an intervening AN. For example: zhè fáng.zi "this house", zhè cháyè "this tea".

3. .A here does not indicate a question. It serves to summon the attention of the person addressed. On Xiǎo Lǐ, see Culture Note 6, Unit II, Lesson 1.

4. The .le here is a "new situation" .le. Note that it follows the time expression liǎng.ge yuè "two months", whereas the "completed action" .le at the end of the previous lesson (note 20) preceded the time expression. The two .le tell you different things. The .le in the previous lesson indicates that the two years of

living in China have been completed, and from the context we know that the whole
two years were in the past:

        Wǒ zài Zhōng.guó zhù.le liǎng-nián.   I lived two years in China.

The "new situation" .le, following the time expression, tells you that the action
has been going on for some time and **is still continuing in the present**:

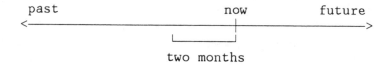

        Nǐ lái Měi.guó liǎng.ge yuè .le.   You have been in America two months
                                                now.

Sometimes **both** kinds of .le will appear in the same sentence, each with basically
the same implication as in the above examples.

        Wǒ zài Zhōng.guó zhù.le   I have been living in China for two
          liǎng-nián .le.   years (and am still in China).
        Xué.shēng wánr.le sān-tiān .le.   The students have been playing for
                                               three days.

When the verb in such sentences has an object, there are two ways to insert it.
You can put it between the time expression and the final .le:

        Tā xiě.le yì-tiān zì .le.   She's been writing characters for one
                                               (or the whole) day.

Or you can put the verb and object right after the subject, repeating the verb:

        Tā xiě-zì xiě.le   She's been writing characters the
          yì-tiān .le.   whole day.

5. Guò "to pass", here has the extended meaning "to pass (time)—to live".

6. Guò.de-guàn .guò.bú.guàn? is the choice-type question for the potential complement
    guò.de-guàn. (Review II.1.18 on potential complements.) Other examples:

        Nǐ hē.de-guàn .hē.bú.guàn?   Can you get used to drinking it?
        Xué.shēng tīng.de-dǒng   Can the students understand (from
          .tīng.bù.dǒng?   listening)?

Note that the syllables of the negative alternative (like .hē.bú.guàn and
.tīng.bù.dǒng) are normally in the neutral tone.

7. Bié.de hái hǎo, ... "everything else was okay, (but) ...".

8.   *Jiàn* is an AN for "thing", whether it be *shi.qíng* or *dōng.xī* (see I.5.25).

9.   *Búdà* "not greatly, not very": *Dà*, normally an adjective, here functions as an adverb modifying an adjective. It can be used in this way only in the negative.

10.   *Xíguàn* here is an adjective meaning "be accustomed to". In the previous sentence *guàn* is used alone, with the same meaning, as a verbal complement. *Xíguàn* can also be a noun meaning "habit" or "custom".

11.   **Predicative Complements and Potential Complements.** *Shuō .de tài kuài* might appear, at first, to be a potential complement (see II.1.18). But in fact it is a predicative complement, which is something quite different. You must learn to distinguish clearly between predicative and potential complements.

      About Predicative Complements: As you have learned in I.2.6, phrases like *shuō .de* can be used as substantives. The nouns that normally would follow are understood. If the understood noun is *huà*, then *shuō .de* means "that which is said". But if the understood noun is "manner" or "style" (which it very frequently is), then *shuō .de* means "the manner of speaking". Thus, *tā shuō .de tài kuài* means "his speaking-manner is too fast" or "he speaks too quickly".

      It is convenient, and perfectly all right, to translate predicative complements using adverbs in English. But remember that in Chinese you are not dealing with adverbs, which always must *precede* their verbs. More examples of predicative complements:

Lǎoshī shuō .de *hěn* hǎo.	The teacher said it very well.
Tā xiě .de .hěn duō.	She wrote a lot.
Gǒu pǎo .de kuài-jí.le.	The dog ran extremely fast.

Remember that if an adjective is not modified, but stands by itself, it normally implies comparison (review I.3.7). Thus:

Tā xiě .de hǎo.	She wrote it better (than someone else).
Gǒu pǎo .de kuài.	The dog ran fast(er).

      Distinguishing Predicative and Potential Complements. A problem can arise because sentences such as the two just given sound, in speech, exactly like the following two, which are potential complements that mean something quite different:

Tā xiě.de-hǎo.	She can write it well.
Gǒu pǎo.de-kuài.	The dog can run fast.

But there are five differences between the two patterns that will, in many cases, help you to keep them separate:

(a)   We use a space in predicative complements (*tā xiě .de hǎo*) and a hyphen in potential complements (*tā xiě.de-hǎo*), so that, at least in romanization, you can easily tell the difference. But remember that these spaces and hyphens do not signal any change in the pronunciation.

(b)   You will learn as you go that some vocabulary can be used with only one of the patterns, not both. *Tīng.de-jiàn*, for example, has to be a potential meaning "can hear", because there is no predicative *tīng .de jiàn*.

(c)   Only predicative complements, not potentials, can take modifiers:

> *Tā xiě· .de hěn* hǎo.   She wrote it very well.
> *Gǒu* pǎo .de tài kuài.   The dog ran too fast.

(d)   All *negative* complements are clearly different, because *bù* or *bú* **is added** alongside *.de* in predicatives, but **substitutes** for *.de* in potentials:

Predicative	Potential
Tā xiě .de bùhǎo.	Tā xiě.bù-hǎo.
(She wrote it poorly.)	(She can't write it well.)
Gǒu pǎo .de búkuài.	*Gǒu* pǎo.bú-kuài.
(The dog didn't run fast.)	(The dog can't run fast.)

(e)   All choice-type questions are different as well:

Predicative	Potential
Tā xiě .de hǎo .bù.hǎo?	Tā xiě.de-hǎo .xiě.bù.hǎo?
(Did she write it well?)	(Can she write it well?)
Gǒu pǎo .de kuài .bú.kuài?	*Gǒu* pǎo.de-kuài .pǎo.bú.kuài?
(Did the dog run fast?)	(Can the dog run fast?)

In the example in the text, the V-O compound *shuō-huà* appears before the verb and predicative complement *shuō .de tài kuài*. This repetition of the verb must be done whenever an object is present. The pattern is:

$$\text{S   V-O   V   }.de\text{   (modifier)   Adj.}$$

Other examples:

> Tā xiě-zì xiě .de bùhǎo.   She doesn't write well.
> Wǒ hē kāfēi hē .de tài duō.   I drink coffee too much.
> Nǐ ná dāo-chā ná .de búduì.   You hold a knife and fork
>   incorrectly.

12.   *Yǒu shí.hòur* "there are times—sometimes".

13.   *Yǐwéi* means "think", usually implying "think incorrectly":

> *Nǐ* yǐwéi wǒ bù dǒng   You thought (mistakenly) that I
>   Zhōng.guó-huà, shi .bú.shi?   didn't understand Chinese, didn't
>   you?

14.   *Tīng-dǒng* "listen with the result of understanding" is a verb and resultative complement (see I.5.12). The negative of *tīng-dǒng.le* "has understood from

listening" is *méi tīng-dǒng* "didn't understand from listening" (see note 16). The choice-type question is:

> Tā tīng-dǒng.le .méi.yǒu?   Did he understand from listening?

With an object, it would be:

> Tā tīng-dǒng.le lǎoshī .de   Did he understand (from listening)
>   huà .méi.yǒu?   what the teacher said?

Note that the *.méi.yǒu* always comes at the end and is in neutral tones.

15. *Qíshí* is used to correct a mistaken opinion. It is like the word "actually" in the English sentence, "I thought it was raining, but actually it wasn't." To translate the word "actually" when it reinforces a correct opinion, as in the sentence, "I thought it was raining and it actually was," you have to use the Chinese word *díquè*, which will appear in Unit 4, Lesson 1.

16. *Méi tīng-dǒng* "did not understand (from listening)". Both *bù* (*bú*) and *méi* (or *méi.yǒu*) are adverbs for negation, but *bù* (*bú*) can negate both verbs and adjectives whereas *méi* can negate only verbs. *Méi* (or *méi.yǒu*) is used before a verb to mean "did not [verb]" or "have not [verbed]", provided that the verb is of the kind that uses a completed action *.le*—i.e., one that refers to specific actions, not to habitual actions or mental states. To negate a verb that refers to habitual actions or mental states (either past or present), **or** to negate a verb that refers to present or future **or** to negate an auxiliary verb, use *bù* (*bù*) before the verb or auxiliary verb:

> Zuó.tiān tā méi lái (past   He did not come yesterday.
>   and specific).
> Míng.tiān wǒ bù lái (future).   I am not coming tomorrow.
> Wǒ bù hē qìshuǐr (habitual).   I don't drink soda.
> Zuó.tiān wǒ búhuì yòng   Yesterday I didn't know how to hold
>   dāo-chā, xiànzài huì .le.   a knife and fork, and now I do.
>   (*Huì* is an auxiliary verb.)
> Jīn.tiān zǎo.shàng tā bùzhīdào wǒ This morning she didn't know my
>   jiào Dīng Xīn, xiànzài ta   name is Dīng Xīn. Now she does.
>   zhī.dào .le. (*Bùzhīdào* refers to
>   a mental state.)

Note that *méi.yǒu* can be shortened to *méi* only when it is followed by another word. When it stands alone or occurs at the end of a sentence, it cannot be shortened to *méi*. "Has he come?" is *Tā lái.le .méi.yǒu?*, not *Tā lái.le méi?*. The answer to the question can be either *Tā méi lái* or simply *méi.yǒu*.

17. "Knife", as an independent word, is *dāo.zi*, and "fork" is *chā.zi*. *Dāo-chā* is a contraction meaning "knife and fork". There are many such contractions in Chinese.

18. **Verbal Expressions in Series.** *Yòng dāo-chā* and *chī-fàn* are both verb-object expressions that could stand independently as predicates:

> Wǒ yòng dāo-chā.   I am using a knife and fork.
> Wǒ chī-fàn.   I am eating.

When the two are strung together, as they are here, we call the first a First Position Verb (see II.1.8). Frequently, you will use a prepositional phrase to translate them into English:

Wǒ yòng dāo-chā chī-fàn.	I eat with a knife and fork.
Tā zài Měi.guó xué Zhōngwén.	She is studying Chinese in America.
Tā.mén gēn .wǒ dào fànguǎnr	They are going with me to the
.qù chī Zhōng.guó-fàn.	restaurant to eat Chinese food.
Wǒ duì lǎoshī shuō Zhōng.guó-huà.	I speak Chinese to the teacher.

19. *Zěm.me?*, literally "how?", here indicates puzzlement. Cf. "How's that?" "What's this?" in English.

20. *Ná* "take, hold". *Ná dāo-chā* and *yòng dāo-chā* are equivalent. When an auxiliary verb like *huì* is involved, V + *shi* + V constructions (see I.3.23) have three equivalent possibilities:

    Huì ná shi huì ná, kě.shi ...
    Ná shi huì ná, kě.shi ...   I know how to hold (them), yes,
    Huì shi huì ná, kě.shi ...   but ...

21. *Jiāo* "teach". *Jiāo.x* is an example of V *.i* V. See II.1.9.

22. Note that in English we say "You use *your* right hand to hold the knife". In cases like this, the "your" is always omitted in Chinese. It is taken for granted that you will use your own right hand. Similarly, to say "I write with my right hand" and "he parked his car in front of the store", "my" and "his" are omitted in Chinese. *Do not* add *wǒ.de*, *nǐ.de*, or *tā.de* to such sentences.

23. Review the use of *zèm(.me)* and *nèm(.me)* before verbs (II.1.22). *Zèmyàngr* and *nèmyàngr* can be substituted for *zèm(.me)* and *nèm(.me)* in this usage.

24. *Wán* "finish" is a common resultative complement: *qiē-wán* "finish slicing", *xiě-wán* "finish writing", *dǎ-wán* "finish beating", etc.

    .Le here exemplifies a new use of the completed action *.le*. It follows one verb and precedes one or more others giving the pattern:

$$\text{Subj.} + V_1 + .le, + V_2 \ (V_3, \text{ etc.})$$

Such cases can be translated "After V_1-ing, V_2, (V_3, etc.)":

    Qiē-wán.le, fàng.xià dāo.zi.   After finishing slicing, I (or
                                             someone) put down the knife.

Note that this use of *.le* has nothing to do with the past tense, but only with the order in which actions occur.

25. *Zài* "and then" indicates a second action after a first has occurred: "Put down your knife, *and then* take your fork in your right hand." This *zài* is an entirely different word from *zài* meaning "be in or at" (II.1.19).

26. The pattern *yi*-AN *yi*-AN *.de* "one after another, one by one" is adverbial and always precedes a verb:

yí-kuài yí-kuài .de chī   eat it piece by piece
yì-zhāng yì-zhāng .de xiě   write one sheet after another

This "adverbial *.de*" is the fourth use of *.de* you have learned. Review the others at I.1.6, II.1.18, and II.2.11.

The kinds of expressions that can modify verbs with the "adverbial *.de*" are limited, so you should not just try anything, but learn examples as you go. *Yi-AN yi-AN .de* is your first example.

27. *Shi .bú.shi?* "is it or isn't it (the case)?" can follow a statement and make it a question. As with the French *n'est-ce pas?*, the speaker often expects an affirmative answer to *shi .bú.shi?*

28. *Dui ni*, literally "facing you", is like "to you" or "for you" in English.

29. *.Ke* is used here for emphasis. This meaning is derived from the previously introduced *ke.shi* meaning "but, however".

30. *Nào* "cause a ruckus, make a scene" goes with *xiào.huà* "joke". *Nào-xiào.huà* "make a laughing scene" in this context means "make a dumb mistake".

31. *Guò*, as a main verb, means "cross". But frequently, as in the case here, it is used as a verb suffix to mean "have had the experience of (once or more in the past)":

Tā yòng.guò dāo-chā.   She has (once or more times) used a
                                 knife and fork.

32. *Ci* "time, instance" is an AN for verbs. The number of times an action occurs is inserted after the verb, but before the object (if there is one):

Wǒ hē.guò liǎng-ci   I have had Chinese tea twice.
Zhōng.guó chá.

33. Just as *yǒu shí.hòur* means "sometimes" (note 12), *yǒu yí-ci* means "one time, once".

34. This is the *yi* of the *yi (yí) ... jiù* pattern (see I.4.22).

35. **Bound Phrase Complement** *Dào*, originally "arrive, reach", can be a complement in the neutral tone *.dào* (often shortened to *.de*) to tell where the action of the verb ends up. *Diào .dào...bēi.zi.li* "fall into...cup". The words *dào* and *zài* (see I.5.23,24) share an important grammatical requirement, regardless of whether they are used in the modifier position (before the verb) or the complement position (after the verb): **they must be followed by Place Words.** On Place Words, review I.5.22. *Dào* (or *zài*) + PW attached to a verb is called **Bound Phrase Complement.**[3]

---

[3] Y.R. Chao, **A Grammar of Spoken Chinese** (Univ. of California Press, 1968) p. 352.

The .*de* that can replace .*dào* in the complement position can also replace .*zài* in that position. The difference between using .*dào* and using .*zài* is that .*dào* implies *motion*, which may still be continuing:

      diào .dào (.de) tāng.li   fall into the soup
      zǒu .dào (.de) wū.zi.li   walk into a room

Whereas .*zài* implies lack of motion:

      zuò .zài (.de) wū.zi.li   sit in a room

This is the fifth use of .*de* you have learned. Each of the five is grammatically distinct, so you should always be clear which you are using. Refer to the following list whenever you need to:

(a)   **The Modification .de** [modifier + .*de* + noun] is used to modify nouns:

      hěn hǎo .de cháyè   very good tea leaves
      xǐ.huān chī lóngxiā .de rén   people who like to eat lobster

A special use of this .*de* is the "possessive": *nǐ.de bēi.zi* "your cup", *lǎoshī .de péng.yǒu* "the teacher's friend", etc. Review I.1.6.

(b)   **The potential .de** [verb + .*de* + complement] is used in potential complements to mean "can": *kàn.de-jiàn* "can see", *tīng.de-dǒng* "can understand (from listening)", etc. Review II.1.18.

(c)   **The predicative .de** [verb + .*de* + (modifier) adjective] tells the manner in which the verb is done: *zǒu .de hěn kuài* "walk very fast", *hē qishuǐr hē .de tài duō* "drink soda excessively—drink too much soda". Remember that English translations of this .*de* often involve an adverb. Review II.2.11.

(d)   **The adverbial .de** [repeated or polysyllabic adjective + .*de* + verb] also tells the manner of the verb: *yí-kuài yí-kuài .de chī* "eat (it) piece by piece", *mànmānr .de zǒu* "walk (nice and) slowly". Review II.2.26. This .*de* is also used between onomatopoeic words and a verb:

      qī.likuālā .de zǒu   clatter along
      pā! .de yì-shēng diào .dào   fall into the soup with a plop!
        tāng.li .le.

(e)   **.De replacing .dao or .zai** in the complement position [verb + .*de* + place word]: *diào .de (.dào) kāfēi bēi.zi.li* "fall into a coffee cup"; *zuò .de (.zài) yǐ.zi.shàng* "sit on a chair".

In writing Chinese characters, the following uses are customary:

      的   for the modification .*de*

      地   for the adverbial .*de*

得 for the potential *de* and the predicative *.de*[4]

.Dào and *.zài* are still written 到 and 在 , even when they are pronounced *.de*.

.De is pronounced the same in all of its five uses, and regardless of which character is used to write it.

36.   *.Lǐ* "inside" is a localizer. Here it makes *bēi.zi* "cup" into a Place Word. Review I.5.22.

Wǒ yì qiē, jī jiù tiào .de hěn gāo, diào .dào wǒ pángbiānr nèi.ge rén .de kāfēi bēi.zi.lǐ .le.

Culture Note 7: How to Address and Refer to People II

Addressing acquaintances with whom you are less familiar. In the first half of the 20th century, the standard Chinese equivalent of "Mr." was *xiān.shēng*. "Mrs." was *tài.tài*, and "Miss" was *xiǎo.jiě*. Thus:

Dīng *Xiǎo*.jiě	Miss Dīng
Zhāng Tài.tài	Mrs. Zhāng

---

[4] Historically 的 has been used for the predicative *.de*, and this usage appears to be preferable from a grammatical point of view as well. But 得 has now become so widespread for the predicative *.de* that we adopt it in this text as conventional.

      Gāo Xīan.shēng   Mr. Gāo

These terms of address are still common in Taiwan, Hong Kong, and overseas Chinese communities. But in the People's Republic their use was opposed, beginning in the 1950s, because of "bourgeois" connotations. *Xiǎo.jiě* and *tài.tài* have now all but disappeared in the PRC, except for use with foreign visitors. *Xīan.shēng* is still occasionally used to address senior intellectuals (primarily men but also women).

    Another common means of formal address is to use a person's title or position together with the *xìng*. We do this sometimes in English (Professor Jones, President Bush, etc.), but it is much more common in Chinese. For example:

        Wáng Kēzhǎng   Section Chief Wáng

        Lǐ Bùzhǎng   Minister Lǐ

        Zhāng Liánzhǎng   Company Commander Zhāng

In the 1950s in the People's Republic, the word *tóngzhì* ("comrade") began to substitute for the name of a person's position, as well as for the terms *xīan.shēng*, *tài.tài*, and *xiǎo.jiě*. *Tóngzhì* was appropriate for both sexes and all ages (except ·children):

        Dīng Tóngzhì   Comrade Dīng

        Wáng Tóngzhì   Comrade Wáng

Sometimes a person's occupation, instead of the *xìng*, is used with *tóngzhì*:

        sījī tóngzhì   comrade driver

        shòuhuòyuán tóngzhì   comrade salesclerk

In the post-Mao years, there has been a general popular reaction against the excessive politicization of earlier years, and a consequent decline in the use of *tóngzhì*. The term is particularly out of place when used by, or in reference to, a foreigner.

    The problem of addressing and referring to married women deserves special note. Before 1949, and still today in Taiwan, Hong Kong, and overseas Chinese communities, the standard way of doing this has been to use the husband's *xìng* plus *tài.x*:

        Zhāng tài.x   Mrs. Zhāng

        Lǐ tài.x   Mrs. Lǐ

But *tài.x* is no longer appropriate in the People's Republic, where *ài.rén* "loved one" has been promoted as a sex-neutral term for "spouse". *Ài.rén*, however, is used only when no *xìng* is attached:

        Zhè.shi wǒ ài.rén.   This is my spouse.

        Dīng Xīn shi tā ài.rén.   Dīng Xīn is his spouse.

Ài.rén CANNOT be used with a *xing* attached. Do not try to say *Tā shi Zhāng Ài.rén* "She is spouse Zhāng". To address a married woman in formal contexts in the PRC, you should use her own family name (not her husband's) plus an appropriate title. If you do not know a title, the term *nǚshi* "lady, madam" can be used as a polite and formal term of address, with *xing* attached, whether or not a woman is married:

        Wáng nǚshì   Madam Wáng

In referring to a woman, the term *nürén* should be used with care, if at all. The term can have vulgar connotations, especially when stressed. Terms you can use instead include: *nǚshì*, *nǚhái.zi*, (for young people), *nǚtóngzhi* (for formal contexts in the PRC), *nǚshēng* (used in Taiwan, even for people who are not young or students).

Exercises

In-class exercises:

1.   Fill in the blanks and read aloud.

    A.   V-O Constructions

        1.   ná ... (knife)
        2.   ná ... (fork)
        3.   yòng ... (left hand)
        4.   qiē ... (meat)
        5.   xué ... (Chinese language)
        6.   nào ... (joke; make a fool of oneself)
        7.   fàng.xià ... (cup)
        8.   shuō ... (English)
        9.   xiě ... (Chinese characters)
       10.   hē ... (one cup of tea)
       11.   chī ... (two eggs)

    B.   Use the above V-O constructions in complete sentences.

    C.   Fill in the missing nouns.

        1.   Wǒ.de Yīngwén ... búgòu gāo. (level)
        2.   Zhèi.ge rén .de ... *hěn* hǎo. (Chinese)
        3.   Zhèi.ge xuéxiào .de ... *hěn* yǒumíng. (teachers)
        4.   Wǒ.men sùshè .de ... *hěn* hǎo. (food, meal)
        5.   Zhèi-jiān wū.zi .de ... hěn liàng. (window)
        6.   Zhèi.ge fànguǎnr .de ... *hěn* yǒumíng. (lobster)
        7.   Jīn.tiān wǎn.shàng .de ... tài lǎo, ... tài shēng, wǒ dōu bù xi.huān. (beef; egg)
        8.   Wǒ.men sùshè .de ... hěn dà, kě.shi ... *hěn* xiǎo. (bed; desk)

    D.   Fill in the blanks.

        1.   Nǐ ... hē chá hái.shi ... hē kāfēi? (like)
               Wǒ ... dōu xǐ.huān (hē). (both)

   2.   Nǐ ... Zhōngwén hái.shi ... Yīngwén? (study)
        Zhōngwén Yīngwén wǒ ... xué. (both)

   3.   Tā shuō ... ? Tā shuō .de shi Zhōngwén hái.shi Yīngwén? (what?)
        Tā shuō .de huà, wǒ dōu méi ... . (hear)

   4.   Nǐ yào wǒ shém shí.hòur lái? Shàng.wǔ lái ... xià.wǔ lái? (or)
        Nǐ ... lái dōu xíng. (morning or afternoon)

   5.   Nǐ yào yòng dāo-chā hái.shi kuài.zi (chopsticks)?
        Dāo-chā huò.zhě ... dōu xíng. (chopsticks)

   6.   Nǐ xiǎng chī xiǎo fānqié ... dà fānqié?
        Xiǎo fānqié ... dà fānqié ... xíng.

E.   *yǐwéi ... qíshí ...*

     Complete the following sentences.

     1.   *Wǒ* yǐwéi tā shi Zhōng.guórén, ...
     2.   *Wǒ* yǐwéi jīn.tiān xià.wǔ tā yǒu sān-táng kè, ...
     3.   ..., qíshí wǒ méi qù.guò Zhōng.guó.
     4.   ..., qíshí xué.shēng dōu méi dǒng.

2.   Answer the following questions according to the clues given.

     A.   Nǐ chī.guò Zhōng.guó fàn .ma? (many times)
     B.   Nǐ nào.guò xiào.huà .ma? (only once)
     C.   Zhèi-zhǒng kuài.zi nǐ yòng.guò .ma? (have not)
     D.   Nǐ zài nèi-jiā fànguǎnr chī.guò fàn .ma? (many   times)

Homework:

1.   The following diagrams are modeled after the ones in Note 4 in this lesson. Use
     the actions listed below to write sentences in the same pattern as the ones in the
     note.

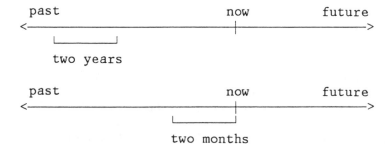

     A.   zhù (zài Zhōng.guó)
     B.   xué Zhōngwén
     C.   hē qīngchá
     D.   zhù (zài zhèi.ge sùshè.li)
     E.   xué Yīngwén

2.   Translate the following sentences into Chinese.

A.   For you it is quite easy; for me it is hard.

B.   Sometimes the teacher speaks too fast in class. I can't understand.

C.   Now you are pretty good with a knife and fork, I suppose.

D.   She doesn't like the food at school, so she eats at a restaurant.

E.   He writes very well, but when he is tired or when he has to write a lot, he (then) does not write so well.

F.   I wanted to hold the lobster with my hands, but the lobster jumped into my girlfriend's purse.

G.   He has already come twice this afternoon.

H.   Can you teach me how to steep tea the Chinese way?

I.   As soon as he says he wants to have lobster, his mother jumps very high.

J.   As soon as I get (have) money, I invite my friends to eat Chinese food.

K.   I can say it, yes, but I don't say it correctly.

Classroom/Homework exercises:

1.   Read the questions aloud and answer them.

A.   *Xiǎo* Li lái Měi.guó yǐ.jīng jǐ.ge yuè .le?

B.   Tā guò.de-guàn .guò.bú.guàn?

C.   *Yǒu* jǐ-jiàn shì.qíng *Xiǎo* Li bù xíguàn? *Qǐng* .ni shuō .yì.shuō shi shém shì.

D.   Yòng dāo-chā chī-fàn duì Zhāng Rúsī nán .bù.nán? Wèishém.me?

E.   *Xiǎo* Li yòng dāo-chā nào.guò jǐ-cì xiào.huà .le?

F.   *Xiǎo* Li dìyī-cì nào.le shém xiào.huà, *qǐng* .ni shuō .yì.shuō.

G.   Yào.shi ni xiànzài zhù .zài Zhōng.guó, *nǐ xiǎng* yǒu shém shì.qíng ni hui jué.de bù xíguàn? Wèishém.me?

2.   Fill in the blanks and then expand into a dialogue.

A: Ni hē ... .bù.hē? (coffee)

B: Wǒ ... hē kāfēi, kě.shi hái búdà xíguàn. (sometimes)

A: Měi.guórén ... hē kāfēi, bù hē kāfēi jiù ... bùshū.fú. (everyday; feel)

B: ....

A: ....

LESSON 3

Vocabulary

tóngxué	同學	schoolmate	zhùyì	注意	notice, pay attention to
yíkuàir	一塊兒	together	cái	才	only then
shēngcài	生菜	lettuce salad	cā	擦	to wipe
fānqié	番茄	tomato	xià	下	'a stroke', AN for verbs
jìrán	既然	since, given that...	(xiàr)	下兒	
búyòng	不用	don't have to, don't need to	kàn.jiàn	看見	see
yǎo	咬	to bite	gāng	剛	just, recently
zhī	汁	juice	dào	到	arrive
(zhīr)	汁兒		wài.guó	外國	foreign countries
jiàn	濺	to splash	zǒng	總	always, generally speaking
liǎn	臉	face	(zǒng.shi)	總是	
piào.liàng	漂亮	pretty	zhǒng	種	type or kind
yī.fú	衣服	clothes	jì.de	記得	remember
dào	倒	contrary to one's expectations	jiā	家	home
			kuài.zi	筷子	chopsticks
			jiā	夾	clench
kè.qì	客氣	polite	pā	啪	plop!
hǎo.xiàng	好像	it seems	....de yì-shēng	的一聲	sound of...
wánquán	完全	entirely	tāng	湯	soup
méi-shìr	沒事兒	it's nothing (it doesn't matter)	wǎn	碗	bowl
....shì.de	…似的	it seems (see Grammar Notes)	mèi.x	妹妹	younger sister
			shǒu	手	hand
yì-huǐr	一會兒	a moment, a while	shēn.shàng	身上	on the body

búyàojǐn	不要緊	unimportant		kě.yǐ	可以	may, can	
méi guān.xì	沒關係	doesn't matter		gěi	給	give	
tàng	燙	scalding		duì.le	對了	yes; right, cor-rect	
wèntí	問題	problem					

Vocabulary Classified by Type

Nouns
tóngxué
shēngcài
fānqié
zhī (zhīr)
liǎn
yī.fú
wài.guó
jiā
kuài.zi
tāng
wǎn
mèi.x
shǒu
wèntí

Verbs
yǎo
jiàn
zhùyì
cā
dào
jì.de
jiā

Auxiliary Verbs
búyòng
kě.yǐ

First Position Verbs
gěi

Adjectives
piào.liàng
kè.qì
tàng

Adverbs
yíkuàir
dào
wánquán
cái
gāng
zǒng (zǒng.shi)

Sentential Adverbs
(Moveable Adverbs)
jìrán

ANs
zhǒng

ANs for Verbs
xià (xiàr)

Time Words
yì-huǐr

Place Words
shēn.shàng

V-Cs
kàn.jiàn

Onomatopoeia
pā

Idiomatic Expressions
hǎo.xiàng....shì.de
méi-shìr
....de yì-shēng
búyàojǐn
méi guān.xì

Grammar Notes

1. *Yíkuàir*, literally "(in) one lump", is an adverb meaning "together".

2. *Shēngcài*, literally "raw vegetables", also means "salad". This term is applied to salads made with lettuce and other raw vegetables. Other salads, such as potato salad, are generally called *shālā*.

3. Here *ge* is short for *yí.ge* "one". In ordinary casual speech, *yí* often drops out after a verb and before an AN.

4. This sentence is an example of **Place Word + yǒu + Noun** (review I.5.25), and therefore the reference to *xiǎo fānqié* "cherry tomato" is indefinite: "a", not "the", cherry tomato was in the salad.

5. *Jirán* meaning "since" or "it being the case that", is always followed in a second
    clause by *jiù* "then", or by a question. *Jirán* resembles *yào.shi* "if", except that
    the speaker does not know whether the clause introduced by *yào.shi* is true or not,
    whereas the clause introduced by *jirán* is assumed to be true:

    > Tā yào.shi bùdǒng Zhōngwén, *ni*   If he doesn't understand Chinese,
    > zěm gēn .tā shuō-huà .ne?   how will you talk with him?

    > Jìrán tā.de Zhōngwén nèm hǎo,   Since his Chinese is so good, you
    > ni *kě*.yǐ gēn .tā shuō   can speak Chinese with him.
    > Zhōng.guó-huà.

    Both *jirán* "since" and *yīn.wèi* "because" can be translated using the word "since"
    in English, but this similarity **is misleading**. *Jirán* is different from *yīn.wèi*.
    Whereas *jirán* normally takes *jiù* in the clause that follows, *yīn.wèi* normally
    takes *suǒ.yi*, and the two clauses indicate cause and effect:

    > Yīn.wèi tā shi Zhōng.guórén,   He is Chinese, so of course he can
    > *suǒ*.yi tā dāngrán huì shuō   speak Chinese.
    > Zhōng.guó-huà.

6. *Búyòng*, literally "no use to", is an auxiliary verb meaning "don't have to".

    > Fānqié búyòng qiē.   (I or some other subject) don't
    >   have to cut the tomato.

    The choice-type question uses *yòng .bú.yòng*:

    > Fānqié yòng .bú.yòng qiē?   (Do I) have to cut the tomato?

    But note that a positive statement does not use *yòng* but another word, *děi*:

    > Fānqié děi qiē.   (I) have to cut the tomato.

7. *.Shàng* "on, on top of" is another example of a **localizer**. (Other localizers you
    have had are *.zhèr*, *.nàr*, and *.lǐ*.) In this sentence *.dào* requires a place word
    and therefore *.shàng* is attached to the noun *liǎn* "face" to form one.

8. *Dào*, originally "invert, turn upside-down", here means "turning one's expectations
    upside-down—contrary to what one would expect". It is not the same word as *dào*
    "arrive".

9. *Méi-shìr* (Peking pronunciation for *méi-shì*) can mean "have nothing (to do)—have
    leisure" (see II.1.4). Here, however, it means "have nothing (to worry or argue
    about)—it doesn't matter". *Méi-shìr*, which has become very common in Peking, can
    be used in a wide variety of contexts, usually as a response to an apology,
    thanks, etc. Depending on the context, it might be translated as "that's all
    right", "never mind", "you're welcome", or "forget it".

10. *Hǎo.xiàng* inserted before a predicate, and *.shi.de* added after a predicate, both
    mean "it seems that...". *Hǎo.xiàng* and *.shi.de* can appear in the same sentence,
    as they do here, or either of them can be used alone.

11. *Guò.le yi-huǐr* "after a moment". *Guò* as explained in II.2.5 means "to pass (time)". The *.le* here is the completed action *.le* as explained in II.1.20. *Yi-huǐr* is a moment or a while—anything from a few seconds to a few hours, depending on context.

12. *Cái*, an adverb, can be understood literally as "only then": "When he saw that I wasn't noticing him, **only then** did he wipe his face." It indicates that an action happens later than one expected. If you think about it, you will realize that in English we often use "not...until", with a reversed order of the clauses, to express the same idea: "He didn't wipe his face until he saw that I wasn't paying attention." Some other examples:

Lǎoshī xià.wǔ cái shàng-kè .ne. The teacher doesn't hold class until afternoon.

Ni xué .diǎnr Zhōngwén cái néng gēn Zhōng.guó tóngxué tán-huà. You won't be able to chat with your Chinese classmates until you learn a bit of Chinese.

13. *.Xià* (or *.xiàr*) "stroke, time" is used like *ci* (II.2.32) as an AN for verbs. But *.xià* is more colloquial than *ci* and often refers to more casual actions.

14. **Past Action with a Quantified Object.** Note the similarity in the following phrases:

jiā *yí*-kuài ròu   clench a piece of meat
chī liǎng-zhī lóngxiā   eat two lobsters
hē sān-bēi kāfēi   drink three cups of coffee
cā *yí*-xià liǎn   give the face a wipe

All of the objects in these examples are "quantified", meaning that they are preceded by No. + AN (although the number can drop out in the case of *yi* (*yí*)).

Now review the uses of the "completed action" *.le* that you have learned thus far (II.1.20, II.2.14, and II.2.24). We have stressed that *.le* is by no means a general marker of the past tense. But it **does** make a sentence refer to the past when it appears with one of these "quantified objects". Thus:

jiā.le yí-kuài ròu   clenched a piece of meat
chī.le liǎng-zhī lóngxiā   ate two lobsters
hē.le sān-bēi kāfēi   drank three cups of coffee
cā.le yí-xià liǎn   gave the face a wipe

IMPORTANT: It is **only** with this kind of verb-plus-quantified-object (V + No. + AN + N) that *.le* definitely makes a sentence past. Other sentences using *.le* may or may not refer to the past. For example *qiē-wán.le* in the previous lesson means "after cutting...(in general, at any time)". Remember that the point of the completed action *.le* is to indicate only "completion"—that an action was completed, is completed, or will be completed, but *not* necessarily that it is past. At all costs, DO NOT simply add *.le* when you want to "make" a sentence past. This will ruin your Chinese.

15. *Kàn* means "look at"; *.jiàn* is a complement expressing successful perception. Thus *kàn.jiàn* is "see". *.Jiàn* can also be used with the verb *tīng* "listen" to make *tīng.jiàn* "hear".

16. *Wài.guó*, literally "outside country", means "foreign country". (See Culture Note 13, Unit IV, Lesson 3.)

17. *Yào* "want" can also mean "will..." or "be bound to...". Review other uses of *yào* at I.4.11 and I.5.21.

18. *Zhǒng*, like *yàngr* (see II.1.14), means "kind, sort, type". When preceded by numbers, *zhǒng* and *yàngr* are used in exactly the same way:

       sān-zhǒng dōng.xī
       sān-yàngr dōng.xī   three kinds of things

When *zhǒng* and *yàngr* are preceded by *zhèi* or *nèi* and immediately followed by a noun, a *.de* must be added after *yàngr*, but cannot be added after *zhǒng*:

       zhèi-zhǒng dōng.xī
       zhèi-yàngr .de dōng.xī   this kind of thing

19. Two words are understood in this sentence. One is the subject, "you" or "one" or "a person". The second is the word *shì* that would appear between *zǒng* and *yào*, if it had been included in the sentence. It is the *shì* of the *shì....de* pattern (see II.1.23).

20. Review the last three examples in II.2.11. According to what was said there, the sentence here should read: *Wǒ yīn.wèi* **ná** *kuài.zi na .de bùhǎo....* But the first *ná* can be omitted. Similarly, in the examples in II.2.11, *xiě* and *shuō* could have been omitted:

       Tā (xiě) zì xiě .de bùhǎo.   She doesn't write well.
       Lǎoshī (shuō) huà shuō .de tài   The teacher speaks too quickly.
       kuài.

21. *Zhù* is a resultative complement indicating that the verb it follows "takes hold". Thus *jiā-zhù* could be translated "clench fast" or "grab hold". Similarly *ná-zhù* "hold firmly", *jì-zhù* "commit solidly to memory". We have already learned *zhù* as a main verb meaning "live or stay (in a certain place)". You will appreciate the connection if you think of "latching on" to the world in a certain place.

22. This is the "adverbial" *.de* that lets certain expressions modify verbs (see II.2.26). Onomatopoeia (such as *pā*) are among the kinds of expressions that can precede this *.de*.

23. *Yì-shēng* is short for *yí.ge shēng.yīn* "one sound". The short form is always used in this kind of sentence. The phrase *X .de yì-shēng* is used as an adverb similarly to the English "with an X", where X represents a sound.

24. *Tāngwǎn* "soup bowl". Words like *wǎn* "bowl" and *bēi.zi* "cup" are normally nouns. When used as nouns, they take ANs: *yí.ge wǎn* "one bowl", *liǎng.ge bēi.zi* "two cups". But they also can be used as ANs themselves:

       yì-wǎn tāng   a bowl of soup
       liǎng-bēi chá   two cups of tea

When used in this way, they are called "temporary ANs". Note that the suffix -.*zi* drops from *bēi* when it is used as a temporary AN.

Wǒ jiā.le yí-kuài ròu, méi jiā-zhù, "pā" .de yì-shēng diào .dào tāngwǎn.lǐ .le.

25. *Shēn.shàng* "on the body". The word for "body" alone, without the localizer .*shàng*, is *shēn.tǐ*.

26. *Búyàojǐn* and *méi guān.xi* are both very common expressions meaning "it doesn't matter" or "don't worry about it". More literally, *búyàojǐn* means "it's not urgent" and *méi guān.xi* means "there are no (negative) implications or consequences" (*guān.xi* originally means "relation").

27. *Tàng* means "hot" when there is an imminent potential to scald, as in *shuǐ hěn tàng* "the water is hot". The more general word for "hot" is *rè*, which appears in the previous line of the text. Both words are distinct from *là*, meaning "(spicy) hot" when referring to food.

28. *Kě.yǐ* "may, be permitted", which is often used as an auxiliary verb, also means "can" in the sense of "it is permitted (by someone or by a situation)".

29. *Gěi .nǐ kàn* "show you". *Gěi* originally means "give": *Tā gěi .le .wǒ sān-kuài qián* "He gave me three dollars". But here *gěi* is a First Position Verb meaning give "to" or "for". Thus *gěi .nǐ kàn*, literally "give to you to look at", means "show you". Other examples:

    gěi .wǒ kàn   show me
    gěi lǎoshī kàn   show the teacher

When *gěi* [someone] *kàn* follows a verb of action, it has the sense of demonstrating or proving the action to someone. Thus *wǒ ná kuài.zi .gěi .nǐ kàn* "I demonstrate the holding of chopsticks for you"—in the sense of either "I show you how to do it" or "I show you that I can do it". The general pattern is:

Subject + Action Verb + *.gěi* + $\begin{Bmatrix} \text{noun} \\ \text{pronoun} \end{Bmatrix}$ + *kàn*

Wǒ xiě .gěi .nǐ kàn.	I'll show you how to write it (or that I can write it).
Tā qiē .gěi .wǒ kàn.	She showed me how to cut it (or that she could cut it).
Nǐ tiào .gěi .tā kàn.	Show him how to jump (or that you can jump).

Tīng "listen to, hear" can be used in this pattern similarly to *kàn*:

Tā chàng (sing) *.gěi .wǒ.mén tīng.*	She sings for us (to listen to).
Qǐng nǐ shuō .gěi .wǒ tīng.	Please say it for me (to hear).

Culture Note 8:   Food and Dining I

Eating family style.[5]   In family meals all the dishes are placed in the center of the table, and everyone has his or her own bowl of rice. Normally people eat from an individual rice bowl by lifting it in the left hand while using chopsticks with the right. Each person helps himself from the dishes in the middle. Only a small amount is taken at a time, because the rice in the individual bowls is considered one's main food, and the dishes only an accompaniment. A common pattern is to have four dishes and one soup. The soup bowl is placed in the middle, surrounded by the four dishes. (This explains why, in Unit II, Lesson 3, the American managed to splash soup all over his friend's sister when he dropped a piece of meat in the central soup bowl.)

You may notice that a Chinese meal is slightly more lively than a Western-style meal because of some of the different ways of eating. For example, soup is sipped off the spoon rather than the spoon's being put inside the mouth. A small slurping sound is permissible, but just as in American manners, a certain discretion is appropriate.

Eating banquet style. At banquets, usually ten to twelve people sit at a round table and, as in family style, help themselves from dishes in the center of the table. Sometimes "serving chopsticks" are used for transferring food from the main dishes to individual bowls.

The main dishes at banquets are not laid out all at once, but are served one after another in sequence. The only exceptions are the cold dishes (typically four) that are set out simultaneously at the beginning. Sometimes these cold delicacies are arranged on one large platter, in which case the number of items can be extended from four to six or more. After the cold dishes come two to four stir-fried ones, followed by three or four other hot dishes that are larger than the stir-fried ones and are considered the main courses. These main courses can be seafood (such as shark's fin, sea cucumber,

---

[5] The following material, from here through "Adaptations to the American environment" below, is taken from Yung-chi Chao Chen, **Harmony of Flavors: A Chinese Cookbook** (Princeton, N.J., 1976), pp.13-14.

fish or shrimp), a whole chicken or duck, or pork, beef, or lamb. They can be cooked in a variety of ways: stewed, roasted, deep-fried, red-cooked, steamed, etc.

Adaptations to the American environment. Traditionally, sweets (one or two) were served in the middle of the sequence of courses, but nowadays in America it has become common to serve a sweet dish at the end as a "dessert". Traditionally in China soup has been the last course, but again, in America, it now comes either before the dessert or even first—which is its traditional place in Western cuisine.

The role of rice has also changed somewhat. For American eaters of Chinese food, rice is not as essential as it traditionally has been in China. Even among Chinese who live in the West, rice is increasingly losing its importance at both banquets and family meals. In China, the cold and the stir-fried dishes at a banquet have traditionally been viewed as dishes to accompany the wine, whereas some of the main dishes, especially the red-cooked ones, were dishes to accompany the rice—called "rice chasers" in the inventive phrase of Mrs. Buwei Yang Chao.[6]   "Rice chasers" naturally require that there be some rice to be chased, and many Chinese diners would feel a meal to be incomplete without some rice. Wine-lovers, half-intoxicated near the end of a banquet, find it extremely satisfying to have a small bowl of rice with some hot soup and a few pickles, which are felt to have a "mouth-clearing" function because most of the courses in a banquet are heavy and rich.

Nowadays, however, the division at a banquet between "dishes for wine" and "dishes for rice" has been almost completely lost. At many Chinese restaurants in the West, rice is not even served unless you ask for it. The amount of rice consumed at family meals seems to be declining as well.

Exercises

In-class exercises:

1.   Translate the following phrases, paying close attention to using the correct AN.

   A.   seven students
   B.   four tables
   C.   three chairs
   D.   one dog
   E.   nine events
   F.   those six pieces of meat
   G.   these two classes
   H.   that bed

2.   Fill in the blanks and read aloud.

   A.   *Jìrán ... jiù ...*   Since ... then ...

      1.   Jìrán zhèi.ge ... zèm xiǎo, jiù búyòng ... .le. (tomato; cut)

---

[6] Buwei Yang Chao, **How to Order and Eat in Chinese** (New York: Vintage Books, 1974), p. 9.

2.   Nǐ.de qián ... gòu, nà wǒ.mén ... chī lóngxīa .ba.
3.   Jìrán ni jīn.tiān ... méi shém shì, zá.mén jiù tán.x .ba. (afternoon)
4.   Jìrán ni bù ... , jiù hē .diǎnr ... .ba. (drink tea; coffee)
5.   Jìrán ni yòng.bú-guàn kuài.zi nà ... yòng dāo-chā .ba.

B.   *Gēn*

   1.   Meaning 'with'.

      a)   Zuó.tiān gēn .ni ... chī-fàn .de nèi.ge nǔ xué.shēng shi shéi?
           (together)
      b)   *Wǒ* ... gēn .ni tán.x. (want to)
      c)   Nǐ.de Zhōngwén zèm hǎo, shi gēn shéi ... .de? (study, learn)

   2.   Meaning 'and'.

      a)   Ni gēn wǒ dōu.shi ... . (students)
      b)   Nèi-zhāng zhuō.zi gēn nèi-*bǎ* yǐ.zi dōu.shi ... . (mine)
      c)   Fānqié zhī ... .dào nèi-wèi nǔ tóngxué .de liǎn.shàng gēn
           piào.liàng .de yī.fú.shàng .le. (splash)

C.   *Qíshí* in fact

   1.   Tā yǐwéi wǒ bù dǒng Zhōng.guó-huà, qíshí ... wǒ dōu dǒng. (what he
        said)
   2.   Tā shuō, "búyàojǐn, méi guān.xì, bú tàng bú tàng," qíshí wǒ zhī.dào
        nèi.ge ... hěn tàng. (soup)
   3.   Chī-fàn .de shí.hòur, tā *gěi* .wǒ dāo-chā, qíshí wǒ huì yòng ... .
        (chopsticks)
   4.   *Wǒ* yǐwéi yòng kuài.zi jiā ... hěn róng.yì, qíshí hěn nán. (eggs)

3.   *Hǎo.xiàng* ... (.*shì.de*)

A.   Ná kuài.zi ... duì tā hěn róng.yì ... ; tā zhǐ xué.le yí-cì jiù ná .de *hěn*
     hǎo .le.
B.   Nèi-bēi kāfēi ... hěn tàng .shì.de, tā yì hē jiù tiào .de hěn gāo.
C.   Zhèi.ge xuéxiào ... shi Zhōngwén xuéxiào, xuéxiào.lǐ .de lǎoshī zhǐ shuō
     Zhōngwén, bù shuō Yīngwén.
D.   Tā.de Yīngwén shuǐpíng ... hěn gāo, lǎoshī shuō .de huà tā wánquán
     tīng.de-dǒng.
E.   Tā ... *hěn* xǐ.huān nèi.ge nǔ xué.shēng ... , tā zǒng.shi qǐng .tā chī-fàn.

4.   Use of '*dào*' (contrary to someone's expectation).

     Example:
          A: Wǒ jué.de zhèi.ge cài (dish) zhēn bùhǎochī, ni jué.de .ne?
          B: Wǒ dào jué.de zhèi.ge cài *hěn* hǎochī. Nǐ .de yāo.qiú
              tài gāo.le.

A.   Wǒ jué.de zuó.tiān wǎnfàn .de niúròu tài shēng .le.
B.   Wǒ.mén.de xīn lǎoshī tài ǎi .le, zhēn bùhǎokàn, duì .bú.duì?
C.   Nǐ yòng kuài.zi yòng .de nèm hǎo, *nǐ* yě huì xiě Zhōng.guó-zì .ma?
D.   Tā *hěn* hǎokàn, tā.de mǔ.qīn hǎokàn .bù.hǎokàn?

Homework:

1.   Translate the following sentences into Chinese.

   A.   When I first got to the United States, I didn't know how to use a knife and
         fork. Now, of course, I don't have any problem.
   B.   Although the hot soup splashed onto her face, she was very polite, as though
         nothing had happened.
   C.   When one arrives in a foreign country for the first time, one is always apt
         to make that kind of dumb mistake.
   D.   That person's clothes are very pretty.

Classroom/Homework exercises:

1.   Read the following questions aloud and then answer them.

   A.   *Xiǎo* Lǐ dì'èr-cì nào.le shém xiào.huà? *Qǐng* .nǐ shuō .yì.shuō.
   B.   Nǐ jué.de *Xiǎo* Lǐ .de nǚ tóngxué kè.qì .bú.kè.qì? Wèishém.me?
   C.   Wèishém *Xiǎo* Lǐ .de nǚ tóngxué kàn *Xiǎo* Lǐ bú zhùyì .de shí.hòur cái cā.le
         .yí.xiàr liǎn?
   D.   Zhāng Rúsī yòng kuài.zi .de shí.hòur nào.le shém xiào.huà? *Qǐng* .nǐ shuō
         .yì.shuō.
   E.   Zhāng Rúsī xiànzài ná kuài.zi ná .de hǎo .bù.hǎo?
   F.   Nǐ shém shí.hòur *kě*.yǐ shuō "búyàojǐn", "méi guān.xì"?

2.   Oral Substitution

   Given: Tā bù xǐ.huān chī lóngxiā.

   Response: Jìrán tā bù xǐ.huān chī lóngxiā, nà wǒ.mén jiù chī bié.de .ba.

   A.   *Wǒ xiǎng qǐng* .nǐ chī wǎnfàn, kě.shi wǒ.de qián búgòu.
   B.   *Wǒ* xiǎng yòng kuài.zi chī Zhōng.guó-fàn, kě.shi wǒ yòng kuài.zi hái yòng .de
         bùhǎo.
   C.   Běnlái wǒ.mén xiǎng yíkuàir shàng Niǔyuē (New York) .qù, kě.shi tā xiànzài
         yǒu .diǎnr bùshū.fú.
   D.   Jīn.tiān xià.wǔ wǒ hái yǒu yì-táng kè, *suǒ*.yǐ bùnéng qù pǎo-bù.
   E.   *Wǒ* xiǎng hē niúròu tāng, kě.shi tāng tài tàng .le.

LESSON 4

Vocabulary

bìng (bù, méi)	並不,没	actually (not)	yíng	贏	to win
zhǐ yào	只要	provided that, so long as	shū	輸	to lose
liàn.xí	練習	to practice, to exercise	yǐqián	以前	in the past
			mǎ.lāsōng	馬拉松	marathon
xiāngxìn	相信	to believe	fēicháng	非常	extremely
jǐ	幾	several	hòulái	後來	later (in the past)
lǐbài	禮拜	week			
gòu	够	enough	tuǐ	腿	leg
wèn	問	ask	shuāi	摔	to slip and fall
yì-tiān-dào-wǎn	一天到晚	all day	shāng	傷	to wound, injure
			mànmānr.de	慢慢兒地	slowly, unhurriedly
niàn-shū	念書	to study			
yùn.dòng	運動	(physical) exercise; to exercise	lǐ	哩	mile (see Grammar Notes)
			duàn.liàn	鍛煉	to exercise, work out
qǐng	請	to request			
bāng-máng	幫忙	to help	.jiù.shi.le	就是了	that's all
zǎo.chén	早晨	morning	jiē	街	street
pǎo	跑	to run	míng.tiān	明天	tomorrow
bǐsài	比賽	compete, competition, race, to race	kāishǐ	開始	begin
			děi	得	have to
...qián	前	(time) ago	zǒu	走	to walk; to leave
kěndìng	肯定	for certain	míng.tiān jiàn	明天見	see you tomorrow

Vocabulary Classified by Type

Nouns		Auxiliary Verbs	V-O Compounds
lǐbài	zǒu		niàn-shū
yùn.dòng		**Auxiliary Verbs**	bāng-máng
mǎ.lāsōng		děi	
tuǐ			**Time Words**
jiē		**Adverbs**	yì-tiān-dào-wǎn
		bìng (bù, méi)	zǎo.chén
Verbs		gòu	yǐqián
liàn.xí		kěndìng	hòulái
xiāngxìn		fēicháng	míng.tiān
wèn		mànmānr.de	
yùn.dòng			**Compound Particles**
qīng		**Sentential Adverbs**	.jiù.shi.le
pǎo		(Moveable Adverbs)	
bǐsài		zhǐ yào	**V-Cs**
yíng			shuāi-shāng
shū		**ANs**	
shuāi		lǐ	**Numerals**
duàn.liàn			jǐ
kāishǐ			

Grammar Notes

1. *Bìng* "actually (not)" can precede only *bù (bú)* or *méi*:

> Tā bìng bú.shi Zhōng.guórén.   Actually he is not Chinese.
> Lǎoshī yǐwéi wǒ.men dōu yǒu shū,   The teacher thought we all had books,
>   qíshí bìng méi.yǒu.   but actually we didn't.

Qíshí, which also means "actually", can appear in the same sentence as *bìng*, but does not have to.

2. *Zhǐ yào...jiù...* is used in the following pattern to mean "provided that (or so long as)...then...":

$$Zh\check{i}\ y\grave{a}o + Subject_1 + Verb_1, Subject_2 + ji\grave{u} + Verb_2$$

> Zhǐ yào nǐ bù shuō-huà, wǒ jiù   So long as you don't talk, I'll
>   gěi .nǐ qián.   give you money.
> Zhǐ yào nǐ tiānx tīng lùyīndài   Provided you listen to tapes every
>   (tape), nǐ jiù kě.yǐ shuō   day, you will be able to speak
>   .de hěn hǎo.   very well.

Zhǐ yào and Subject$_1$ can change places:

> *Nǐ* zhǐ yào bù shuō-huà, wǒ jiù   So long as you don't talk, I'll
>   gěi .nǐ qián.   give you money.

If the subjects are clearly understood, they can be omitted from the pattern:

Zhǐ yào tiānx tīng lùyīndài, jiù   Provided you (or I or someone)
 kě.yi shuō .de *hěn* hǎo.   listens to tapes every day, then
                                             (that person) will be able to
                                             speak very well.

Naturally, if the subjects are *different*, they cannot be omitted.

3. *Liàn.xí* is a verb meaning "exercise". With *xí* in the full tone it can also be a
    noun, *liànxí* meaning "an exercise" or "exercises". *Duō* here is used adverbially:
    duō liàn.xí means "do much (or more) practicing".

        In general, *duō* + Verb means "do much (or more) Verb-ing" and *shǎo* + Verb
    means "do little (or less) Verb-ing".

        Duō tīng, duō shuō, duō xiě, duō   You will learn fast if you do a lot
        kàn, nǐ jiù *kě*.yi xué .de   of listening, speaking, writing, and
        hěn kuài.   reading.

    Sometimes, *duō* + V implies "too much V-ing" and *shǎo* + V implies "too little
    V-ing":

        Nèi.ge xué.shēng *shǎo* xiě.le   That student wrote one character too
          yí.ge zì.   few.
        Wǒ duō qiē.le yí.ge xiǎo fànqié.   I cut one cherry tomato too many.

4. *Xiāngxin*, "believe" or "believe in", is a fuller form of *xin* (I.4). In sentences
    like this one, which tell what it is that the speaker believes, the full form
    xiāngxin must be used.

5. Review the use of *zài* "and then" in II.2.25. The same adverb *zài* here has the
    sense of "more":

        zài guò jǐ.ge lǐbài   in a few more weeks (after a few more
                                             weeks have passed)

    You will understand the connection between these two uses of *zài* if you think of
    them both as meaning "additionally".

6. **Topic-Comment Sentences.** Note that *nǐ ná dāo-chā*, which could be a sentence by
    itself, here serves as the subject for the following predicate. It is a "topic"
    on which the predicate "comments". This kind of topic-comment structure is very
    common in Chinese. The topic serves as a substantive, but it does not have to be
    a noun or noun phrase. It can also be an adjective, a verb, a full predicate, or
    a whole sentence.

        In meaning, the relation between topic and comment is also quite flexible,
    rather like the English "As for [topic], say [comment]". In the example in the
    text, the topic is *nǐ ná dāo-chā* (as for your holding of knife and fork) and the
    comment is *wánquán méi.yǒu wèntí .le* (no problem at all any more).

    Study the following examples:

Topic	Comment

1. Shuō Zhōng.guó-huà   bìng bù nán.

Literal translation: As for speaking Chinese, it's not really hard.
Natural translation: It's not really hard to speak Chinese.

2. *Nǐ* xiě .de shū   wǒ bù xiǎng kàn.

Literal translation: As for the book you wrote, I don't feel like reading it.
Natural translation: I don't feel like reading the book you wrote.

3. Fáng.zi dà   hǎo.

Literal translation: As for the building's being large, that's good (or better).
Natural translation: It's better that the building is large.

If you can master the idea of topic-comment sentences, certain of the patterns already introduced will seem more natural. For example, the first V (or Adj.) in the V-*shi*-V construction can be thought of as a topic, and the *shi*-V a comment (see I.3.23).

7. This is another topic-comment sentence. The topic of tea was introduced by the preceding question *nǐ.de chá .ne?* Now B is giving a topic-comment answer: *chá* (as for my tea) *wǒ hē-wán.le* (I've finished it).

8. *Yì-tiān-dào-wǎn* "one-day-reach-night—from dawn to dusk". Sayings in literary style, such as this one, should be memorized as whole units.

9. *Niàn-shū*, literally "read book", means "study". It is an intransitive Verb-Object (V-O) and a complete predicate, whereas *xué* "to learn, study" is a transitive verb which usually takes an object.

10. **Question Word + dou.** When *dou* "in all cases" follows a question word such as *shéi* "who?", *shém* "what?", *nǎr* "where?", *něi* "which?", etc., the meaning becomes "every..." or "any...". For example:

    Shéi dōu zhī.dào.   Everyone knows.
    Shém dōu xíng.   Anything will do.

The question word does not have to be the subject of the sentence:

    Tā shém dōu huì.   She can do anything.

Remember that *dōu* is an adverb and therefore must come **right before** the verb. If the question word is *něi*, an AN must follow immediately, and a noun might follow as well. In such cases both AN and noun must come before *dōu* so that *dōu* can come right before the verb. For example:

    Něi.ge dōu hǎo.   Any one is fine.
    Něi-jiān jiàoshì dōu xíng.   Any classroom will do.

Similarly, the question word *shém.me* can also be followed by a noun. When this happens, *dōu* again must follow the noun and come right before the verb:

> Tā shém chá dōu hē.   He drinks any tea.

Yě often substitutes for *dōu* in this pattern, especially when the verb is negative:

> Tā shém yě bù xiǎng chī.   She didn't feel like eating anything.
> Tā *nǎr* yě méi qù.guò.   He hasn't been anywhere.

11. *Bāng-máng*, literally "help busy-ness", is an intransitive V-O meaning "help". *Máng* by itself is an adjective meaning "busy":

> Tā jīn.tiān hěn máng.   He's very busy today.

To say "help [someone]", use *bāng* [someone] *.de máng*, for example *bāng wǒ.de máng* "help me", *bāng nǐ.de máng* "help you", etc. To say what action someone is given help in doing, use the pattern:

> S + *bāng* [someone] + V

> *Qǐng* .nǐ bāng .wǒ xiě.   Please help me write it.

12. *Xiǎng (.ge) fá.zi* means "think of a way, figure out how to...". On this use of *shém*, review I.5.2.

13. The abbreviation "*vx*" indicates that the two previous syllables are repeated in the neutral tone. Note that *yùn.dòng* here is a verb, whereas at note 9 (in the text) it was a noun.

14. Adding *.hǎo .bù.hǎo?* to the end of a Chinese sentence is like adding "okay?" to the end of an English sentence.

15. This *.a* indicates enthusiasm for the suggestion that is being accepted.

16. This sentence means, "Do you run fast?". The sentence "Can you run fast?" would be *Nǐ pǎo.de-kuài .pǎo.bú.kuài?* (review II.2.11).

17. *Bǐsài* can be a verb meaning "compete" or a noun meaning "competition".

18. *Qián* or *yǐqián* following a time expression means "in the past, ago". In this sentence *wǔ-nián qián* "five years ago" should be understood subjunctively: "(Had it been) five years ago, I could have competed with you."
    Note that there is no special marker of the subjunctive in Chinese. Although a statement may be contrary to fact (as in the above example), the verb form does not change and even the "*yào.shi*" (if) is omitted as usual.

19. *Kěndìng* "it is certain that" is commonly used in making confident predictions.

20. Here, *shì* means "it is (or was or will be) a case of...".

21. See I.3.16 on this use of *.yòu*.

22. *Yǐqián* can be used as a time word (like *jīn.tiān*, etc.) meaning "in the past". Remember that time words are moveable (see I.3.4). Thus:

> *Yǐqián wǒ shi pǎo mǎ.lāsōng .de.*
> *Wǒ yǐqián shi pǎo mǎ.lāsōng .de.*   I used to run the marathon.

If you want to specify **how far** in the past you are referring to, add a time expression before *yǐqián*:

> sān-tiān yǐqián   three days ago

As we saw in note 18 above, *yǐ* can sometimes drop out: *wǔ-nián qián* and *wǔ-nián yǐqián* are equivalent.

   Yǐhòu "in the future" can be a time word just like *yǐqián* "in the past". For example, *sān-tiān yǐhòu* means "three days from now" or "after three days".

23. *Mǎ.lāsōng*, like *kāfēi*, is a transliteration of a Western word. The *shi....de* in this sentence is the one discussed in II.1.23.

24. *Fēicháng*, literally "not usual", means "extremely".

25. *Lǐ*, an AN written 里 , is a traditional Chinese measure of distance equal to approximately one-third of a mile. *Lǐ* (哩) here means a mile. *Shí-jǐ* means "a few more than ten".

26. *Hòulái* is a time word meaning "later" or "later on", but it **always** refers to events in the past. To express "later (on)" in the future, use *yǐhòu*.

27. *Mànmānr.de* "slowly" is an adverb created by duplicating the adjective *màn* "slow" and adding the "adverbial" *.de*. In Běijīng Mandarin the second syllable always changes to first tone and adds the retroflex *-r* ending; hence *mànmàn.de* becomes *mànmānr.de*.

   The same can be done with a few other adjectives, such as *kuài* "fast" and *lǎn* "lazy". Thus: *kuàikuāir.de* "quickly", *lǎnlānr.de* "lazily".

   Note that this is a third way you have learned to use the "adverbial" *.de*, the first two being *yì-AN yì-AN + .de* (see II.2.26) and onomatopoeia + *.de* (see II.3.22).

   There is an implied "or" in phrases like: *liǎng-sān-lǐ* "two or three *lǐ*". Similarly, *liǎng-sān-bǎ yǐ.zi* "two or three chairs", *wǔ-liù.ge rén* "five or six people", etc.

28. *.Jiù.shi.le*, as a compound particle at the end of a sentence, means "and that's it" or "and that's all there is to it".

29. This is a somewhat idiomatic use of *dōu*. It still has its basic adverbial meaning "in all cases". The flavor of the sentence as a whole is like the English, "Where all do you run?".

30.   *Jiù* here means "merely, simply", or "right" as in "right on the street".   It
      indicates the immediate or commonplace nature of the action.

31.   *Děi* "must, have to".   Review II.3.6.   WARNING: Never say *bùděi*.   Use *búyòng* or
      búbì.

32.   The phrase *míng.tiān jiàn* (or *míngr jiàn*) "see you tomorrow" is extremely common.
      Here the speaker has added *zǎo.shàng* "morning" to be more specific about the time.
      (See Culture Note 4, Unit I, Lesson 4.)

Culture Note 9: Beverages

The most common Chinese beverage is tea.   As you know from Unit I, Lesson 5, there
are both green and black teas.   In South China, green tea is more common.   In North
China, jasmine tea (*huāchá* or *xiāngpiàn*) is more common.   As mentioned in II.1, there is
a Chinese way of steeping tea.   Traditionally, Chinese tea was always loose—never in a
teabag.[7]   Tea leaves are placed in a cup and rapidly boiling water is poured over
them.   The drinker waits until the leaves have sunk to the bottom, and then drinks.   Tea
is served at any time of day in China; afternoon "tea time" is an English custom.

In China, whether in homes, hotels, dormitories, or even railroad trains, the custom
of tea-drinking makes the thermos bottle an important item.   When you check into a
hotel, often the first thing you receive in your room is a thermos of hot water.   In
dormitories, students often have two or three thermos bottles each, which they fill in
the morning and use during the day.

Chinese who are accustomed to drinking hot beverages sometimes find the drinking
habits of Americans hard to get used to.   For example in American hotels, the first
thing you get might be ice water.   This helps explain why the Chinese student in Unit
II, Lesson 2 said he had trouble "getting accustomed to" American life.

Conversely, for Americans in China, drinking hot tea and hot water can sometimes be a
problem.   One American student, after spending a warm summer at a Chinese university,
jokingly remarked that he had had no time to study because he had spent all his time
trying to cool down the hot water.   Of course, younger Chinese people now drink soda as
well as tea.

Exercises

In-class exercises:

1.   Fill in the blanks and read aloud.

      A.   *Liàn.xí* ...   practice ...

            1.   Liàn.xí ...   (speaking Chinese)

---

[7] You may have noticed that you can now get Chinese tea in teabags in the West.

    2.   Liàn.xí ... (writing Chinese characters)
    3.   Liàn.xí ... (using knife and fork to eat)
    4.   Liàn.xí ... (holding chopsticks)
    5.   Liàn.xí ... (jogging)
    6.   Liàn.xí ... (running marathon)

B.   *Xiāngxìn* believe

    1.   Wǒ xiāngxìn zhǐ yào zài ... , nǐ jiù néng yòng kuài.zi jiā-zhù ròu .le. (practice few more times)
    2.   Wǒ bù xiāngxìn nǐ ... niàn-shū, shém bié.de shì dōu bú zuò. (from morning till night)
    3.   ... *nǐ* měi-tiān zǎo.chén dōu pǎo-bù, wǒ xiāngxìn nǐ yídìng pǎo .de hěn kuài. (if)

C.   *Yǐqián ... , xiànzài ...* Formerly ... , now ...

    1.   Yǐqián *wǒ* pǎo .de ..., xiànzài pǎo.bú-kuài .le. (very fast)
    2.   Yǐqián wǒ yòng.bú-guàn ..., xiànzài wǒ yòng.de-guàn .le. (knife and fork)
    3.   Yǐqián wǒ bùzhīdào "xiā" .zì *zěm* xiě, xiànzài wǒ ... xiě .le. (know how to)
    4.   Yǐqián wǒ shém yùn.dòng dōu méi.yǒu, xiànzài wǒ yào ... pǎo-bù .le. (start to)

D.   Reduplication of verbs and adverbs

    1.   Yǒu yí-jiàn shì wǒ yào ... .nǐ. (ask)
    2.   *Wǒ xiǎng qǐng* .nǐ ... . (help me out)
    3.   Pǎo .de kuài .bú.kuài méi guān.xì, zhǐ yào měi-tiān ... jiù xíng .le. (exercise)
    4.   Xiànzài *wǒ* měi-tiān zǎo.shàng ... *pǎo* liǎng-sān-lǐ. (slowly)

E.   *Děi ...* must, have to ...

    1.   Yì-tiān-dào-wǎn ... bùhǎo, *nǐ* děi yùn.dòng vx. (study)
    2.   ... *wǒ děi* zǒu .le. (now)
    3.   Yào xiǎng xué-huì ... , jiù děi duō chī jǐ-cì Zhōng.guó-fàn. (using chopsticks)
    4.   ... *wǒ* yǒu wèntí, *nǐ* děi bāng wǒ.de máng. (if)

F.   *Méi shém(.me)* ...

    1.   Xiànzài wǒ yòng dāo-chā chī-fàn, méi shém ... .le. (problem)
    2.   *Wǒ* měi-tiān ... pǎo-bù, zǎo.chén jiē.shàng méi shém rén. (on the street)
    3.   Wǒ méi shém bùshū.fú, kě.shi *yǒu* .diǎnr ... . (hungry)
    4.   Zhèi-jiān wū.zi méi shém bùhǎo, kě.shi ... búgòu dà. (window)

2.   Comment on the truth of the following statements.

    A.   *Pǎo* mǎ.lāsōng .de rén děi tiān.x liàn.xí, měi-tiān dōu *děi pǎo* liǎng-sān-lǐ.
    B.   Wài.guó shū.li yǒu Zhōng.guó-zì.

C.   Yòng *zuǒ*.shǒu bùnéng xiě Zhōng.guó-zì.
D.   Yòng *zuǒ.shǒu* xiě-zì .de rén yě yòng *zuǒ*.shǒu ná kuài.zi.
E.   *Pǎo* mǎ.lāsōng .de rén dù.zi dōu hěn dà.

3.   Answer the following questions according to the clues given.

A.   *Nǐ* pǎo .de kuài .bú.kuài? (fēicháng)
B.   *Nǐ* wǎnfàn chī .de duō .bù.duō? (bútài)
C.   Zhōng.guó-zì *nǐ* xiě .de hǎo .bù.hǎo? (bìng bù)
D.   Ni kàn, wǒ ná dāo-chā ná .de duì .bú.duì? (wánquán)

Homework:

1.   Translate the following into Chinese.

A.   I like to eat everything but I don't like to eat a loss.
B.   She can't drink anything. She can only drink cold water.
C.   Now I understand completely what you said. I don't have any questions.
D.   So long as you believe running the marathon is a good sport, whether you win
       or lose the competition does not matter.
E.   He likes to exercise very much. I remember that when we lived together in
       the college dormitory, we used to exercise together every day.
F.   Do you write characters fast?
       No, I don't. I like to write slowly.
G.   Do you eat fast?
       Yes, I do. I eat very fast.
H.   Can you run fast?
       No, I cannot.

Classroom/Homework exercises:

1.   Read the following questions aloud and then answer them.

A.   Zhāng Rúsī jué.de ná kuài.zi nán .bù.nán?
B.   *Xiǎo* Lǐ wèn Zhāng Rúsī shém wèntí? *Qǐng* .nǐ shuō .yì.shuō.
C.   Zhāng Rúsī zěm bāng *Xiǎo* Lǐ .de máng?
D.   Zhāng Rúsī néng .bù.néng gēn *Xiǎo Lǐ* bǐsài? Wèishém.me?
E.   Tā.mén xiǎng zài *nǎr* pǎo-bù?
F.   Tā.mén wèishém zǎo.chén pǎo-bù?
G.   *Nǐ* xǐ.huān .bù.xǐ.huān pǎo-bù? *Nǐ* pǎo .de kuài .bú.kuài?

2.   Oral Substitution

Given: Xiě Zhōng.guó-zì fēicháng nán.

Response: Qíshí xiě Zhōng.guó-zì bìng bù nán; zhǐ yào duō liàn.xí jǐ-cì jiù xíng.

A.   *Pǎo* mǎ.lāsōng fēicháng nán.
B.   Yòng kuài.zi jiā fānqié fēicháng nán.
C.   Yòng *zuǒ.shǒu* xiě-zì fēicháng nán.
D.   Pào Zhōng.guó chá fēicháng nán.

UNIT III

LESSON 1

Vocabulary

kè.rén	客人	guest		érqiě	而且	moreover
fáng.zi	房子	house, building		kāi-dēng	開燈	turn on the light or lamp
kǒngpà	恐怕	afraid; perhaps (see Grammar Notes)		*hǎojǐ*...	好幾...	quite a few...
fángjiān	房間	room		zhǎn	盞	AN for light or lamp
...hào	...號	number...		dēng	燈	lamp
bǐ	比	to compare		kāi	開	turn on, open
....yìdiǎnr	...一點儿	a little bit (more or less)		fángdǐng	房頂	ceiling, roof
....de duō	...得多	much (more)...		búhuì	不會	is not likely to, will not
...duō.le	...多了					
chà.bùduō	差不多	almost, about the same		bùtóng	不同	different; difference
chuāng.zi	窗子	window		zěmyàng?	怎麼樣	how about...?
yíyàng	一樣	the same		juédìng	決定	decide

Vocabulary Classified by Type

Nouns
kè.rén
fáng.zi
fángjiān
chuāng.zi
dēng
fángdǐng
bùtóng

Verbs
bǐ
juédìng
kāi

Auxiliary Verbs
búhuì

Adjectives
chà.bùduō
hǎojǐ...

Adverbs
yíyàng

Conjunctions
érqiě

ANs	**Complements**	**Idiomatic Expressions**
...hào	...yìdiǎnr	kǒngpà
zhǎn	....de duō	zěmyàng
	...duō.le	
V-Os		
kāi-dēng		

Grammar Notes

1. *Kàn-fáng.zi* "look at housing", where "housing" can be a room, an apartment, or a house.

2. *Zá.mén liǎng.ge rén* "we two people--the two of us". Similarly, *ni.mén sān.ge rén* "the three of you", *tā.mén sì.ge rén* "the four of them", etc.

3. *Kǒngpà* "I'm afraid". *Pà* by itself is a verb meaning "fear" or "be afraid", as in *wǒ pà gǒu* "I'm afraid of dogs". *Kǒngpà*, however, is an adverb. It carries the mild sense of "afraid" in sentences like:

    Kǒngpà tā búhuì lái.   I'm afraid he won't come.

    DO NOT, therefore, use *kǒngpà* to describe genuine fear.

    Note also that the subject of *kǒngpà* is always an understood *wǒ* "I", and *not* the subject of the main sentence. This is true whether *kǒngpà* appears before or after the subject. For example the sentence above could also be:

    Tā kǒngpà búhuì lái.   He—I'm afraid—won't come.

    The second sentence **cannot** mean "He is afraid he won't come". The two versions the sentence are identical in meaning.

4. Notice the topic-comment structure of this sentence, which actually has layers. First, *zhèi-jiān wū.zi* is a topic for which the rest of the sentence is the comment. Then that comment can be further understood as a topic-comment where *liǎng.ge rén zhù* (itself a clause with a subject and predicate) is the topic and *tài xiǎo .le* is the comment.

    The final *.le* in this sentence is basically a new situation *.le*. It reinforces *tài* "too much", indicating that (on an imaginary scale, if you will, of different-sized rooms) with this room we have reached a "new" case of its being simply too small.

5. *Kě .bù.kě.yǐ* is short for *kě.yǐ .bù.kě.yǐ*. Similarly, *xǐ.huān .bù.xi.huān* can be shortened to *xǐ .bù.xi.huān*. Such shortenings are possible with some other two-syllable verbs and adjectives, but not all.

6. *Sān-hào* "number three". Ordinal numbers can be made by putting *dì* in front of the number (*dìsān*), by putting *-hào* after the number (*sān-hào*), or by using both (*dìsān-hào*). *Hào*, though, is grammatically an AN, so it cannot occur when there is another AN, as in *dìsān.ge mén* "the third door".

7.   *Bǐ* "compare". To compare two nouns, use:

                              A   *bǐ*   B   Adj.

Other examples:

Zhèi-zhāng zhuō.zi bǐ nèi-zhāng gāo. This desk is taller than that one.

Wǒ.de gǒu *bǐ* ni.de gǒu hái   My dog is even uglier than your
    nánkàn.   dog.

The *hái* in the second example can be inserted to give the sense of "even".
Nánkàn, literally "difficult to look at", means "ugly". It is the opposite of
hǎokàn "good-looking" (see I.3.15). (Similarly, *nántīng* "ugly-sounding" is the
opposite of *hǎotīng*; *nánchī* "bad-tasting" is the opposite of *hǎochī*.)

    NOTE: The normal way to express the opposite of the "A *bǐ* B Adj." pattern is
to use *méi.yǒu* as introduced in note 11 below. But sometimes you will want
specifically to negate an "A *bǐ* B" sentence by inserting *bù* or *bìng bù*. When this
happens, *bù* or *bìng bù* must come before *bǐ*, **not** before the Adj. For example:

Sān-hào bìng bù *bǐ* wǔ-hào dà.   No. 3 actually is *not* bigger than
                                    no. 5.

8.   The use of the adjective *dà* without a preceding *hěn* implies comparison: this room
is larger. Review I.3.7.

9.   *Dà .yì.diǎnr* "a bit bigger". WARNING: The pattern "Adj. *.yì.diǎnr*" is
importantly different from "*yǒu yìdiǎnr* Adj.". This is a tricky point that often
causes problems for beginning students.

    "Adj. *.yì.diǎnr*" always **implies comparison** with something else. This is
because a sentence of the form "A Adj. *.yì.diǎnr*" is just the shortened form of "A
bǐ B Adj. *.yì.diǎnr*" in which "*bǐ* B" is understood. For example:

Zhèi-jiān wū.zi dà .yì.diǎnr.   This room is a bit bigger (than some
                                        other one).

Nǐ chī .de nèi.ge fānqié xiǎo   That tomato you ate was a little
    .yì.diǎnr.   smaller (than some others).

But "*yǒu yìdiǎnr* Adj.", although it sometimes implies the idea of "too much", does
not imply comparison with specific other things:

Zhèi-jiān wū.zi yǒu yìdiǎnr dà.   This room is a bit (too) big (in
                                        general).

Wǒ.de chuáng yǒu yìdiǎnr ruǎn.   My bed is a bit too soft.

In **both** the "Adj. *.yì.diǎnr*" pattern and the "*yǒu yìdiǎnr* Adj." pattern, it is
very common for the yì to drop out: *Zhèi.ge fángjiān dà .diǎnr, wǒ.de chuáng yǒu
.diǎnr ǎi*, etc. Note that when yì drops out, *yǒu* must change to second tone.

10.   To say something "is **a bit** more Adj.", you use "Adj. + *(.yì).diǎnr*" (see previous
note). To say it "is **much** more Adj.", use "Adj. *duō.le*" or "Adj. *.de duō*":

Zhèi-jiān wū.zi dà .de duō.   This room is much larger (than some

Ni.de gǒu nánkàn duō.le.   other one).
                                              Your dog is much uglier (than
                                                 unspecified others).

Do not try to analyze the *.de* in *.de duō* or the *.le* in *duō.le*. Just memorize them as set phrases.

.Yi.diǎnr, *duō.le*, and *.de duō*, all of which imply comparison, easily combine with the *bǐ* pattern (note 7), in which comparison is explicit:

A *bǐ* B Adj. $\begin{Bmatrix} (.yi).di\check{a}nr \\ du\bar{o}.le \\ .de\ du\bar{o} \end{Bmatrix}$ a bit more
                                                          much more
                                                          much more

Zhèi-jiān wū.zi bǐ nèi-jiān dà   This room is a bit larger than
   .diǎnr.   that one.
Wǒ.de wū.zi bǐ zhèi-jiān dà   My room is much larger than this one.
   duō.le.
Zhèi-jiān bǐ nèi-jiān dà .de   This room is much larger than that
   duō.   one.

11.   Review note 7 on the pattern "A *bǐ* B Adj.". To say the reverse, that A is *less* than B in some respect, use:

A *méi.yǒu* B (*nèm.me*) Adj.

Nèm.me (or *nèm*) is in parentheses because it is optional. Examples:

Tā méi.yǒu nǐ (nèm) gāo.   He is not as tall as you.
X-dà méi.yǒu Y-dà nèm yǒumíng.   X university is less famous than
                                        Y university.

In normal rapid speech, *méi.yǒu* can be shortened to *méi*.

12.   *Chà* "fall short". *Chà.bùduō*, literally "cannot differ by much", is an adjective meaning "about the same".

13.   From notes 7 and 11, we know how to say "A is **more** (note 7) or **less** (note 11) than B in some respect". To say that A and B are **the same**, use:

A *gēn* B *yíyàng*

Wǒ.de wū.zi gēn nǐ.de yíyàng.   My room is the same as yours.

To specify **in what respect** A and B are the same, simply add an adjective:

A *gēn* B *yíyàng* Adj.

Wǒ.de wū.zi gēn nǐ.de yíyàng dà.   My room is the same size as yours
                                         (literally, "equally as big as
                                         yours").
Nǐ.de gǒu gēn tā.de gǒu yíyàng   Your dog and her dog are equally
   nánkàn.   ugly.

14. *Érqiě*, "moreover" or "what's more", is always used at the beginning of a clause.

15. Note the topic-comment structure here: *búliàng* "not being bright" (topic) + *búyàojìn* "not important" (comment) = "It doesn't matter if it's not bright."

16. *Zhèr* "here" and *nàr* "there" are Place Words (see I.5.22). The sentence *zhèr yǒu dēng* is therefore an example of "PW *yǒu* N" implying indefinite reference (see II.3.4).

17. *Zhǎn* is an AN for lamps. *Hǎojǐ-zhǎn dēng* is "a good number of lamps" or "quite a few lamps". Similarly, *hǎojǐ.ge rén* means "quite a few people", etc.

18. **Voicelessness of Chinese Verbs.** There is no distinction between "active" and "passive" voice in the use of Chinese verbs. The "direction" of action is inferred from context. Here, since the lamp cannot turn on something else, *dēng kāi .le* has to mean "the lamp is turned on".

19. *Kàn* "look at" is a very common way to say "think" (cf. English "as I see it ..."). In many contexts, it is more natural than *xiǎng*.

20. *Fángdǐng* can be either "ceiling" (indoors) or "roof" (outdoors).

21. Even though *bǐ* does not appear in this sentence, there is no question that *ǎi .yi.diǎnr* **implies comparison**: "a bit lower (than some other ceiling)". Review note 9 above.

22. The pattern "A *méi.yǒu* B (*nèm.me*) Adj." (see note 11) makes a choice-type question this way:

A *yǒu méi.yǒu* B (*nèm.me*) Adj.?

 Zhèi-zhāng zhuō.zi yǒu méi.yǒu nèi- Is this table as big as that one?
  zhāng dà?
 Ná kuài.zi yǒu méi.yǒu ná chā.zi   Is holding chopsticks as easy as
  nèm róng.yì?   holding a fork?

In this pattern *yǒu méi.yǒu* is a set unit, similar to *shì .bú.shì*. Therefore *méi.yǒu* cannot be shortened to *méi*.

23. *Bùtóng* can be an adjective meaning "different" or a noun meaning "difference". As an adjective, it is often used in the pattern:

A *gēn* B *bùtóng*

to mean "A is different from B":

 Ni.de wū.zi gēn wǒ.de bùtóng. Your room is different from mine.

NOTE: You can use *bùtóng* in this pattern, but never *tóng* alone. To say that A and B are the same, use "A *gēn* B *yíyàng*" (note 13).

When *bùtóng* is used as a noun, it can be used with *yǒu* (or *méi.yǒu*) in a pattern that **always takes a modifier** like *shém* "what?", *yi.diǎnr* "a bit of", *hěn dà .de* "very big", etc:

A *gēn* B *(méi)yǒu* [modifier] *bùtóng*

Nǐ.de gǒu gēn wǒ.de yǒu shém   What difference is there between
   bùtóng?   your dog and mine?
Niǔyuē gēn Běijīng *yǒu* hěn   There are big differences between
   dà .de bùtóng.   New York and Peking.

In the sentence in the text, *shém* is used indefinitely (see II.1.7). *Búhuì yǒu shém bùtóng* means "are not likely to have any (important) differences".

24.   The final *.de* here is part of a *shì....de* construction with the *shì* omitted. (It would come before *búhuì* if it appeared in the sentence.) This use of *.de* frequently accompanies *huì* meaning "likely".

25.   *Kàn* as mentioned in note 19 means "think". *Zěmyàng* means "how is something (or someone)?". *Nǐ kàn zěmyàng* "what do you think?" is used to solicit someone's opinion:

   Nǐ kàn zhèi-běnr shū zěmyàng?   What do you think of this book?

Zěmyàng can precede *.de* N to mean "what kind of?":

   Tā shi zěmyàng .de yí.ge rén?   What kind of person is he?

Zěmyàng? can also be used, among close acquaintances, as a greeting roughly equivalent to "How's it going?" in English.

26.   *Juédìng* "decide". *Jiù zèm juédìng .le* "let's decide this way, let's settle on this". In general, *jiù zèm* V *.le* means "let's (or I'll) just V in this way". *Jiù zèm bàn* (manage) *.le* "let's just do it this way", *jiù zèm shuō .le* "let's just leave it (our talk) at that".

Culture Note 10:   "Fānqié" and Names for Other Imported Things

In traditional China "foreign lands" generally meant Central Asia, not lands across the ocean. The people who lived there were thought of as *hú* "uncivilized, barbarian", and the things they brought to China were often labeled using this word. Thus the Chinese began to call carrot *hú luó.bō*, literally "barbarian turnip". Other examples are *hú.qín* "(Chinese) fiddle"; *hújiāo* "pepper". Things imported from Central and South America were called *fān*, for example: *fānshǔ* "potato" (literally "barbarian sweet potato"); *fānqié* "barbarian eggplant—tomato". (In Peking the tomato is also called *xīhóngshì*, literally "Western red persimmon".)

Beginning in the 19th century, when people and things from Western countries began to arrive in China in large numbers, the word *yáng* "ocean" was used as a similar prefix because the newcomers had come from across the ocean. New words entered the Chinese language: *yángrén* "ocean person—Westerner"; *yánghuǒ* "ocean fire—matches"; *yángfáng* "Western (-style) house"; *yángcōng* "onion"; and many others. When bicycles were brought to Sìchuān they were first called *yángmǎ* "ocean horses".

Although *hú*, *fān*, and *yáng* were derogatory when they were first used, in time their derogatory use became obsolete. Today *fānqié* and *hújiāo* are just names for tomato and pepper. Nobody attaches any particular meaning to *fān* and *hú*. Similarly, people no longer think of "ocean" when they use the word *yáng*; it simply means "Western" or "foreign". For example the famous term "foreign devil", which comes from the Chinese word *yánggui.zi* "ocean ghost", was indeed derogatory in its origins. But in the latter half of the 20th century it has lost its sting. When children use it they mean no harm. Adult Chinese sometimes use it in jest, as do Westerners in self-satire.

Exercises

In-class exercises:

1.   Fill in the following blanks and read aloud.

    A.   *Kǒngpà* afraid that ... , perhaps

        1.   Wū.zi zèm xiǎo, zá.mén liǎng.ge rén zhù kǒngpà ... .ba. (not big enough)
        2.   Zhuō.zi tài ǎi, chuáng tài ruǎn, kǒngpà bù ... .ba. (comfortable)
        3.   Chuāng.zi tài xiǎo, kǒngpà ... .ba. (not bright enough)

    B.   Comparison.

        1.   Explicit.

            a)   Zhèi-jiān wū.zi bǐ nèi-jiān ... . (bigger)
            b)   Zhèi-zhāng chuáng bǐ nèi-zhāng ... . (harder)
            c)   Zhāng Sān *bǐ* Lǐ Sì ... . (much taller)

        2.   Implicit.

            a)   Zhèi-jiān wū.zi .de fáng*dǐng* hǎo.xiàng ... . (a bit lower)
            b)   Jīn.tiān wǎn.shàng .de niúròu ... . (a bit harder, over-cooked)

        3.   Equally Adj.

            a)   Zhèr .de wū.zi dōu yíyàng ... . (tall, high)
            b)   Měi-jiān wū.zi .de chuāng.zi dōu yíyàng ... . (large)
            c)   Wǒ mèi.x .de yǎn.jīng ... *wǒ* mǔ.qīn.de ... piào.liàng. (equally)
            d)   Érqiě wǒ mèi.x .de bí.zi yě ... *wǒ* mǔ.qīn.de ... gāo; *suǒ.yǐ* nǐ *kě*.yǐ shuō tā.mén liǎng.ge rén ... hǎokàn. (equally)

        4.   As Adj. as

            a)   Zhèi-jiān wū.zi yǒu méi.yǒu nèi-jiān ... liàng? (that, so)
            b)   Zhèi-jiān .de fángdǐng méi.yǒu nèi-jiān ... gāo. (that, so)

C.   *Jué.de* to feel, to think

     1.   Wǒ jué.de ... búgòu dà. (this room)
     2.   Wǒ jué.de ... fēicháng nán. (writing Chinese characters)
     3.   Wǒ jué.de Zhōng.guó-fàn ... . (very tasty)
     4.   Wǒ jué.de nǐ shuō .de huà ... . (very strange)
     5.   Wǒ jué.de zhèi-jiān wū.zi gēn ... chà.bùduō. (that one)
     6.   Nǐ jué.de ... ? (How? How about it?)

D.   *Juédìng* to decide

     1.   Wǒ juédìng míng.tiān ... liàn.xí pǎo-bù. (start)
     2.   Zá.mén jiù juédìng ... zhèi-jiān wū.zi .ba. (take, place order for)
     3.   Zhèi-jiān shì ... kuài .diǎnr juédìng. (we have to, we must)
     4.   Hǎo, jiù zèm.me ... .le. (decide)

2.   Omissions of the equivalent expressions

Given: Zhèi-jiān wū.zi .de chuāng.zi gēn nèi-jiān wū.zi .de chuāng.zi yíyàng dà.

Response: Zhèi-jiān wū.zi .de chuāng.zi gēn nèi-jiān (.de) yíyàng dà.

A.   Zhèi-jiā fànguǎnr .de fángdǐng bǐ nèi-jiā fànguǎnr .de fángdǐng gāo.
B.   Tā.de liǎn gēn wǒ.de liǎn yíyàng hóng.
C.   Jīn.tiān .de zǎofàn gēn zuó.tiān .de zǎofàn yíyàng nánchī.

Homework:

1.   Translate the following sentences into Chinese.

A.   This window is much bigger than that one.
B.   This window is bigger.
C.   This window is not as big as that one.
D.   This window is about the same size as that one.
E.   Shrimp is more tasty than chicken.
F.   Shrimp is a bit more tasty.
G.   Chicken is not as tasty as shrimp.
H.   Shrimp is as tasty as chicken.

Classroom/Homework exercises:

1.   Read the following questions aloud and answer them.

A.   Tā.mén kàn.le *něi*-liǎng-jiān fángjiān?
B.   Tā.mén xǐ.huān .bù.xǐ.huān wǔ-hào fángjiān? Wèishém.me?
C.   Wǔ-hào fángjiān dà hái.shi sān-hào fángjiān dà?
D.   Tā.mén juédìng zhù něi-jiān fángjiān?
E.   Sān-hào shi .bú.shi méi.yǒu wǔ-hào nèm liàng?
F.   Xué.shēng A wèishém shuō fángjiān búliàng yě búyàojǐn?
G.   Zhèr .de fángdǐng dōu yíyàng gāo .ma?
H.   Yào.shi nǐ .qù kàn-fáng.zi, nǐ zhùyì shém shì? *Qǐng* .nǐ shuō .yì.shuō nǐ jué.de shém.me yàojǐn, shém.me búyàojǐn.

I.   *Nǐ* xǐ.huān yí.ge rén (alone) zhù hái.shi gēn péng.yǒu yíkuàir zhù? Wèishém.me?

J.   Nǐ xiànzài .de xuéxiào gēn yǐqián .de xuéxiào yǒu shém bùtóng?

LESSON 2

Vocabulary

luàn	亂	in disorder, in a mess, in confusion		zhī.dào	知道	know
yuè...yuè...	越…越…	the more...the more...		xīnwén	新聞	news
shū	書	book		túshūguǎn	圖書館	library
búdàn... érqiě...	不但… 而且…	not only...but also...		cóng (TW) qǐ	從…起	starting from (TW)
běn (běnr)	本　本ㄦ	AN for book		dìng	定	set up
bùdéliǎo	不得了	'has-no-end', extremely		gōngzuò	工作	work
zhěng.lǐ	整理	to tidy up		shíjiān	時間	time
dào...PW...lái	到…來	come to...PW		shíjiānbiǎo	時間表	timetable, schedule
dào...PW...qù	到…去	go to...PW		xīngqī	星期	week
duì.bùqǐ	對不起	I'm sorry		sǎo-dì	掃地	to sweep the floor
wàng.le	忘了	forget		zuì hǎo	最好	had better...
fàng	放	to put		bǎ	把	pretransitive (see Grammar Notes)
shūjià.zi	書架子	bookshelf		zhǐ	紙	paper
bào	報	newspaper		ránhòu	然後	and then
kàn-bào	看報	to read a newspaper		tiē	貼	to paste, to stick
				qiáng	牆	wall

Vocabulary Classified by Type

Nouns		Verbs	
shū	gōngzuò	zhěng.lǐ	tiē
shūjià.zi	shíjiānbiǎo	wàng.le	
bào	xīngqī	fàng	
xīnwén	zhǐ	zhī.dào	
túshūguǎn	qiáng	dìng	

Pretransitives
bǎ

          ránhòu

Sentential Adverbs
cóng (TW) qǐ

Conjunctions
búdàn...érqiě...

ANs
běn (běnr)

V-Os
kàn-bào
sǎo-dì

Idiomatic Expressions
bùdéliǎo
duì.bùqǐ

Adjectives
luàn

Adverbs
yuè...yuè...
zuì hǎo

Grammar Notes

1. *Yuè* is an adverb used in pairs, often translatable as "the more...the more...". The common pattern is:

    Subject *yuè* Predicate$_1$ *yuè* Predicate$_2$

    Nèi-*zhǒng* gǒu yuè dà yuè   The bigger that kind of dog is the
       nánkàn.   uglier it is.

    The "predicates" can be either verbs or adjectives. If the verb or adjective in question is negative, you will need to use "the less" instead of "the more" to translate *yuè*:

    Wǒ yuè tīng yuè bù dǒng.   The more I listen the less I
                                     understand.

    Wǒ yuè bù dǒng yuè búyào tīng. The less I understand the less I want
                                     to listen.

    When the predicate is a verb that has an object, it is normal to *prepose* the object before subject, in topic-comment fashion:

    Object Subject *yuè* Predicate$_1$ *yuè* Predicate$_2$

    Zhōng.guó-zì tā yuè xiě yuè   The more she writes Chinese
       hǎo.   characters the better they get.
    Lóngxiā wǒ yuè chī yuè   The more I eat lobster the more
       xi.huān chī.   I like it.

    WARNING: The English phrases "the more" and "the less" precede nouns and pronouns. But *yuè* is an adverb. Therefore it must directly precede a verb, and **never** precedes a noun or pronoun. Never let yourself say something like "*yuè wǒ*..." or "*yuè lóngxiā*...".

    Sometimes you will want to say that just **one** verb or adjective is getting "more and more" (or "less and less"), without measuring it against the progress of another verb or adjective. How, for example, would you say "my Chinese is getting better and better"? You still use *yuè...yuè...*, but employ *lái* "come" as a "dummy predicate" to go with the first *yuè*:

    Subject *yuè lái yuè* Predicate

Wǒ.de Zhōngwén yuè lái yuè hǎo.   My Chinese gets better and better.
Wū.zi.li yuè lái yuè luàn.   It's getting messier and messier in
                                     the room.

Yuè can also be used with two different subjects:

Subject₁ *yuè* Predicate₁, Subject₂ *yuè* Predicate₂

Wǒ yuè hē-chá, dù.zi yuè è.   The more I drink tea, the hungrier
                                     I get.

Tā yuè shuō wǒ yuè bù dǒng.   The more he talks about it the less
                                     I understand.

2.   *Yì-tiān bǐ yì-tiān luàn* "messier day by day" exemplifies the pattern:

yì-AN *bǐ yì*-AN Adj.

Xīn sùshè.li .de wū.zi yì-jiān   The rooms in the new dorm are (seem)
   bǐ yì-jiān dà.   each bigger than the next.
Tā.de sì.ge mèi.x yí.ge bǐ yí.ge   Each of her four younger sisters is
   piào.liàng.   prettier than the next.

"Nǐ.de yī.fú yuè lái yuè duō, zá.mén zhè wū.zi yì-tiān bǐ yì-tiān luàn."

3.   *Bù shǎo*, literally "not few", means "quite a lot".

4.   The *.a* indicates mild reproach.

5. *Búdàn* "not only" frequently precedes a second clause containing *érqiě* to form the pattern:

$$\text{S } \textit{búdàn } V_1 \textit{ érqiě } V_2$$

Bìngqiě can substitute freely for *érqiě*. Examples:

Tā búdàn huì shuō Zhōng.guó-huà, érqiě huì xiě Zhōng.guó-zì.	She not only can speak Chinese, but also can write characters.
Zhèi.ge sùshè búdàn wū.zi dà, bìngqiě chuáng *yě* hěn shū.fú.	Not only are the rooms big in this dormitory, but its beds are comfortable as well.

Érqiě and *bìngqiě* can also be used without a preceding *búdàn* clause. See III.1.13 (in text) for an example.

6. *Běnr* is the Běijīng retroflex version of *běn* "volume", which is the AN for books. *Dōng yì-běnr, xī yì-běnr* "one at the east, one at the west" is like the English "one here, one there"--i.e., "all over the place".

7. *Jiǎnzhí*, literally "simple and straight", often implies a bit of exasperation, as in the English word "downright", or "simply" in the phrase "simply outrageous".

8. *Bùdéliǎo*, literally "not reaching an end", can be used by itself to mean "wonderful" or "amazing" or "awful" or just "wow!". But in the very common usage "Adj..de bùdéliǎo" (where the *.de* can be understood as short for *.dào* "to the point of"), *bùdéliǎo* means "extremely", or "unbelievably". Thus *rè .de bùdéliǎo* "extremely hot", *hǎo .de bùdéliǎo* "great!", etc.

9. *Guò* here is not the suffix *.guò* "have had the experience of" described in II.2.31. It is a resultative complement (as in I.5.12) to the verb *zhěng.lǐ*, and means "have finished" or "already done". The pronunciation of the two *guò* is also different. While the suffix *.guò* is always pronounced in neutral tone, for the complement *guò* the neutral tone is optional. It is often pronounced in the full fourth tone. The complement *guò* is also a special case of the resultative complement, because, unlike the regular resultative complement, no *.de* or *.bú* can be inserted to form a potential complement. (It is incorrect to say *zhěng.lǐ .de guò* or *zhěng.lǐ .bú guò*.)

10. This sentence is actually an example of the use of *yuè* with two different subjects (see the last part of note 1, above), because the subject *shū* is implied before the second *yuè*.

11. This is an example of the pattern "*dào* Place Word *lái*" (review I.5.23). *.Shàng* "on" is the localizer that makes *chuáng.shàng* a Place Word.

12. *Duì.bùqǐ* and *duì.búzhù* mean "I'm sorry" or "Excuse me". Literally they are potential complements meaning "cannot raise (my head) to face (you)" and "cannot face (you) and hold that position".

13. Determinatives (like *zhèi*) and numbers (like *jǐ*) normally both take an AN (see I.1.11). But they can also share an AN: *zhèi-jǐ-běnr shū* "these few books", *nèi*

sān.ge rén "those three people", etc. Note also the operation of tone *sandhi* in the phrase *zhèi-jǐ-běnr wǒ...* . *Jǐ*, of course, changes to second tone because of *běnr*. But because there could be a short pause between *běnr* and *wǒ*, *běnr* does not necessarily change to second tone.

14. *Wàng* "forget" rarely stands alone. It almost always is used with *.le* (*wàng.le*) or *.jì* (*wàng.jì*).

15. This *.le* indicates a new discovery of an existing situation (see I.3.9). *Fàng .dào shūjià.zi.shàng* is an example of Bound Phrase Complement, i.e., *.dào* + Place Word in the complement position (see II.2.35 and II.3.7).

16. *Yǐhòu* "in the future" is a moveable time word like *yǐqián*. On this point and the contrast with *hòulái*, see II.4.22 and 26.

17. In Unit I (I.5.24), you learned that *zài* "be in, at, on" could be a main verb followed by a Place Word, as in *X zài zhèr* "X is in this place". Here, *kàn-bào* is the main verb and *zài* is the First Position Verb (FPV); *zài wū.zi.li* is in the adverbial position (before the verb) to tell where the action of the main verb takes place. (See also note 27 below.)

18. Note that both the subject and the conditionality (if...then...) are implied in this sentence.

19. *Túshū* "books (collective term)", and *guǎn* "establishment" make *túshūguǎn* "library". *Guǎn* (or *guǎnr*) is used for many kinds of "establishment". Because the "diminutive suffix" *-r* tends to be used more with small or informal things, *guǎnr* is often used in such words as *fànguǎnr* "restaurant", *cháguǎnr* "teahouse", and *kāfēiguǎnr* "coffeehouse" (although *fànguǎn*, *cháguǎn*, and *kāfēiguǎn* are also common). But **only** *guǎn*, not *guǎnr*, is used for larger, more formal establishments: *túshūguǎn*, *bówùguǎn* "museum", *dàshǐguǎn* "embassy".

Note that the pattern used here is "*dào* Place Word *.qù*" (see I.5.23). *Túshūguǎn* acts as a Place Word even though there is no localizer attached. This is possible with certain polysyllabic nouns.

20. Here *.qù* is part of the "*dào* PW *.qù*" pattern, but it also works with the following verb (*kàn*) to mean "in order to": *.qù kàn-bào* "go (in order) to read the paper". *.Qù* in this usage can come before the verb, after the verb, or both places:

        Wǒ dào sùshè .qù ná yī.fú.
        Wǒ dào sùshè ná yī.fú .qù.   I'm going to the dormitory to
        Wǒ dào sùshè .qù ná yī.fú   get my clothes.
          .qù.

21. *Cóng jīn.tiān qǐ* "from-today-begin—starting today". Other time words can substitute for *jīn.tiān* in the same pattern.

22. *Gōngzuò shíjiānbiǎo* "job-time-chart—schedule of chores".

23. *Xīngqī*, literally "star period", and *lǐbài*, literally "(weekly) religious worship" are both standard words for "week". Probably because of its religious (and specifically Christian) connotations, *lǐbài* is not used in the People's Republic

of China in any formal or official contexts, including most printed materials. It continues in very wide use colloquially, however. In Taiwan and overseas Chinese communities, both *lǐbài* and *xīngqī* are common.

Xīngqīyī-sān-wǔ is a contraction for *xīngqīyī gēn xīngqīsān gēn xīngqīwǔ*. *Xīngqī* itself can also be omitted, so that *yī-sān-wǔ* means "Monday-Wednesday-Friday" and *èr-sì-liù* means "Tuesday-Thursday-Saturday".

24. *Lái* "come" can stand in for another verb so that *nǐ lái* means "you do it". (Cf. the role of *lái* as a "dummy predicate" in the *yuè* pattern, note 1 above.)

25. *Zuì* "most" is used to make a superlative of the adjective that follows: *zuì dà* "biggest", *zuì qíguài* "strangest," etc. But here *zuì hǎo* has a special adverbial use, meaning "had better" or "had best".

26. **The pretransitive bǎ.** We have seen that Chinese objects frequently follow verbs in the familiar order:

Subject + Verb + Object

Zá.mén zuì hǎo xiě gōngzuò shíjiānbiǎo.

(S)   (V)   (O)

We have also seen that complements follow verbs in the pattern:

Subject + Verb + Complement

Zá.mén zuì hǎo xiě .zài zhǐ.shàng.

(S)   (V)   (C)

A problem can arise when **both** an object and a complement go with the same verb. It would appear that a "traffic jam" might result behind the verb. And indeed, Chinese does avoid having both the complement and the object after the verb. In such cases the pretransitive *bǎ* is used to move the object up **before** the verb, leaving the complement after the verb and thus solving the "traffic jam". The pattern is:

Subject + *bǎ* + Object + Verb + Complement or other elements

(This formula is adapted from **Modern Chinese Reader**, Peking: Epoch Publishing House, 1963.)

Zá.mén zuì hǎo bǎ gōngzuò shíjiānbiǎo xiě .zài zhǐ.shàng.
‾‾‾‾‾   ‾‾‾‾‾‾‾‾‾‾‾‾‾‾‾‾‾‾‾ ‾‾ ‾‾‾‾‾‾‾‾‾‾‾
(S)   (O)   (V)   (C)

The minimum "other element" that can follow the verb is a simple *.le*.

Note that adverbs (in this case *zuì hǎo*) come before the *bǎ*. This is quite natural because *bǎ* itself is, originally, a verb. In fact you can sometimes think of it as meaning "take" (as if you were saying, "we had best 'take' the work

schedule and write it down on paper"). But it will usually be an overtranslation
to use "take" in your English translation. Study the following examples:

> *Qǐng* .nǐ bǎ shū fàng.dào   Please put the books onto the
>   shūjià.zi.shàng .qù.   bookshelf.
> Wǒ zuó.tiān bǎ wū.zi.lì .de   I straightened up all the things in
>   dōng.xī dōu *zhěng*.li guò.le.   the room yesterday.
> Bǎ lóngxiā chī-wán, .hǎo .bù.hǎo?   How about finishing the lobster?

The best way to master the *bǎ* usage (or any point of grammar, for that matter) is
to memorize and imitate examples, not to study theoretical rules. But just as a
check on your imitative efforts, we offer the following rules about *bǎ*:

   (1) The object has to be a definite object, not an indefinite object. If you
say:

> Wǒ yào .dào túshūguǎn .qù   I want to go to the library to read
>   kàn-shū.   some books.

you are talking about "a" book or "some" books (an indefinite object). But if you
say:

> Wǒ yào .dào túshūguǎn .qù bǎ   I want to go to the library to
>   shū kàn-wan.   finish reading the book.

then you are talking about a certain book or certain books (a definite object).

   (2) You *must* have something else (usually a complement) after the verb in
order to use *bǎ*.

   (3) *Bǎ* is not used with potential complements. (See II.1.18 to review
potential complements.)

   (4) *Bǎ* is not used with complements containing *jiàn*, such as *kàn.jiàn* "see",
tīng.jiàn "hear", etc.

27. In note 17 above, you saw how "*zài* + Place Word" could **precede** a verb to tell
where it happened. Here, in the phrase *xiě .zài zhǐ.shàng*, you see "*zài* + Place
Word" **follow** the verb *xiě* to tell its result:

Adverbial Position		Complement Position
(tells location)		(tells result)
zài + Place Word	VERB	.*zài* + Place Word

Example of adverbial position:

> Bié zài wū.zi.lì kàn-bào.   Don't read the newspaper in the room.

Example of complement position:

> *Qǐng* .nǐ xiě .zài zhǐ.shàng.   Please write it down on paper.

Similarly, the phrase "*dào* + Place Word + *lái/qù*" can also appear either before or after the main verb. There is an important distinction of meaning between the two usages:

> Tā dào jiē.shàng .qù pǎo-bù.   He's going out onto the street to jog.
> Tā pǎo .dào jiē.shàng .qù.   He's running out onto the street.

Before the main verb, "*dào* + Place Word + *lái/qù*" tells where the subject is going in order to do the main verb. **After** it, the phrase tells the result (destination) of the main verb

Note that there are two places in this sentence ("zuì hǎo bǎ" and "shíjiānbiǎo xiě") where third-tone syllables appear next to each other, yet we have not indicated tone *sandhi* by italics in the text. In both cases this is because there can be a slight pause between the two third-tone syllables, preventing tone *sandhi* from applying. In the case of "zuì hǎo" there may not be a following pause, but in that case "hǎo" would become neutral tone, not second tone.

28. *Ránhòu* "and then" can be used to refer, either in the past or the future, to an event that came, or will come, *after another event*. You should review clearly the distinctions among *yǐhòu* (note 16 above), *hòulái* (II.4.26), and *ránhòu*.

29. In III.1.7 you saw how to compare **nouns** using *bǐ*. To compare **verbs** (as in "you write better than I"), you can use the pattern:

$$S_1 \quad V\text{-}O \quad V \ .de \quad bǐ \quad S_2 \ Adj.$$

> *Nǐ* xiě-zì xiě .de *bǐ wǒ* hǎo.   You write better than I.

Note that the verb is said twice—first paired with the object (*xiě-zì*) and then paired with the predicative complement (*xiě .de hǎo*). The verbs and objects in the pattern are not limited to standard V-O compounds like *xiě-zì* and *shuō-huà*, but can be any verbs or objects that make sense:

> Tā shuō Yīngwén shuō .de *bǐ wǒ* hǎo.   She speaks English better than I.

There is an alternate position for the "*bǐ* S_2" element in this pattern:

$$S_1 \quad V\text{-}O \quad bǐ \quad S_2 \quad V \ .de \ Adj.$$

> Tā shuō Yīngwén *bǐ* wǒ shuō .de hǎo.   She speaks English better than I.

In the example in the text, note that the first V, the one that goes with the O, is omitted. This omission is entirely natural in either of the formulas given above, and implies no change of meaning whatsoever. Thus the following are also normal patterns:

$$S_1 \quad O \quad V \ .de \quad bǐ \quad S_2 \ Adj.$$

> Tā Yīngwén shuō .de *bǐ wǒ* hǎo.   She speaks English better than I.

$$S_1 \quad O \quad bǐ \quad S_2 \quad V \ .de \ Adj.$$

> Tā Yīngwén *bǐ wǒ* shuō .de hǎo.   She speaks English better than I.

Sometimes no object is involved at all, either because the verb has no object or because the object is an implied "it" (review I.4.24). In this case the alternative patterns are simply:

$$S_1 \text{ V } .de \text{ } bĭ \text{ } S_2 \text{ Adj.}$$

Tā shuō .de *bĭ wŏ* hǎo.   She speaks (it) better than I.

$$S_1 \text{ } bĭ \text{ } S_2 \text{ V } .de \text{ Adj.}$$

Tā *bĭ* wŏ shuō .de hǎo.   She speaks (it) better than I.

30.   This *lái* is similar to the *lái* at note 24, although here it accompanies, rather than replaces, the main verb. *Nĭ lái xiĕ* would be similar to "you do the writing" in English.

Exercises

In-class exercises:

1.   Fill in the following blanks and read aloud.

   A.   *Yuè* A *yuè* B

       1.   Tā.de Zhōng.guó-huà yuè ... yuè ... . (speak; fast)
       2.   *Xiǎo* gǒu yuè ... yuè ... . (jump; high)
       3.   Nǐ chī .de yuè duō dù.zi ... . (getting bigger)
       4.   Niàn-shū, ... (the more you study) yuè hú.tú (confused).

   B.   *Yuè lái yuè* ... more and more ...

       1.   Yī.fú yuè lái yuè ... . (many, more)
       2.   Wū.zi yuè lái yuè ... . (messy)
       3.   Xué.shēng yuè lái yuè ... . (few)
       4.   Fàn yuè lái yuè ... . (bad)
       5.   Zhōngwén yuè lái yuè ... . (difficult)
       6.   Tā.de Yīngwén shuǐpíng yuè lái yuè ... . (high)

   C.   Change the sentences in Exercise B using *yì-tiān bǐ yì-tiān*.

   D.   *Dōng yì-... , xī yì-...*

       1.   Dōng yì-běnr, xī yì-běnr, dōu.shi tā.de ... . (books)
       2.   Dōng yí-jiàn, xī yí-jiàn, dōu.shi tā.de ... . (clothes)
       3.   Dì.shàng *yǒu* hěn duō ... , dōng yì-zhāng, xī yì-zhāng. (newspaper)
       4.   ... hěn luàn, dōng yì-bǎ xī yì-bǎ. (chairs)

   E.   *Zěm.me* how

       1.   Bú kàn-bào zěm zhī.dào ... ? (news)
       2.   Bù ... zěm kàn.de-jiàn? (turn on the light)

3.   Nǐ bù qǐng .tā chī-fàn, tā zěm huì ... ? (help you)
4.   Bù tiānx ... zěm xiě .de hǎo? (practice)

F.   *Cóng ... qǐ* (kāishǐ) starting from ...

1.   Cóng jīn.tiān qǐ zá.mén dìng yí.ge ... . (work schedule)
2.   Cóng míng.tiān qǐ zá.mén yíkuàir ... , .hǎo .bù.hǎo? (jog)
3.   Cóng xiànzài qǐ zá.mén yào ... yùn.dòng. (every day)
4.   Cóng ... kāishǐ zá.mén zhǐ shuō Zhōng.guó-huà, bù shuō Yīngwén.
     (tomorrow)

G.   *Wàng.le* forget

1.   Bié wàng.le, míng.tiān ... zá.mén yíkuàir qù pǎo-bù. (morning)
2.   Bié wàng.le bǎ shū fàng .dào ... .shàng .qù. (book shelf)
3.   Tā shi shéi? Wǒ wàng.le tā.de ... jiào shém.me .le. (name)
4.   *Qǐng* .nǐ xiě ... .de "xiā" .zìr (.zì) *gěi* .wǒ kàn, .hǎo .bù.hǎo?
     .Ai.ya, wǒ wàng.le zhèi.ge zì zěm xiě .le. (lobster)

H.   *Zuì hǎo*

1.   Nǐ yuè lái yuè pàng (fat) .le, nǐ ... cóng jīn.tiān qǐ bié chī
     bīng.qílíng (ice cream) .le.
2.   Tā jīn.tiān hěn máng, méi.yǒu kòngr gēn .nǐ tán, nǐ ... míng.tiān ...
     lái .ba.
3.   Nǐ yào.shi jué.de bùshū.fú, ... xiū.xí (rest), bié chū.qù .le.
4.   Wū.zi tài luàn .le, wǒ.mén ... zhěng.lǐ vx.

Homework:

1.   Translate the following sentences into Chinese.

A.   Do you know where the library is?
B.   Who put the books on my bed? (Use the *bǎ* construction.)
C.   You said that I didn't tidy up the room very well. Well then, you do it.
D.   Look at your clothes—one piece here, one piece there; it's a total mess.
     (AN for clothes is *jiàn*.)
E.   I am sorry. I have pasted the work schedule on your lamp. (Use the *bǎ*
     construction.)
F.   I didn't have breakfast this morning, and I ran over ten miles. I am simply
     starving.
G.   He writes Chinese characters slower than I do, but he eats lobster much
     faster than I do.

Classroom/Homework exercises:

1.   *Búdàn ... érqiě ...*

Combine the two sentences into one, using *búdàn* and *érqiě*.

A.   Chuāng.zi dà. Chuāng.zi liàng.
B.   Zhāng Rúsī huì shuō Zhōng.guó-huà. Zhāng Rúsī huì shuō Yīngwén.

C.   Yīn.wèi wǒ .zài Zhōng.guó zhù.guò suǒ.yi wǒ huì yòng kuài.zi chī-fàn.
      Yīn.wèi wǒ .zài Zhōng.guó zhù.guò suǒ.yi wǒ huì yòng Zhōng.guó fá.zi
      pào-chá.
D.   Pǎo mǎ.lāsōng .de rén děi tiānx liàn.xí pǎo. Pǎo mǎ.lāsōng .de rén děi zuò
      bié.de yùn.dòng.

2.   Use the given verbs (with objects) and complements to form sentences using the "bǎ
      construction."

      Example:
            zhěng.lǐ wū.zi; hǎo
            Jīn.tiān wǒ děi bǎ wū.zi zhěng.lǐ hǎo.

A.   hē jītāng; wán
B.   xiě "xiā" zhèi.ge zì; zài zhǐ.shàng
C.   xiě míng.zì; duì

3.   Omissions of the equivalent expressions

      Given: Nǐ xiě-zì xiě .de bǐ wǒ xiě-zì xiě .de hǎo.

      Response: Nǐ xiě-zì xiě .de bǐ wǒ hǎo.
                 Nǐ zì xiě .de bǐ wǒ hǎo.

A.   Nǐ shuō-huà shuō .de bǐ wǒ shuō-huà shuō .de kuài.
B.   Tā ná kuài.zi ná .de bǐ wǒ ná kuài.zi ná .de hǎo.
C.   Wǒ kàn Zhōngwén shū kàn .de bǐ lǎoshī kàn Zhōngwén shū kàn .de duō.
D.   Tā pào Zhōng.guó chá pào .de bǐ wǒ pào Zhōng.guó chá pào .de hǎo.

LESSON 3

Vocabulary

tǐng	挺	rather, pretty
pián.yí	便宜	inexpensive
lí	離	"distanced" from
jìn	近	close to, near
xiàng... zhèyàngr	像...這樣ㄦ	as...as this
chángx (cháng)	常常 常常	often, frequently
chídào	遲到	arrive late
yóuqí	尤其	especially
suǒ	所	AN for buildings
zuì	最	the most...; ...-est
suàn	算	be considered as
gèng	更	even more...
búguò	不過	but; however
yīnggāi	應該	should, ought to
zuò	做	to do
shuō.qǐ.lái	說起來	(see Grammar Notes)
zuò.qǐ.lái	做起來	(see Grammar Notes)
....qǐ.lái	起來	begin to...
jiǎndān	簡單	simple
lóuxià	樓下	downstairs
fēng	封	AN for letter

xìn	信	letter
ná	拿	take
duōxiè	多謝	many thanks
zāogāo	糟糕	what a mess, gosh!
qīn.qī	親戚	relative
fùjìn	附近	vicinity
zhāodài	招待	entertain
mǎshàng	馬上	immediately
búbì	不必	needn't
jǐn.zhāng	緊張	tense, uptight
xià	下	next
zuò-shì	做事	do things
xiànglái	向來	all along
màn	慢	slow
cónglái (bù, méi)	從來不沒	never
wù-shì	誤事	cause delay, bumble matters
guài	怪	to blame
lìkè	立刻	right away
dòng-shǒu	動手	'move-hand', begin to
bùxíng	不行	will not do
kǎoshì	考試	test, exam
kàn-shū	看書	to read

Vocabulary Classified by Type

Nouns	jǐn.zhāng	shuō.qǐ.lái
xìn	màn	zuò.qǐ.lái
qīn.qī		
kǎoshì	**Adverbs**	**V-Os**
	tǐng	zuò-shì
Verbs	chángx (cháng)	wù-shì
lí	yóuqí	dòng-shǒu
chídào	zuì	kàn-shū
suàn	gèng	
zuò	mǎshàng	**Place Words**
ná	xiànglái	lóuxià
zhāodài	cónglái	fùjìn
guài	lìkè	
		Exclamations
Auxiliary Verbs	**ANs**	zāogāo
yīnggāi	suǒ	
búbì	fēng	**Determinatives**
		xià
Adjectives	**Conjunctions**	
pián.yí	búguò	**Idiomatic Expressions**
jìn		xiàng...zhèyàngr
jiǎndān	**Verb Complements**	
zāogāo	....qǐ.lái	

Grammar Notes

1. *Yào*, meaning "want", can also mean "soon will" or "is going to". Review other meanings of *yào* at I.4.11 and I.5.21.

2. *Tǐng* "pretty, rather". *Tǐng shū.fú* "rather comfortable"; *tǐng yǒu yì.sī* "pretty interesting", etc.

3. *Lí* is used to indicate the distance between two things. The pattern is:

    $$A \; \textit{lí} \; B \; \textit{.hěn} \begin{Bmatrix} \textit{jìn.} \\ \textit{yuǎn.} \end{Bmatrix} \qquad A \; \text{is} \begin{Bmatrix} \text{close to} \\ \text{far from} \end{Bmatrix} B.$$

    To say how many miles (or *lǐ*) one thing is from another, you can use:

    $$A \; \textit{lí} \; B \; X \; \textit{lǐ} \qquad\qquad A \text{ is } X \textit{ lǐ} \text{ from } B$$

4. *Xiàng* (someone or something) *zhèyàngr* Verb (or Adj.) means Verb-ing in the manner of (someone or something).

5. *Yóuqí* "especially" is an adverb. It must, therefore, precede a verb or adjective. *Yóuqí děi zhù .de jìn* "especially needs to live close by"; *yóuqí shū.fú* "especially comfortable".

6. *Cái xíng* (literally, "only then will it do") reinforces the sense of *děi* "must". *Nǐ děi zhù .de jìn .yì .diǎnr cái xíng* means "you must live closer by".

7. *Suàn*, originally "calculate", commonly means "reckon, regard", or "be regarded as, be considered to be". Thus, *bùnéng suàn.shi* means "can't be considered to be" or "can't be regarded as". WARNING: The opposite of *bùnéng suàn.shi* is *kě.yi suàn.shi* (not *néng suàn.shi*).

> Wǒ.mén .de wū.zi bùnéng suàn.shi   Our room can't be considered the
>   zuì luàn .de.   messiest.
> Wǒ.mén .de wū.zi *kě*.yi suàn.shi   Our room can be considered the
>   zuì luàn .de.   messiest.

8. *Gèng* precedes adjectives to mean "even more (Adj.)" Thus *gèng luàn* "even messier", *gèng pián.yí* "even less expensive", etc.

9. *Gēn huài.de bǐ* "compare with the bad ones". In general, *gēn* X *bǐ* = "compare with X".

10. As a verbal complement, *.qǐ.lái* can mean "begin" or "set about". Thus *shuō.qǐ.lái* has the sense of "when one first speaks of it", while *zuò.qǐ.lái* in the next line means "when one sets about doing it". The sentence as a whole is similar in spirit to the English phrase "easier said than done".

> If the verb to which *.qǐ.lái* is attached has an object, it splits *.qǐ* and *.lái*: *shuō.qǐ huà .lái* "begin speaking"; *xiě.qǐ zì .lái* "begin writing characters"; etc.

11. *Ná.shàng.lái*, literally "take + up (the stairs) + come (toward you)" is called a directional complement. We will study these in detail in IV.2.8. For now, learn *ná.shàng.lái* as "bring up (stairs)".

12. *Zāogāo*, literally "messy-cake", is a very lively, but not obscene, expression of alarm or disgust at something.

13. *Xìn* "letter", uses the AN *fēng*. *Lái* "come" and *qù* "go" can be used with *xìn* to mean "send (a letter)":

> Tā *gěi* .wǒ lái.le yì-fēng xìn.   She wrote me a letter.
> *Wǒ* gěi .tā qù.le yì-fēng xìn.   I wrote her a letter.

14. **Pivot sentences.** Consider the following sentences:

> A. *Wǒ* yǒu .ge qīn.qī.   I have a relative.
> B. Qīn.qī zhù .zài fùjìn.   The relative lives nearby.

In sentence A, *qīn.qī* is the object. In sentence B, it is the subject. While A and B can both stand on their own as independent sentences, they can also be combined, as they are in the text, by "pivoting" on *qīn.qī*. The resulting sentence means "I have a relative *who* lives nearby." In the following examples, the pivot word is in **boldface**:

> *Wǒ* yǒu .ge **péng.yǒu** huì shuō   I have a friend who can speak

Zhōng.guó-huà.   Chinese.
Wǒ kàn.jiàn.guò **gǒu** yòng   I have seen a dog eat with
kuài.zi chī-fàn.   chopsticks.

15. *Búbi* "no need to" precedes adjectives or verbs. *Nǐ búbi jǐn.zhāng* means "You need
not be nervous—don't worry". *Bì* cannot be used alone, but only in the negative
búbi. To say the opposite of *búbi*, use *děi* "must". To summarize:

        must or have to V = *děi* + V
        don't have to V = *búbi* or *búyòng* + V
        should or ought to V = *yīnggāi* + V
        shouldn't or ought not to V = *bù yīnggāi* + V

16. *Jǐn.zhāng* "tense, nervous" has, in recent years in the People's Republic of China,
taken on the meaning "to be in short supply": *Běijīng .de fáng.zi hěn jǐn.zhāng*
means "housing in Běijīng is 'tense'—i.e., hard to get."

17. For the distinction between *lǐbài* and *xīngqī*, review III.2.23. The days of the
week are:

        Monday   *lǐbàiyī*   or   *xīngqīyī*
        Tuesday   *lǐbài'èr*   or   *xīngqī'èr*
        Wednesday   *lǐbàisān*   or   *xīngqīsān*
        Thursday   *lǐbàisì*   or   *xīngqīsì*
        Friday   *lǐbàiwǔ*   or   *xīngqīwǔ*
        Saturday   *lǐbàiliù*   or   *xīngqīliù*
        Sunday   *lǐbàitiān*   or   *xīngqītiān*
                or   *lǐbàirì*   or   *xīngqīrì*

"Next week" is *xià(.ge) lǐbài* or *xià(.ge) xīngqī* (literally, "the week below");
"last week" is *shàng(.ge) lǐbài* or *shàng(.ge) xīngqī* ("the week above"). To specify a certain day in the next or last week, simply add the number of the day of
the week:

        shàng(.ge) lǐbàisān   Wednesday of last week
        xià(.ge) xīngqīwǔ   Friday of next week

Be careful not to equate these usages with the common English phrases "last Wednesday" or "next Friday". When we say "next Friday" in English we mean the next
Friday to arrive—which may or may not be the Friday of next week. In the example
in the text, it is clear that *xīngqīwǔ* is not "next Friday".

18. *Cái* is used between a Time Word and a verb to give the sense of "later than
expected." *Tā xià.ge xīngqīwǔ cái lái* means "He's coming a week from Friday (and
that's later than you were expecting)". The meaning is similar to the English "He
won't come until a week from Friday".

19. *Yí.ge duō lǐbài* "more than one week (but less than two)". The pattern:

                    No. + AN + *duō* + Noun

means "more than the given number (but less than the next highest)". It is normally used only for the numbers below 10:

| sān.ge duō yuè | more than three months (but less than four) |
| sì-nián duō | more than four years (but not five) |

Note that this pattern works only with nouns that are easily divisible, such as months and years. If you say *sān.ge duō rén* you will not be understood.

With higher numbers, you can use the pattern:

$$\text{No.} + duō + \text{AN} + \text{Noun}$$

to mean "several more than the given number". In this pattern, the number is a multiple of ten and *duō* stands for an indefinite additional number of units. For example:

| èr.shí duō (.ge) lìbài | more than twenty weeks (maybe twenty-two or twenty-three) |
| sānbǎi duō (.ge) rén | over three hundred people |

Note that the second pattern can use any kind of noun, whether easily divisible or not.

20. *Xiànglái* "always have (Verb-ed)" or "always have been (Adj.)".

21. Review note 18 above on the use of *cái*. *Jiù* has an exactly parallel use that conveys the sense of "sooner than expected", or "right on time". *Nǐ zuì hǎo xiànzài jiù kāishǐ* means "you'd better start now (sooner than you expected)". Study the pattern:

$$\text{Subject} + \text{Time Word} + \left\{ \begin{array}{c} ji\grave{u} \\ c\acute{a}i \end{array} \right\} + \text{Verb}$$

Whether *jiù* or *cái* (or neither) is used does not affect the basic fact that a certain action happens at a certain time. *Jiù* or *cái* tells only whether the action was sooner or later than somebody expected. For example, if I was expecting two letters to arrive on Wednesday, but one came on Tuesday and the other on Thursday, I might say: *Dìyī-fēng xìn lǐbài'èr jiù lái .le, dì'èr-fēng lǐbàisì cái dào.*

22. *Cónglái* "always have (not)" should be studied together with *xiànglái* (note 20). They differ in that *cónglái* must be followed by a negative, either *méi(.yǒu)* or *bù (bú)*. *Cónglái méi(.yǒu)* takes *.guò* after the verb:

| Wǒ cónglái méi kàn.jiàn.guò tā. | I've never seen him. |
| Tā cónglái méi.yǒu xiě.guò Zhōngwén xìn. | She's never written a letter in Chinese. |

The implication of such sentences is that the action has not happened in the past, although it might happen in the future. Using *bù (bú)* with *cónglái*, the implication is slightly different. It suggests that the speaker has a kind of policy or resolve that has prevented action in the past and probably will continue to prevent it in the future:

| Wǒ cónglái bù hē kāfēi. | I don't drink coffee (now or in the past). |

> Tā cónglái bù xǐ.huān gǒu.   She is not a dog-lover.

In examples using *bù*, *xiànglái* can be substituted for *cónglái*. But *xiànglái* cannot stand in for *cónglái* in the examples that use *méi....guò*.

23. *Guài* is normally an adjective meaning "peculiar, queer". *Guàirén* means "strange person—an eccentric". Here *guài* is used transitively: "to find (someone) peculiar," which comes to mean "to blame".

24. "*Hái.shi* + Verb + *.ba*" has the sense "it would be better (after all, all things considered) to Verb".

25. *Zài shuō*, literally "and speak of it again", can follow Time Words to mean "wait until (a certain time) before doing anything".

Culture Note 11: More on Chinese Names

In addition to regular *xìng* and *míng.zi*, (see Culture Note 1, Unit I, Lesson 1), Chinese names have traditionally included a variety of other kinds.

Many children are given "childhood names" (*xiǎo míngr*). For boys, these are often drawn from names of (1) animals: *Xiǎo Niú* "Little Cow", *Xiǎo Gǒu.zi* "Little Dog"; or (2) solid things: *Shí.tóu* "Stone"; *Zhù.zi* "Pillar". Girls' names are often of (3) ornaments: *Jīn chuànr* "Golden Bracelet"; *Xiǎo Yù* "Little Jade"; or (4) just *Xiǎo mèi* "Little Sister"; *Niū.x* "Little Girl"; etc. Both sexes have used (5) poundage at birth: *Qī-jīn* "Seven pounds"; *Jiǔ-jīn* "Nine pounds".

In the past, among uneducated people, "childhood names" could stick for a lifetime—sometimes being modified to account for having grown up, e.g., *Xiǎo Niú* might become *Dà Niú* "Big Cow". But if children registered for school, they would use their formal *míng.zi*.

The common people have also often used, as informal names, "Surname plus number": *Zhāng Sān* "Zhāng Number Three"; *Lǐ Sì* "Lǐ Number Four"; *Wáng Èr* "Wáng Number Two".

Among the literate classes, names also included *zì* and *hào*, which in English have been referred to as "courtesy names" or "style names" (*zì*) and "studio names" (*hào*).

Zì. In ancient times, *zì* were given to a boy when he reached manhood (at 20) and to a girl when she attained maturity (at 15). Often an honorable guest who attended the ceremonies celebrating these occasions (i.e., manhood or maturity) was requested to select a *zì* for the boy or girl. In later times such formalities became obsolete, and a child's *zì* came to be chosen by the parents just as the *míng.zi* was. *Zì* normally consisted of two characters. Their meanings were often chosen to supplement or complement the meaning of the *míng.zi*. For example, if the *míng.zi* were "(be) excellent and superb", then the *hào* might be "(be) humble and modest".

In traditional China, *zì* were actually used more than *míng.zi*, because *míng.zi* were only for formal situations such as in school, in court, or in business, while *zì* were used for addressing friends, schoolmates and relatives on social occasions and in daily life. It was considered extremely impolite, and even a breach of decorum, to address someone using a *míng.zi*. Only one's superiors, such as the emperor or one's parents, could use one's *míng.zi* for address. (This is why *zi* has been rendered as "courtesy name" in English—because it is "courteous" to use it instead of the *míng.zi*.)

The only common use for *míng.zi* was in referring to oneself—because courtesy to oneself was unnecessary. In writing letters or sending out invitations, one would always sign a *míng.zi*, not a *zi*. For example, Sun Yatsen's *míng.zi* was *Wén*, and his *zi* was *Yi-xiān* (Cantonese: Yatsen). Therefore in public letters to the Chinese people, he always signed himself *Sūn Wén*, while others often referred to him as *Sūn Yi-xiān* (or *Sūn Zhōng-shān*, *Zhōng-shān* being the name of his home county).

In the past, it was common to use "honorific" (i.e., polite) ways of asking a person's name. For *xìng*, one used *guìxìng*; for *míng.zi*, one used *dàmíng*; and for *zi*, one used *táifǔ*. Of these, only *guìxìng* has remained common in the late twentieth century.

Hào. Also called *biéhào*, these names were used by scholars, poets, calligraphers, painters, and others who chose to give themselves one. (The connection with art or creativity explains why they are called "studio" names in English.) *Hào* were typically two to five characters in length, and had meanings that were poetic, idealistic, or eremitic, such as:

Bàn-shān	半山	Halfway in the Mountain
Zhú-yǒu	竹友	Friend of Bamboo
Wǔ-liǔ Xiān.shēng	五柳先生	Master of Five Willows
Bái-yún Xiān.shēng	白雲先生	Master of White Clouds
Dōng-pō Jūshì	東坡居士	Master of the Eastern Slope

In the late twentieth century most of these old conventions have become obsolete. The use of *zi* has disappeared; people born after 1920 have not even had them. The same is true of *hào*, except that painters, especially those who work in the traditional Chinese style, have continued to use *hào* to sign their paintings. But although *zi* and *hào* are obsolete in contemporary China, they remain essential basic knowledge for students of traditional China. Biographical dictionaries for earlier periods regularly list *zi* and *hào*.

Exercises

In-class exercises:

1.   Multiple choice   (Read aloud the whole sentence after the choice has been made.)

   A.   Zá.mén zhè wū.zi luàn shi luàn, _____ tǐng shū.fú.
            a) dāngrán   b) kě.shi   c) *yěxǔ*   d) yídìng
   B.   Chángx chídào .de rén _____ děi zhù .de lí xuéxiào jìn .diǎnr cái xíng.
            a) *suǒ*.yi   b) yīn.wèi   c) yào.shi   d) yóuqí
   C.   Wū.zi tài luàn .le. Zá.mén _____ mǎshàng *zhěng*.lǐ vx.
            a) děi   b) děng   c) dōu   d) bié
   D.   Nǐ búbì jǐn.zhāng, tā xiànzài búhuì lái, xià.ge xīngqīwǔ _____ lái .ne.
            a) jiù   b) cái   c) zǎo   d) gāng

2. From each pair of Chinese sentences, choose the one you prefer (grammatically or idiomatically).

    A. Zhōngwén nán, zhēn.de, kě.shi *tǐng* yǒu yì.sī (yǒu yì.sī = interesting).
        Zhōngwén nán shi nán, kě.shi *tǐng* yǒu yì.sī.

    B. Zhèi-jiān wū.zi hái bùnéng xiǎng.shi zuì luàn .de, yīn.wèi sān-hào gèng luàn.
        Zhèi-jiān wū.zi hái bùnéng suàn.shi zuì luàn .de, yīn.wèi sān-hào gèng luàn.

    C. Tā shuō .de yìdiǎnr kuài.
        Tā shuō .de *yǒu*.diǎnr kuài.

    D. Wǒ bùzhīdào tā huì .bú.huì lái.
        Wǒ bùzhīdào yào.shi tā huì lái.

    E. Nǐ yào chī-ròu hái.shi yào hē-tāng?
        Nǐ yào chī-ròu huò.zhě yào hē-tāng?

    F. Wǒ bù xiǎng tā huì kàn Zhōngwén bào.
        Wǒ xiǎng tā búhuì kàn Zhōngwén bào.

    G. Wǒ.de qīn.qī bù lái .le. Zá.men bùděi *zhěng*.lǐ wū.zi .le.
        Wǒ.de qīn.qī bù lái .le. Zá.men búbì *zhěng*.lǐ wū.zi .le.

    H. *Qǐng* .nǐ bāng-máng wǒ xiě yì-zhāng gōngzuò shíjiānbiǎo.
        Qǐng .nǐ bāng .wǒ xiě yì-zhāng gōngzuò shíjiānbiǎo.

3. Fill in the blanks and read aloud.

    A. *Yóuqí*

        1. *Wǒ* xǐ.huān chī Zhōng.guó-cài ... shi Sì.chuān (Szechuan) cài. [cài: a dish (of food)]
        2. Tā.de sān.ge mèi.x dōu hěn piào.liàng, ... shi zuì xiǎo .de mèi.x.
        3. Wǒ shém yùn.dòng dōu bù xǐ.huān, ... bù xǐ.huān pǎo-bù.
        4. Wǒ jué.de tā *hěn* hǎokàn. Tā .de yǎn.jīng ... hǎokàn.
        5. Wǒ bù xǐ.huān *zhěng*.lǐ wū.zi. Wǒ ... bù xǐ.huān sǎo-dì.

    B. *Cónglái bù* (*bú*); *cónglái méi*

        1. Wǒ ... qù.guò Zhōng.guó, *suǒ*.yǐ *hěn* xiǎng qù.
        2. Wǒ ... kàn.guò Zhōng.guó bào, *suǒ*.yǐ wǒ bùzhīdào kàn Zhōng.guó bào nán .bù.nán.
        3. Wǒ bù xǐ.huān chī là (hot, pungent) .de, *suǒ*.yǐ wǒ ... chī Hú.nán (Hunan) cài.
        4. Nèi-jiā fànguǎnr .de dōng.xī búdàn guì érqiě bùhǎochī, *suǒ*.yǐ wǒ ... zài nàr chī-fàn.

    C. *Děi* ... *cái xíng* vs. *zhǐ yào* ... *jiù xíng*

        1. Pào Zhōng.guó chá bù róng.yì, búdàn *děi yǒu* hǎo cháyè gēn hěn tàng .de shuǐ, hái děi yòng tèbié (special) .de fá.zi ... .
        2. Pào Zhōng.guó chá hěn róng.yì, ... bǎ cháyè gēn rè shuǐ fàng .zài yíkuàir ... .le.
        3. Yào bǎ Zhōngwén xué-hǎo ... dào Zhōngguó qù ...
        4. Yào bǎ Zhōngwén xué-hǎo hěn róng.yì, ... shàng jǐ-táng Zhōngwén-kè ...

4. *Děi* vs. *búbì*

A.   Wǒ jīn.tiān ... niàn-shū, yīn.wèi míng.tiān *yǒu* kǎoshì.
     Wǒ ... niàn-shū; wǒ xià.ge xīngqī cái *yǒu* kǎoshì.
B.   Zá.mén ... xiànzài *zhěng*.lǐ wū.zi; kè.rén mǎshàng ... lái .le.
     Zá.mén ... xiànzài dòng-shǒu, yīn.wèi kè.rén míng.tiān ... lái.
C.   Nǐ ... kāi-dēng; wū.zi búgòu liàng bùnéng kàn-shū.
     Xiànzài wǒ bú kàn-shū, *suǒ*.yǐ ... kāi-dēng.
D.   Nǐ.mén liǎng.ge rén zhù zhèi-jiān wū.zi tài xiǎo .le; wǒ kàn .nǐ.mén ...
     kàn.x dà .yì.diǎnr .de fángjiān.
     Wǒ jué.de zhèi-jiān wū.zi *hěn* hǎo, *suǒ*.yǐ wǒ.mén ... kàn bié.de wū.zi .le.

5.   *Gèng*

A.   Zhèi-jiān wū.zi hěn dà, dàn.shi nèi-jiān bǐ zhèi-jiān ... dà.
B.   Zuó.tiān hěn rè; jīn.tiān bǐ zuó.tiān ... rè.
C.   Nǚ xué.shēng .de sùshè hěn luàn; nán xué.shēng .de sùshè bǐ nǚ xué.shēng .de
     ... .

Homework:

1.   Translate the following sentences into Chinese.

A.   There was a letter for you downstairs; I've brought it up (for you).
B.   How can we receive guests in a room as messy as ours?
C.   Since you're always slow in doing things, we had better start tidying things
     up right now.
D.   I have a test tomorrow; I have to go to the library and study.
E.   You shouldn't just compare (yourself) with elementary school students, you
     should compare (yourself) with college students (and only then it will do).
F.   What you said is correct; but it's easy to say, hard to do.
G.   I have a test tomorrow. (As for) the matter of cleaning up the room, let's
     put it off for a few days (wait several days and then do it).
H.   He is the tallest student in the school.
I.   I like this house because this house is closer to the library and (it) is
     also less expensive.
J.   I have a relative who never reads newspapers.

Classroom/Homework exercises:

1.   Comment on the truth of the following statements.

A.   Chángx chídào .de rén děi zhù .de lí xuéxiào jìn .diǎnr cái xíng.
B.   Bù xǐ.huān chī jī .de rén cónglái bù chī jī.
C.   Yīn.wèi wǔ-hào bǐ sān-hào luàn, *suǒ*.yǐ zhù .zài sān-hào .de rén bǐ zhù .zài
     wǔ-hào .de rén shū.fú.
D.   Jīn.tiān shi xīngqīwǔ, *suǒ*.yǐ zuó.tiān shi xīngqīliù.
E.   Míng.tiān shi lǐbàiliù, *suǒ*.yǐ zuó.tiān shi lǐbàiwǔ.
F.   Jīn.tiān shi èr-yuè sān-hào xīngqīsān, *suǒ*.yǐ míng.tiān shi èr-yuè sì-hào
     xīngqīsì.
G.   Shàng.ge lǐbàiliù shi qī-hào, zhèi.ge lǐbàiliù shi shísì-hào.
H.   Zhèi.ge lǐbàitiān shi shí-hào, *suǒ*.yǐ xià.ge lǐbàitiān shi shíwǔ-hào.

LESSON 4

Vocabulary

dòng	動	to move		hébì	何必	why must?
lǎn	懶	lazy		shàng.wǔ	上午	morning
zhǐ hǎo	只好	(the) only good (thing to do is)		xìng.kuī	幸虧	fortunately
piàn	騙	to trick, deceive, to fool		jìn.lái	進來	come in
				liú	留	to leave (behind)
yáyī	牙醫	'teeth-doctor', dentist		tiáo.zi	條子	note
gāngcái	剛才	just a while ago, just now		...diǎn zhōng (...diǎn)	點鐘 點	o'clock
zài-jiā	在家	be at home		kè	刻	quarter (hour)
hǎo-jiā.huǒ	好傢伙	'good-utensil', Oh boy! Goodness gracious! My goodness!		děng	等	to wait
				jí	急	nervous
				shíyàn	實驗	experiment, lab (class)
bàn	半	half		qù	去	to go
zhōngtóu	鐘頭	hour		fàng-xīn	放心	'put down heart', rest assured, relax
(zhōngtóur)	鐘頭儿					
.he	喝	interjection expressing surprise		shàng	上	attend (class)
gān.jìng	乾淨	clean		yídìng	一定	surely (see Grammar Notes)
zěm huí shì	怎麼回事	what's this? what's the matter?		fēi...bùkě	非…不可	must... (see Grammar Notes)
huí	回	to return		dǎ	打	to strike, to beat
huí.lái	回來	come back				

Vocabulary Classified by Type

Nouns	jí	jìn.lái
yáyī		
zhōngtóu (zhōngtóur)	**Adverbs**	**Time Words**
tiáo.zi	hébì	gāngcái
kè	yídìng	shàng.wǔ
shíyàn	*zhǐ* hǎo	...diǎn zhōng

Verbs	ANs	Interjections
dòng	diǎn	.he
piàn		
huí	**Sentential Adverbs**	**Exclamations**
liú	(Moveable Adverbs)	hǎo-jiā.huǒ
děng	xìng.kuī	
qù		**Numerals**
shàng	**V-Os**	bàn
dǎ	zài-jiā	
	fàng-xīn	**Idiomatic Expressions**
Adjectives		zěm huí shì
lǎn	**Verb-Complements**	fēi...bùkě
gān.jìng	huí.lái	

Grammar Notes

1. *Yìdiǎnr dōu méi dòng*, literally "(even) one bit uniformly did not move", means "didn't move at all". The general pattern is:

$$\text{Subject} + yìdiǎnr + dōu + \begin{cases} méi \text{ Verb ("didn't Verb at all or} \\ \qquad\qquad \text{hasn't Verb-ed at all")} \\ bù\ (bú) \text{ Verb ("do not Verb at all")} \\ bù\ (bú) \text{ Adj. ("is not at all Adj.")} \end{cases}$$

Examples:

Tā yìdiǎnr dōu méi dòng.	He didn't move at all.
Wǒ yìdiǎnr dōu bùdǒng.	I don't understand at all.
Zhèi-zhāng chuáng yìdiǎnr dōu bù shū.fú.	This bed is not comfortable at all.

Yě can substitute for *dōu* in this pattern (and therefore in any of the above examples) with no change in meaning.

If the Verb in this pattern takes an Object, the pattern becomes:

$$\text{Subject} + yìdiǎnr + \text{Object} + dōu/yě + \begin{cases} méi \text{ Verb} \\ bù\ (bú) \text{ Verb} \end{cases}$$

Examples:

Nèi.ge xué.shēng yìdiǎnr shū yě méi kàn.	That student didn't read anything.

> Xiè.x, wǒ yìdiǎnr lóngxiā dōu   Thank you, (but) I don't wish to
>   bù xiǎng chī.   eat any lobster at all.

Note that **all** the above patterns and examples are negative. The pattern does not work with positive verbs or adjectives.

2.   *Zhǐ hǎo*, literally "the only good (way to)", indicates reluctant acceptance of a less than ideal alternative.

3.   On *hòulái*, see II.4.26. Here it is used in parallel with *běnlái* "originally, at the start, in the first place".

4.   *Zǎo* "early" is normally an adjective, but here it is an adverb modifying *lái*. *Zǎo lái.le liǎng-tiān* means "came two days early".

5.   *Gāngcái* "just now, just a moment ago" is a Time Word, and therefore can come either before or after the subject *wǒ*. It is similar in meaning to *gāng* "just, just now". But *gāng*, because it is an adverb, must come after the subject, not before. Hence, the following sentence patterns are all correct:

> *Gāngcái wǒ* + Verb
> *Wǒ gāngcái* + Verb   Just now I (Verb-ed)
>
> *Wǒ gāng* + Verb   I just (Verb-ed); right after I
>   (Verb-ed)...

Note that *kàn* here means "see" in the sense of "visit". *Wǒ xiǎng qù kàn mèi.x* means "I'd like to go visit my younger sister".

6.   *Zài-jiā* "to be at home". Note the use of the completed action *.le* in the first clause of this sentence. It has the sense of "**after** seeing the dentist" or "**having** seen the dentist", and it goes with *jiù* in the next clause, which means "**then** I came to see you". This common use of *.le* paired with *jiù* has nothing to do with tense. It can refer to past or future actions equally well.

7.   *Hǎo-jiā.huǒ*, literally "good utensil", expresses sharp surprise, something like "my goodness!" or "holy mackerel!" in American English.

8.   *Bàn* "half". To say "half of" something, use the pattern:

> *bàn* + AN + N   half a (noun)
>
> bàn.ge zhōngtóu   half an hour
> bàn-zhāng zhǐ   half a sheet of paper
> bàn-kuài jī   half a piece of chicken

Remember that words like *tiān* "day" and *nián* "year" are themselves ANs. Hence:

> bàn-tiān   half a day
> bàn-nián   half a year

To add half to a large number, use:

> No. + AN + *bàn* + N

liǎng.ge bàn zhōngtóu	two and a half hours
sì.ge bàn lǐbài	four and a half weeks
sān-zhāng bàn zhǐ	three and a half sheets of paper
wǔ-nián bàn	five and a half years

"Hǎo-jiā.huǒ! Hái .yǒu liǎng.ge bàn zhōngtóu."

9.   *Zhè.shi zěm huí shì?*, literally "what kind of a matter is this?", is an idiomatic way to say "what's the matter?", "what's going on?", or "how did this happen?". (*Huí* is a special AN for *shì* in this usage; the usual AN is *jiàn*.) *Zhè.shi* often is dropped, in which case *zěm huí shì?* stands on its own with no change in meaning.

10. Review III.3.18 and III.3.21 on the use of *cái* after Time Words.

11. *Huí.lái* "come back, return". *Lái* indicates that the motion is towards the speaker. In a similar way, *qù* is used to indicate motion away from the speaker.

12. The phrase *yí.ge rén* is used here as an adverb meaning "alone, by oneself".

13. Review III.3.21 on *jiù* after Time Words.

14. *Bú.shi ... .ma?* "Isn't (it the case that) ...?"

15. *Guò* here is another example of the complement *guò* as described in III.2.9.

16. Telling time. To tell hours, use the AN *diǎn* "point" plus *zhōng* "clock". Note that *zhōng* can be omitted:

yì-diǎn zhōng (or yì-diǎn)	one o'clock
liǎng-diǎn zhōng	two o'clock
shí'èr-diǎn zhōng	twelve o'clock

To tell half-hours, use *bàn* "half" (and omit *zhōng*):

| yì-diǎn bàn | half past one |
| *liǎng*-diǎn bàn | half past two |

For quarter hours, use *kè* (and omit *zhōng*):

| yì-diǎn yí-kè | quarter past one |
| *liǎng*-diǎn sān-kè | 2:45 |

For minutes, *fēn* is used if the number of minutes is ten or less:

yì-diǎn yì-fēn	1:01
yì-*diǎn* liǎng-fēn	1:02
yì-diǎn shí-fēn	1:10

But *fēn* is usually omitted if the number is higher than ten:

yì-diǎn shíyī	1:11
yì-diǎn shí'èr	1:12
shíyī-diǎn èrshí-sān	11:23

When it is a few minutes *before* an hour, you can use *chà* "fall short" that we learned in the phrase *chà.bùduō* (III.1):

| chà yí-kè *liǎng*-diǎn | quarter to two |
| chà wǔ-fēn sān-diǎn | five minutes to three |

For "a.m." use *shàng.wǔ*, and for "p.m." *xià.wǔ*:

| shàng.wǔ *jiǔ*-diǎn shíqī | 9:17 a.m. |
| xià.wǔ *liǎng*-diǎn wǔ-fēn | 2:05 p.m. |

17. *Yídìng*, "surely" or "must be", is an adverb. It is used when the speaker is not positively certain of something but is making a very reasonable guess. *Zhè yídìng shi nǐ xiě .de* means "(I can't prove it but) you *must* be the one who wrote this". WARNING: *Yídìng* cannot substitute for *dāngrán* "of course". *Dāngrán* implies complete agreement and no doubt. For example:

| A: Zhōngwén bǐ Yīngwén nán. | Chinese is harder than English. |
| B: Dāngrán. (Not *yídìng*!) | Of course. |

In the PRC in recent years, *kěndìng* has been a common substitute for the adverbial *yídìng*:

| Zhè kěndìng shi *nǐ* xiě .de. | You must have written this. |

18. *Fēi* + V + *bùkě* means "absolutely must V". *Fēi*, a word borrowed from classical Chinese, means *bù* or *bú.shi*. *Kě* is short for *kě.yi* "may, can, all right". Thus

the strong imperative tone of this construction is based on a double negative: *fēi dǎ-sǐ .nǐ bùkě* "It won't do not to beat you to death."

Exercises

In-class exercises:

1.   Multiple choice

    A.   Jīn.tiān wǒ.de qián búgòu, _____ xià.cì zài *qǐng* .nǐ chī lóngxiā .le.
            a) zhǐ yào   b) *zhǐ* hǎo   c) yídìng
    B.   Yào tā dòng-shǒu *zhěng*.lǐ wū.zi, _____ xiǎng .ge fá.zi cái xíng.
            a) dōu   b) *hěn*   c) *děi*
    C.   _____ *nǐ qǐng* wǒ, xiànzài *wǒ qǐng* nǐ .le.
            a) yào.shi   b)běnlái   c) yǐ.jīng
    D.   Zhè wū.zi _____ yě méi zèm gān.jìng.guò.
            a) cónglái   b) běnlái   c) yídìng
    E.   Nǐ _____ zhī.dào tā búhuì lái?
            a) suírán   b) zěm   c) shém
    F.   Xiànzài shí.hòur hái zǎo, ni _____ zèm jǐn..zhāng .ne?
            a) hébì   b) yào.shi   c) búbì

2.   Fill in the blanks and read aloud.

    A.   *yìdiǎnr dōu/yě bù/méi*

        A: Tā zuò-shì wǒ zuì fàng-xīn.
        B: Nǐ shuō .de yìdiǎnr ... búduì, tā zuò-shì xiànglái màn, chángx
            wù-shì, *suǒ*.yǐ tā zuò-shì wǒ ... .

        A: Zhèi.ge xué.shēng zhēn lǎn, tā ... (never cleans up his room), *suǒ*.yǐ
            wū.zi.lǐ luàn .de bùdéliǎo.
        B: Qíshí tā yìdiǎnr dōu bù lǎn, jiù.shi tài máng .le, méi kòngr
            zhěng.lǐ.

        A: Bié jǐn.zhāng, kǎoshì hěn róng.yì, ... (not difficult at all)
        B: Wǒ yì*diǎnr* yě bù jǐn.zhāng. Tā dào *hěn* jǐn.zhāng, yīn.wèi tā ... .
            (did not study at all)

Homework:

1.   Answer the following questions.

    A.   A wèishém yào piàn B?

    B.   A yòng shém fá.zi piàn B?

    C.   Shéi bǎ wū.zi *zhěng*.lǐ gān.jìng .le?

    D.   B wèishém shuō "*Wǒ* děng .de jí.sǐ .le"?

E.   B wèishém shuō "Wǒ fēi *dǎ-sǐ* .nǐ bùkě"?

2.   Translate the following sentences into Chinese.

A.   If you want to learn Chinese well, there is only one method and that is to
        keep practicing (practice more).
B.   Fortunately you came to my help; if you hadn't come I wouldn't have known
        what to do.
C.   She has never been late before.
D.   How do you know that he is going to (will likely) believe you?
E.   Please give me half a cup of water.
F.   I studied (books) for one and a half hours today.
G.   I have waited for her for half a day, but she has not come yet.
H.   He always eats breakfast slowly. We have to wait for him.
I.   He never eats breakfast. We don't have to wait for him.
J.   If you go to see him at 4 p.m., he (I am sure) won't be home.
K.   My younger sister has wiped the table clean and swept the floor clean. (Use
        bǎ construction.)
L.   She visits the dentist frequently, therefore her teeth have never decayed
        (become bad).
M.   Your relative is not coming till a week from Friday. We've still got more
        than a week.

3.   Nǐ qù kàn yí.ge péng.yǒu. *Nǐ xiǎng* qǐng .tā chī-fàn, kě.shi tā bú zài-jiā. *Qǐng*
        .nǐ yòng Zhōngwén gěi tā liú yí.ge tiáo.zi.

Classroom/Homework exercises:

1.   Review of *zài*, *jiù*, and *cái*

A.   Xiànzài wǒ tài máng .le, míng.tiān ... tán .ba.
B.   Tā jīn.tiān xià.wǔ bù lái, míng.tiān ... lái.
C.   Chī.le fàn yǐhòu *qǐng* .nǐ lìkè ... dào túshūguǎn .qù *děng* .wǒ.
D.   ... guò liǎng-tiān jiù.shi wǒ mèi.x .de shēngrì (birthday) .le.
E.   Tā měi-cì dōu.shi děng kè.rén kuài lái .de shí.hòur ...   kāi*shǐ zhěng*.lǐ
        wū.zi.
F.   Jìrán *nǐ* yě jué.de zhèi.ge fá.zi búcuò, nà wǒ.mén ... zèm juédìng .le.
G.   Tā yì *yǒu* kǎoshì ... jǐn.zhāng .de bùdéliǎo.
H.   *Wǒ* běnlái yǐwéi yòng kuài.zi jiā dàn hěn róng.yì, jiā.guò yǐhòu ... zhī.dào
        yì*diǎnr* yě bù róng.yì.
I.   Zhǐ yào nǐ bù bǎ zhèi-jiàn shì wàng.le, tā ... búhuì guài .nǐ .le.
J.   Gěi rén liú tiáo.zi .de .shí.hòur yídìng děi jì.de bǎ míng.zì gēn shíjiān
        xiě zài tiáo.zi.shàng ... xíng.

UNIT IV

LESSON 1

Vocabulary

xiào	笑	to laugh (at)
huáng	黃	yellow, brown
qīng.chǔ	清楚	clear
nín	您	you (polite form)
jiǎo	腳	foot
chuān	穿	to wear
xié	鞋	shoe
hēi	黑	black
zìjǐ	自己	self
bùhǎoyì.sī	不好意思	embarrassed
qǐ.lái	起來	get up (from bed)
tiān	天	sky
cuò	錯	wrong, incorrect
zhào	照	according to
shàng	上	previous
suǒ	所	emphatic adverb
jiǎng	講	to lecture, discuss
yì.sī	意思	meaning
dàodǐ	到底	'reach-bottom', after all
hēix .de	黑黑的	darkish (see Grammar Notes)
diàndēng	電燈	electric light
dǒng	懂	understand
yàng.zi	樣子	appearance
díquè	的確	indeed
tèbié	特別	special; peculiar
héshì	合適	suitable

Vocabulary Classified by Type

Nouns	Pronouns	
jiǎo	nín	jiǎng
xié	zìjǐ	dǒng
tiān		
yì.sī	**Verbs**	**Adjectives**
diàndēng	chuān	huáng
yàng.zi	qǐ.lái	qīng.chǔ
	zhào	hēi
		cuò

héix .de   **Adverbs**   **Idiomatic Expressions**
tèbié   suǒ   bùháoyì.sī
héshì   dàodǐ
                               díquè

Grammar Notes

1. *Shí Kělěi* is an example of how a Western name, in this case Claire Smith, can result in an elegant Chinese name. Normally, sound is a basis for picking names: *Kělěi* for Claire and *Shí* for Smith. (To be sure, *shí* and *s* are different initial sounds, and thus not a perfect fit. But the only alternative closer to *s* is a surname *Sī*, which is rare and would give a somewhat peculiar impression.) Besides sound, meaning is important. *Shí* is "stone", *kě* is "may" (as in *kě.yi*), and *lěi* means "a pile of stones". Thus: "stone that may be piled high". *Lěi* also has connotations of "great" or "magnanimous", thus making the name meaningful and elegant: through diligence and intelligence, one can make pebbles into magnificent rocks—implying that a modest start can result in greatness. (See Culture Note 2, Unit II, Lesson 2.)

2. *Nín* is a polite form of *ni*. It acknowledges that the person referred to has higher status than the speaker. For purposes of politeness, it is often used even when the matter of higher status is far from clear.

3. *Huáng* is often translated as "yellow", and correctly so. *Huáng xié*, however, is "brown shoes", meaning dark brown, light brown, or beige shoes. China's famous *Huánghé* "Yellow River" is also obviously not yellow but brown. (Chinese names for colors do not always correspond to the same ranges on the spectrum as English terms.)

4. Review III.3.10 on *.qi.lái* as a verbal complement. Here *qi.lái* is a main verb meaning "to get up (from bed)".

5. *Tiān* "sky" and *liàng* "bright" combine to be *tiān liàng* "the sky brightens—the day breaks, it's dawn". *Dà* "big" here is an adverb meaning "very". Thus *tiān hái méi dà liàng* means "it was not quite fully dawn".

6. *Cuò* "mistaken, incorrect" here is a resultative complement for the verb *chuān* "put on (clothes or shoes)". *Chuān-cuò* means "wear incorrectly". The final *.le* is both a "completed action" *.le* for the verb *chuān-cuò* and a "new situation" *.le* for the very unusual outcome of having put on differently colored shoes. When the two kinds of *.le* occur in the same place, they combine into one.

7. *Zhào*, originally "shine, illuminate", here means "according to". Note, however, that in English we say "according to him", but in Chinese *zhào* cannot be followed by a noun or pronoun alone. Do not say *zhào ta* or *zhào lǎoshī*. You have to say *zhào tā jiǎng .de* "according to what he said" or *zhào lǎoshī .de yì.sī* "according to what the teacher meant", or something similar.

8. *Suǒ*, the same word that is the first part of *suǒ.yi* and an AN for buildings, can also be used as an adverb in the pattern:

                    suǒ + Verb + *.de* + (Noun)

The noun can be stated or implied. In either case the whole phrase is a substantive. The use of *suǒ* is optional in such phrases; when it appears, it has one of the following two senses:

(a) *Suǒ* can add emphasis to an assertion. *Zhào lǎoshī jiǎng .de* ("according to what the teacher said") means the same as *zhào lǎoshī suǒ jiǎng .de*, but the use of *suǒ* implies more confidence and clarity about exactly what the teacher said. Similarly, *wǒ kàn.jiàn .de gēn tā kàn.jiàn .de bùyíyàng* ("what I saw and what he saw are not the same") means the same as *wǒ suǒ kàn.jiàn .de gēn tā suǒ kàn.jiàn .de bùyíyàng*; but the second, using *suǒ*, implies more precision and confidence.

For translation purposes, *suǒ* in such examples is usually comparable to English words like "that" or "whom", which are omittable in the same way *suǒ* is:

Tā (suǒ) chuān .de yī.fú ...	The clothes (that) he wore ...
Wǒ (suǒ) xǐ.huān .de rén ...	The people (whom) I like ...

Note, however, that despite this similarity between *suǒ* and "that" or "whom", *suǒ* is grammatically an adverb and must **always** precede a verb, whereas "that" and "whom" in English precede nouns and pronouns.

(b) *Suǒ* can convey the sense of "all" when followed by *dōu*:

Tā suǒ chuān .de yī.fú dōu.shi hěn guì .de.	All the clothes she wears are expensive.
Tā jīn.tiān suǒ qǐng .de kè.rén dōu.shi Zhōng.guórén.	All the guests he has invited today are Chinese.

An important example of this second case is *suǒ yǒu .de* "all that there is (are)". Again, it must be used with *dōu*. Examples:

Sùshè.lǐ suǒ yǒu .de wū.zi dōu .hěn luàn.	All the rooms in the dorm are messy.
Suǒ yǒu .de xué.shēng dōu zhī.dào .le.	Every one of the students knows about it now.

9. *Hēi* "black" or "dark". *Hēix .de* "darkish, murky". Similarly *liàng* "bright" and *liàngx .de* "rather bright"; *suān* "sour" and *suānx .de* "sourish". The repeated form diminishes the intensity of the word to give the sense of "sort of..." or "...ish". NOTE: Because the intensity is diminished, you cannot add *hěn* or other intensifiers before the repeated form.

10. Review II.2.15 on the difference between *díquè* and *qíshí*.

11. *Tèbié* "special, unusual" and *qíguài* "strange" can both be used as adjectives to describe something out of the ordinary. But *tèbié* implies simply "different", whereas *qíguài* adds the notion of "peculiar" or "weird":

Tā .de yàng.zi .hěn tèbié.	His appearance is unusual.
Tā .de yàng.zi .hěn qíguài.	He looks weird.

As an adverb, *tèbié* is similar to *yóuqí* "especially" (see III.3.5): *tèbié* (or *yóuqí*) *guì* "especially expensive"; *tèbié* (*yóuqí*) *xi.huān* "especially fond of". But *yóuqí* is usually stronger than *tèbié*. *Yóuqí* is used when *all* members of a group are outstanding in some respect, but one or more is especially outstanding. Hence *yóuqí* often appears in the second clause of a sentence:

Zhèr .de fànguǎnr dōu guì,
  zhèi-jiā yóuqí guì.

All the restaurants here are expensive, and this one is especially so.

Tā *hěn* xi.huān Zhōngwén-kè,
  yóuqí xi.huān xiě
  Zhōng.guó-zì.

She loves her Chinese class, especially the writing of characters.

Tèbié is more general; unlike *yóuqí*, it does not tend to appear in the second clauses of sentences. To complain about the high price of a store, you can say, "*Zhèr .de dōng.xi tèbié guì.*" You cannot say "*Zhèr .de dōng.xi yóuqí guì*" without some kind of earlier assertion, either stated or implied.

Another difference between *tèbié* and *yóuqí* is that *tèbié* can be used with *.de* to modify a noun: *tèbié .de fá.zi* "special method". *Yóuqí* cannot be used this way.

Culture Note 12:   Transliteration of the Names of Foreign Countries

Chinese names for foreign countries have generally been based on the sounds of foreign languages. Thus England was originally named *Yīnggélán*; France was *Fǎlánxī*, and Italy *Yìdàlì*. Many such names were later simplified by using the first syllable only and attaching *guó* "country". Thus *Yīng.guó* "England", *Fǎ.guó* "France", and *Yì.guó* "Italy". (This form is also used for the states of ancient China: *Lǔ.guó*, *Qí.guó*, etc.)

In the case of "America", originally *Yàměilìjiā*, the shortened form *Měi.guó* is based on the second syllable *měi*, because the first syllable *yà* is too common and would be ambiguous.

It is sometimes said that Chinese call America *Měi.guó* "beautiful country" because of a partiality to America, or that Chinese do not like Russia and therefore call it *È.guó* (a homonym for "hungry country"). These speculations are groundless. The characters that are chosen to represent foreign names are chosen for their sounds only, not their meanings. Meanings are basically regarded as irrelevant—except only that obviously negative meanings are avoided. (For example, *Měi.guó* could not be *Méi.guó* "mildew-country", *Yīng.guó* could not be *yíng.guó* "fly-country", or *fǎ.guó* be *Fá.guó* "punishment-country".)

Transliterations need not be based on English, of course. For example *Xībānyá* "Spain" is based on Hispania; *Déyìzhì* "Germany" is based on Deutschland. A few transliterations have come via the dialects of China's southern provinces, where contact with modern European countries first occurred. For example Switzerland is *Ruìshì*, whose pronunciation in Cantonese is close to "Suisse".

Exercises

In-class exercises:

1. Fill in the blanks with the words provided.

    A. Dà-xiǎo, qián-hòu, zuǒ-yòu, *zǎo-wǎn*

        1. Nín yì-jiǎo chuān huáng xié, yì-jiǎo chuān hēi xié ... bùyíyàng.
        2. Ni zuó.tiān shuō xi.huān hē-chá, jīn.tiān shuō xi.huān hē-kāfēi, ... bùyíyàng.
        3. Jīn.tiān wǒ cóng jiā.li chū.lái .de shí.hòur hái *hěn* lěng, kě.shi xiànzài zèm rè, ... bùyíyàng.
        4. Sān-hào wū.zi *bǐ* wǔ-hào guì .yì.diǎnr, yīn.wèi ... bùyíyàng.

    B. Kàn.bù-qīng.chǔ, tīng.bù-qīng.chǔ, méi kàn-qīng.chǔ, méi tīng-qīng.chǔ

        1. Ni zì xiě .de tài xiǎo .le, wǒ ... .
        2. Zhèr rén tài duō .le, shuō-huà ... , zá.mén dào bié.de wū.zi .qù .ba.
        3. Ni gāngcái shuō shém.me? Wǒ ... .
        4. Duì.bùqǐ, wǒ ... , *wǒ* kě .bù.*kě*.yi zài kàn.x?

2. Fill in the blanks and read aloud.

    A. *Dàodǐ* + interrogative structure

        1. Zuó.tiān tā shuō tā bā-diǎn lái, jīn.tiān ni yòu shuō tā *liǎng*-diǎn lái, tā ... shém shí.hòur lái?
        2. Wū.zi tài hēi .le, qiáng.shàng xiě .de ... shi shém zì shéi yě kàn.bù-qīng.chǔ.
        3. Tā xiànzài *yěxǔ* zài xuéxiào, *yěxǔ* zài jiā, wǒ bùzhīdào tā ... zài ... .
        4. Ni ... xiǎng chī ... , lóngxiā hái.shi jī? Kuài .diǎnr juédìng .ba, wǒ è-sǐ.le.
        5. Tā.de Zhōng.guó-huà gēn Rìběn-huà (Japanese) shuō .de yíyàng hǎo, *suǒ*.yi wǒ tīng.bù-chūlái tā ... shi Zhōng.guórén ... .

3. *Shém.me dōu bù* ...; *shém.me dōu méi* ...

    A. Zuó.tiān wǒ ... chī, *suǒ*.yi wǒ xiànzài è .de bùdéliǎo.
    B. Shàng.ge xīngqī wǒ shém ... *suǒ*.yi jīn.tiān kǎoshì .de shí.hòur ... jì.de, ... huì xiě.
    C. Tā.de xìng.qíng hěn qíguài *suǒ*.yi tā ... péng.yǒu ... yǒu.
    D. Wǒ gāng dào Zhōng.guó .de shí.hòur, ... tīng.bù-dǒng, *suǒ*.yi nào.le hěn duō xiào.huà.
    E. Nèi.ge túshūguǎn.li ... Zhōngwén shū ... méi.yǒu, *zhǐ* yǒu *jǐ-běn* hěn jiù .de Yīngwén shū, *suǒ*.yi wǒ cónglái ... shàng nèi.ge túshūguǎn .qù.

Homework:

1. Translate the following sentences into Chinese.

A.   Oh no! How embarrassing! I wrote your name incorrectly. (Use the *bǎ* construction.)

B.   This morning I got up very early and it was dark outside; I couldn't see anything.

C.   Please turn on the light. I want to see (take a look) if there is anything on the wall.

D.   According to what that dentist said, you had better not drink hot soup.

E.   Yesterday I invited a relative to have lobster at a famous restaurant. I didn't know there wasn't any money in my wallet until after we finished eating (use *cái*). It was really embarrassing.

F.   He first puts tea leaves into a cup, then pours in (dào) very hot water. This really is a special method of steeping tea.

G.   That dress is too small. It doesn't fit (is not suitable).

H.   I have a friend who always blames others only, never himself.

Classroom/Homework exercises:

1.   Oral Substitution

A.   Given: *Wǒ* bǐ .tā dà.

Response: Yào.shi *nǐ* bǐ .tā dà, tā jiù méi.yǒu nǐ nèm dà.

1.   *Wǒ* bǐ .tā gāo.
2.   Zhèi.ge zì bǐ nèi.ge zì dà.
3.   Tā chī-fàn *bǐ* .wǒ chī .de duō.
4.   Tā Zhōngwén bǐ Yīngwén shuō .de qīng.chǔ.
5.   Jīn.tiān *wǒ* bǐ .tā lái .de zǎo.
6.   Tā xiě .de zì *bǐ nǐ* (xiě .de zì) hǎokàn.

B.   Given: First student: Zuó.tiān wǒ tīng.bú-jiàn.

Response: Second student: Nǐ xiànzài tīng.de-jiàn .tīng.bú-.jiàn?
         First student: Xiànzài wǒ tīng.de-jiàn .le.

1.   Liǎng.ge yuè yǐqián wǒ yòng.bú-guàn dāo-chā.
2.   Yǐqián wǒ chī.bú-guàn Zhōng.guó-fàn.
3.   Wǒ gāngcái kàn.bù-qīng.chǔ.
4.   Yǐqián Zhōng.guó-zì *wǒ* xiě.bù-hǎo.
5.   Tā yǐqián pǎo.bú-kuài.

C.   Given: Zhèi-jiàn yī.fú duì tā hěn héshì.

Response: Zhèi-jiàn yī.fú duì tā díquè hěn héshì. Tā jīn.tiān tèbié piào.liàng.

1.   Nèi.ge xué.shēng *hěn* xǐ.huān xiě-zì.
2.   Zhèi-jiān wū.zi zhēn xiǎo.
3.   Zuó.tiān wǎnfàn .de niúròu zhēn hǎochī.

LESSON 2

Vocabulary

Wáng	王	common surname	guǎn...jiào...	管...叫...	to call... (see Grammar Notes)
dì	地	floor; ground	.ma	嘛	final particle indicating obviousness
hé.zi	盒子	box			
bù	布	cloth	bǐnggān	餅乾	cookie, cracker, biscuit
.diào	掉	(resultative complement) "...off"	huí.qù	回去	go back
			jìn.qù	進去	go in
.A	啊	interjection of minor surprise	kāi	開	to open
tiáo	條	AN for animals and things in strips	chū.lái	出來	come out
			dǐ.xià	底下	bottom, below

Vocabulary Classified by Type

Nouns
dì
hé.zi
bù
bǐnggān

Proper Nouns
Wáng

Verbs
jiào
kāi

Resultative Complements
.diào

V-Directional Complements
huí.qù
jìn.qù
chū.lái
tiáo.chū.lái

ANs
tiáo

Localizers
dǐ.xià

Particles
.ma

Interjections
.A

Pretransitives
guǎn (guǎn...jiào...)

Grammar Notes

1. This sentence is an example of the pattern "PW *shì* N", which has a slightly different sense from the "PW *yǒu* N" pattern that you already know (see I.5.25). Study these two pairs of examples:

Qiáng.shāng yǒu shūjià.zi.   There are bookshelves on the wall.
Qiáng.shāng shi shūjià.zi.   The things on the wall are
                                bookshelves.

Zhuō.zi pángbiānr yǒu dēng.   A lamp is beside the desk.
Zhuō.zi pángbiānr shi dēng.   What's beside the desk is a lamp.

In the first sentences of the two pairs of examples, the full implications of the *yǒu* pattern are: "There might or might not be anything on the wall (or beside the desk), and I am telling you there are bookshelves (or a lamp) there." The full implications of the *shi* pattern are: "It is understood that there is something on the wall (or beside the desk), and I am telling you what that thing is —bookshelves (or a lamp)." *Shi* "is" tells what something is, while *yǒu* "there is" tells **whether** there is anything. In the sentence in the text, the teacher and students all know that something obviously is on the floor, and the teacher is asking what *it is* that is on the floor. Therefore he uses *shi* instead of *yǒu*.

2.   Review II.3.21 on the use of *zhù* "to live, stay" as a resultative complement meaning "take hold". *Diào* as a resultative complement means "off" or "away" and is the opposite of *zhù*. Thus *ná.diào* "take off or away", *cā.diào* "rub off—erase", *wàng.diào* "forget (away)". As a main verb, *diào* means "fall" or "drop".

3.   In I.2 you learned *zhī* as the AN for *gǒu* "dog". *Tiáo* "strip" is another common AN for dogs. It is used for certain other things as well. For example:

yì-tiáo dàjiē   one big street—one avenue
liǎng-tiáo xīnwén   two items of news

In VI.1 we will have *liǎng-tiáo máojīn* "two towels".

4.   In China dogs are sometimes named "*Lái* X", where *lái* is "come" and "X" is some kind of luck that the dog is supposed to bring. For example: *Láifú* "come blessings", *Láifù* "come wealth", *Láixǐ* "come happiness". (In Taiwan, *Láixǐ* is used to translate the name of the famous American dog Lassie. This is a clever choice, since sound and meaning are both appropriate.)

5.   *Guǎn* is a pretransitive (like *bǎ*), but can be used only with the verb *jiào* in the pattern:

Subject *guǎn* A *jiào* B

Měi.guórén *guǎn* Niǔyuē jiào   Americans call New York "the big
   "dà píngguǒ".   apple".
Xiǎoxuéshēng guǎn zhèi-tiáo gǒu The primary school students call
   jiào Láixǐ.   this dog Lassie.

6.   The particle *.ma* is used here for emphasis and indicates obviousness. It suggests that the listener is expected to agree.

7.   *Bǐnggān*, literally "cake-dry", means "cookie" or "cracker".

8.   Directional Complements. In *huí.qù* "go back" and *huí.lái* "come back" (III.4.11) *lái* and *qù* are directional complements, meaning complements that tell the direction in which the action of a verb moves. Directional complements can be simple or compound.

Simple Directional Complements

There are only two simple directional complements, *lái* "come" and *qù* "go". Remember that these two words can be main verbs on their own, as in:

Tā lái.le.	He has come.
Lǎo Wáng qù.guò hěn duō dì.fāng.	Lǎo Wáng has been to a lot of places.

When *lái* and *qù* are used as directional complements, they immediately follow another verb (such as *jìn* "enter", *chū* "exit", *huí* "return", etc.) and tell the direction of the verb's action *from the speaker's standpoint*. *Lái* indicates that the action moves toward the speaker, and *qù* indicates that it moves away from the speaker. Remember that it is only the speaker's position that determines the choice between *lái* and *qù*. Examples:

Tā shàng.lái.le.	He came up.
Tā xià.qù.le.	He went down.
Tā guò.lái.le.	He came over.
Tā chū.qù.le.	She went out.
Tā jìn.lái.le.	She came in.
Tā huí.qù.le.	She went back.

Compound Directional Complements

In compound directional complements, *two* elements follow the main verb:

Main Verb + A + B

Main verb: The main verb can be any verb involving movement in a direction, such as *pǎo* "run", *zǒu* "walk", *tiào* "jump", *zuò* "sit", *dǎ* "hit", and a great many others.

A-elements: These include *jìn* "enter", *chū* "exit", *shàng* "move upward", *xià* "move downward", *huí* "return", *guò* "cross over", or *qǐ* "rise". A-elements indicate the direction of action in an *absolute frame of reference*—that is, without regard to where the speaker is.

B-elements: *Lái* "come" or *qù* "go" indicate (just as in simple directional complements) whether an action moves toward or away from the speaker. This is in a *relative frame of reference*. *Lái* indicates motion "toward the speaker" and *qù* motion "away from the speaker". Examples:

pǎo.jìn.lái	come running in (speaker is inside)
pǎo.jìn.qù	go running in (speaker is outside)
zǒu.chū.lái	walk out (speaker is outside)
zǒu.chū.qù	walk out (speaker is inside)
tiào.guò.lái	jump over (toward speaker)

dǎ.huí.qù	hit (it) back (away from speaker)
ná.shàng.lái	bring (it) up (toward speaker)
zuò.qǐ.lái	sit up

The last example, using *.qǐ*, is an interesting special case. Only *lái* can be used with *.qǐ*, because *.qǐ.qù* does not exist in Mandarin Chinese. Even if you are lying down next to someone and that person sits up in a direction "away" from you, you have to say *tā zuò.qǐ.lái.le* "he sat up".

Note that directional complements, both simple and compound, are usually pronounced in neutral tones. In certain exceptional cases, the *.lái* or *.qù* can be omitted, as in the example *zuò.xià* "sit down" in the next lesson.

9. **Potential Directional Complements.** All directional complements have potential forms that use *.de* indicating "can" or *.bù* (*.bú*) indicating "cannot". When the whole of "Verb + A + B" is present, *.de* or *.bù* comes between the "Verb" and "A":

tiào.de-shàngqù	can jump up (away from speaker)
tiào.bú-shàngqù	cannot jump up (away from speaker)
pǎo.bú-guòlái	cannot run over (towards speaker)
dǎ.de-chūqù	can hit (it) out (away from speaker)

etc.

For Simple Directional Complements, *.de* or *.bù* comes between the verb and *lái/qù*:

chū.de-lái	can come out
guò.de-qù	can go over
huí.bù-lái	cannot come back
jìn.bú-qù	cannot go in

To make choice-type questions using potential directional complements, repeat all the elements in both the *.de* and *.bù* (*.bú*) alternatives:

Tā jìn.de-qù .jìn.bú.qù?	Can she get in (away from speaker)?
Nǐ qǐ.de-lái .qǐ.bù.lái?	Can you get up?
Nǐ tiào.de-shàng.qù .tiào.bú.shàng.qù?	Can you jump up (onto something, away from speaker)?
Tā zǒu.de-guò.lái .zǒu.bú.guò.lái?	Can he walk over (something, toward speaker)?
Nǐ dǎ.de-huí.qù .dǎ.bù.huí.qù?	Can you hit (it) back (there)?

Note that all the elements in the *.bù* (*.bú*) alternative are pronounced in neutral tones. The elements in the *.de* alternative may or may not be neutral tone, depending on the speaker's stress.

10. The first *kāi* here is a main verb "open". The second *kāi* is an adjective "open" acting as a resultative complement. *Kāi.bù-kāi* is the potential form "cannot be opened (up, so that it is open)". Note that the second *kāi* must be full first tone, not neutral tone. *Mén kāi.bù-kāi* means "The door cannot be opened"; *Mén kāi .bù.kāi?* means "Is the door open?" or "Are you open for business?".

11.   *Bǎ* is used here because the verb *kāi* "open" has both an object (*mén* "door") and a complement (*kāi* "open").

12.   *.Dào yǐ.zi.nàr .qù*, literally "to over-by-chair go", is an example of an important pattern:

$$dào \text{ Place Word } \begin{Bmatrix} .l\acute{a}i \\ .q\grave{u} \end{Bmatrix} \quad \begin{Bmatrix} \text{come} \\ \text{go} \end{Bmatrix} \text{ to a place}$$

Review I.5.22 on the precise definition of "Place Word". The above pattern can be used in three ways:

 1) As a main verb. *Nǐ dào yǐ.zi.nàr .qù* "You go over there by the chair"; *Tā dào Měi.gwo lái .le* "She came to America". (Note that *lái* and *qù* can be either full tone or neutral tone, depending on the example and how it is said.)

 2) Before a verb (in the adverb position). *Wǒ dào yǐ.zi.nàr .qù kàn.x* "I'm going over to the chair to have a look"; *Tā dào Měi.gwo lái xué Yīngwén* "She's coming to America to study English".

 3) After a verb (in the complement position, called a Bound Phrase Complement). This is the case presented in the text. *Nǐ zǒu .dào yǐ.zi.nàr .qù* "you walk over by the chair". Note that in the complement position, *.dào* is always neutral tone (and is sometimes abbreviated to *.de*).

 .The difference between (2) and (3) is that (2) tells the location at which the action of the verb takes place, while (3) tells the result (or destination) of the action of the verb. Sometimes the difference between the two is very clear: *Tā pǎo .dào wài.tou .qù* "He ran outside"; but *Tā dào wài.tou .qù pǎo* "He went outside to run".

Exercises

In-class exercises:

1.   (1) Translate the following English questions into Chinese and (2) answer the questions using localizers such as *.zhèr, .nàr, shàng.tou, dǐ.xià, .lǐ*, etc. in your answers.

 A.   Where is my Chinese (language) book?
 B.   How about Lǎo Huáng? Where did he go?
 C.   Where do you find the news? (Where is the news?)
 D.   Where do you want to go jogging?
 E.   Where is the salad?

Homework:

1.   Complete the following sentences using (1) the vocabulary and (2) the sentence pattern specified.

 A.   1.   hé.zi.lǐ   kàn.bú-jiàn   dōng.xī   bùzhīdào   shì   shém.me
   2.   yīn.wèi ... *suǒ*.yǐ ...

B.   1.   Lǎo Huáng   mén   kāi.bù-kāi   jìn.bú-qù
      2.   yīn.wèi ... *suǒ*.yǐ ...

C.   1.   bù   kàn.de-jiàn .le   bǎ   wǒ   ná-diào   nǐ.mén
      2.   yào.shi ... jiù ...

D.   1.   mén   Lǎo Huáng   wǒ   jìn.de-qù .le   kāi.x   bǎ
      2.   yào.shi ... jiù ...

2.   Translate the following sentences into Chinese.

A.   As soon as I opened the door, he came in.
B.   Do you like cookies? I have some cookies for you.
C.   She is my younger sister's good friend. Her name is Huáng Xiǎoqīng.
      Because her face is always sort of red (reddish) we all call her "cherry
      tomato".
D.   There's a big box on the floor. Inside the box are three pairs (shuāng) of
      black shoes, a big red bowl, seven green cups and over thirty sheets of
      paper.
E.   Look, he is jumping out. Now he is jumping in again.
F.   Look, my little dog is running under the table.
G.   Come back, Lassie, I'll give you a piece of beef (to eat).

Classroom/Homework exercises:

1.   Oral Substitution

A.   Given: *Wǒ* bǎ fàn chī-wán .le.

      Answer: *Nǐ* bǎ fàn chī-wán.le, .ne.me tā .ne? Tā chī-wán.le .méi.yǒu?
              Tā *yě* bǎ fàn chī-wán .le.

      1.   *Wǒ* bǎ "dà" zì xiě-duì .le.
      2.   Lǎo Zhāng bǎ Yīngwén xué-hǎo .le.
      3.   *Wǒ* bǎ wū.zi *zhěng*.lǐ-gān.jìng .le.
      4.   Tā bǎ zhèi-liǎng.ge zì xiě-wán .le.

B.   Given: Yīngwén, lái, come

      Response: Yīngwén guǎn "lái" jiào shém.me?
                Yīngwén guǎn "lái" jiào "come", "come" jiù.shi lái .de yì.sī.

      1.   Yīngwén, mǔ.qīn .de mǔ.qīn, grandma
      2.   Běijīngrén, míng.tiān, míngr
      3.   Zhōng.guórén, chī-fàn .de dì.fāng, fànguǎnr
      4.   Zhōng.guórén, hē-kāfēi .de dì.fāng, kāfēiguǎnr
      5.   Zhōng.guórén, hē-chá .de dì.fāng, cháguǎnr
      6.   Zhōng.guórén, kàn-shū .de dì.fāng, túshūguǎn
      7.   Tā.mén, nèi.ge lǎn jiā.huǒ, *lǎn*guǐ (lazy devil) huò.zhě lǎn gú.tóu
            (lazy bones)
      8.   Wǒ.mén, huài jiā.huǒ, huàidàn

LESSON 3

Vocabulary

xiē	歇	to rest	-.zhe (.zhi)	着	suffix for progressive action
zhàn	站	to stand			
dèng.zi	凳子	stool	zuǒ.biānr	左邊ㄦ	left side
pá	爬	to climb; to crawl	yòu.biānr	右邊ㄦ	right side
			qián.tou	前頭	front, in front of...
shàng.lái	上來	come up			
xià.qù	下去	go down	hòu.tou	後頭	rear, in back of...
shì	試	to try	guò.lái	過來	come over
ràng	讓	let	zhèi.huǐr	這會ㄦ	this moment
zhōngjiànr	中間ㄦ	middle	miànqián	面前	'face-front', in front of (a person)
tǎng	躺	to lie (on back or side)			
pā	趴	to lie (on stomach)	zhèng	正	just ...-ing, just in the process of...

Vocabulary Classified by Type

Nouns	Verb Suffixes	
dèng.zi	-.zhe	tiào.xià.qù
		pǎo.guò.lái

Verbs	Adverbs	Localizers
xiē	zhèng	zhōngjiànr
zhàn		zuǒ.biānr
pá	**V-Directional Complements**	yòu.biānr
shì	shàng.lái	qián.tou
ràng	xià.qù	hòu.tou
tǎng	guò.lái	miànqián
pā	zhàn.qǐ.lái	
	pá.shàng.qù	**Time Words**
	pá.shàng.lái	zhèi.huǐr

Grammar Notes

1. *Shì.x .kàn* "try and see—give it a try" is a fixed expression usable in many contexts. *Shì* by itself is often translated as "try", but actually is used much more selectively than "try" in English. This is partly because "try" in English means both "test" and "attempt" whereas *shì* in Chinese means only "test". In English "try" is commonly followed by a verb: "I tried (attempted) to tell him that ..."; "try (make an attempt) to come back before five o'clock". But in Chinese you cannot say *shì gào.sù .tā* ... or *Shì zài wǔ diǎn zhōng yǐqián huí.lái*. You should continue to bear in mind that Chinese and English words are seldom equivalent and that literal translation will lead you into numerous mistakes.

    One common way to say "try to (verb)" in Chinese is to repeat a verb in the neutral tone and add *.kàn*: *xiě.x .kàn* "try to write (it)", *chī.x .kàn* "try eating (it)", *tīng.x .kàn* "try listening (to it)". The repeated verb is originally a temporary AN with *yì (yí)* "one": *tīng .yì.tīng*, literally "listen one listen". This is shortened to *tīng.x*, and the following *.kàn* has the sense of "...and see". Thus, *tīng.x .kàn* becomes "have a listen and see—try listening".

2. Note that here the teacher is telling Old Yaller to *pá.shàng.lái*, but two sentences ago was talking about *pá.shàng.qù*. Why the change from *.qù* to *.lái*? Even without looking at your videotape, you can infer that the teacher has moved. A moment ago the dog was supposed to climb up in a direction away from the teacher. Now, the teacher apparently has moved near to the thing onto which the dog will climb, so that the motion is *toward* him.

3. **Adverb and Complement Uses of Zài and Dào.** Review note 12 of the last lesson on *dào* + Place Word. In this lesson we have *zài* "in, on, at" + Place Word. The two constructions are very similar, except that *.lái* and *.qù* are not used with *zai*. Like *dao*, *zai* has three uses with a Place Word:

    (1) As a main verb. *Wǒ zài chuáng.shàng* "I am in bed."; *tā zài Měi.guó* "she is in America".

    (2) Before a verb (as the First-Position Verb, i.e., in the adverb position). *Wǒ zài chuáng.shàng kàn-shū* "I am reading in bed"; *tā zài Měi.guó xué Yīngwén* "she's studying English in America".

    (3) After a verb (in the complement position). *Lǎo Huáng tǎng .zài chuáng.shàng* "Old Yaller is lying on the bed". When *.zài* is in the complement position, like *.dào* it is always neutral tone and can also be abbreviated to *.de*: *Lǎo Huáng zuò .de yǐ.zi.shàng*.

    As with *.dào*, the distinction in meaning between uses (2) and (3) is often quite clear, that is, the adverb emphasizes manner and the complement emphasizes result. In a few cases, though, the two forms amount to the same meaning. For example, *Chǐng .nǐ màn .yì.diǎnr shuō* (*màn .yì.diǎnr* in adverb position) and *Qǐng .nǐ shuō màn .yì.diǎnr* (*màn .yì.diǎnr* in complement position). Both mean "Please speak a little more slowly".

    If the speaker does want to place emphasis on either manner or result, he or she will make a distinction between the adverb and complement positions. For example, if a woman sees her child write something on her coat with a piece of chalk, she will say, *Zài hēibǎn.shàng xiě, bié zài wǒ yī.fú.shàng xiě* "Write on the blackboard; don't write on my coat." On the other hand, when the same woman sees her husband write some useful information on a piece of paper that could easily be lost, she might say, *Xiě .zài hēibǎn.shàng, bié xiě .zài zhǐ.shàng* "Write it on the blackboard; don't write it on the paper." In the first instance, her attention is focused on the manner of *xiě*, so she puts *zài hēibǎn.shàng* in the adverb position. In the second instance, she cares about the result of *xiě*, i.e., she wants to have the information stay on the blackboard, so she puts *zài hēibǎn.shàng* in the complement position.

In usage (3), the complement position, *.dào* and *.zài* are sometimes interchangeable. If a piece of chicken falls into a coffee cup (as in II.2.35), you can say *diào .dào kāfēi bēi.zi.lǐ* or *diào .zài kāfēi bēi.zi.lǐ* or *diào .de kāfēi bēi.zi.lǐ*—all equally well. But in many cases *.dào* and *.zài* have differing senses. If there is a change of location **onto**, **into**, or **arriving at** a second place, *.dào* is preferred or required: *tiào .dào shuǐ.lǐ* "jump into the water", *pá .dào zhuōr.shàng .qù* "climb up onto the table". When no change of location is involved, *.zài* is preferred or required: *zuò .zài yǐ.zi.shàng* "sit on the chair", *tǎng .zài chuáng.shàng* "lie on the bed", *zhàn .zài hēibǎn qián.tou* "stand in front of the blackboard". (*.De* can still replace *.dào* or *.zài* in any of these examples.)

4. *Xué.shēng qián.tou* is originally *xué.shēng .de qián.tou*. The *.de* almost always drops out before free-word localizers (*qián.tou, hòu.tou, lǐ.tou, wài.tou, wài.biānr, hòu.biānr, pángbiānr, shàng.tou, dǐ.xià*, etc.). Other cases where the *.de* almost always drops are between pronouns and words for relatives: *wǒ fù.qīn* "my father", *tā mā.x* "his mom", *nǐ jiě.x* "your elder sister", etc.

5. "Between A and B" is A *gēn* B *.de zhōngjiànr*. The phrase as a whole is a Place Word, and operates as such in all patterns that call for Place Words.

6. Note that this sentence, *Nǐ xiǎng...yǐ.zi.shàng*, is not grammatically a question. But with *zěm.me* preceding it, it becomes a question with the sense of "How can it be that...?", expressing minor surprise and asking for confirmation. For example, *Nǐ bù dǒng Yīngwén* is a statement, but *Zěm.me, nǐ bù dǒng Yīngwén?* means "How can it be that you don't understand English?".

7. *Zuò.bú-xià.qù* "sit and be unable to go down—can't sit down". The directional complement *xià.qù* is used here in its literal meaning. It also has figurative meanings: (1) "continue", as in *shuō.xià.qù* "continue saying", *kàn.xià.qù* "go on reading", and *tīng.bú-xià.qù* "cannot go on listening". (2) With *chī* "eat", and usually omitting *.qù*, *chī.bú-xià(.qù)* means "cannot eat (it) down—to be full". The unifying sense in these various examples is the presence or absence of an obstacle: (Verb) *.xià.qù* "go on (Verb)-ing free from obstacle"; (Verb) *.bú-xià(.qù)* "encounter an obstacle to continued (Verb)-ing".

8. In English, we "lie on the back" or "lie on the stomach", but in either case "lie". In Chinese *tǎng* is "lie on back" (or, as in Old Yaller's case, "lie on side"), while *pā* is "lie on stomach".

9. *Nǐ jiù pā.zhe* "you just lie there". The actual pronunciation of the suffix -*.zhe* can be either *.zhe* or *.zhi*. It is added to a verb to indicate that an action is progressing, or in a continuing state. Here, it is part of an imperative (a

command or request) to do something and "keep doing" it. Other examples: *Nǐ zuò.zhe!* "Sit (and keep sitting)!"; *(Nǐ) ná.zhe zhèi.ge* "Hold (and keep holding) this"; *Zhàn.zhe!* "Stand (and maintain position)!".

10.   Note, in this long sentence, the contrasting emphases of the "*dào* (or *zài*) + Place Word" phrases when used (1) in the adverb position (emphasizing manner) and (2) in the complement position (emphasizing result).

11.   Note the use here of *guò.lái* as a verb on its own. In the next part of the sentence, *pǎo.guò.lái*, it is a directional complement.

12.   *Zǒu-lái zǒu-qù* "walk back and forth". The pattern "Verb-*lái* Verb-*qù*" works with certain other verbs as well: *pǎo-lái pǎo-qù* "run back and forth, run here and there", *kàn-lái kàn-qù* "look here and there", *xiǎng-lái xiǎng-qù* "think here and think there--think of everything one can", etc.

13.   *Méi fá.zi* (+ Verb) "have no way to (Verb)".

14.   Note the difference between *zǒu .dào fáng.zi pángbiānr .qù* in this sentence and *dào fáng.zi pángbiānr .qù zǒu* in the previous sentence. (Review the last paragraph of note 12 in the previous lesson and note 3 in this lesson.)

15.   **Progressive Action.** To indicate that an action is currently in progress, you can use *zhèng .zài .nàr* "right there" before the verb, with *.ne* after it. *Tā zhèng .zài .nàr zǒu .ne* "He is (right there in the process of) walking." You can also use the -*.zhe* described in note 9 above to reinforce the same idea: *tā zhèng .zài .nàr zǒu.zhe .ne*. In fact the following versions are all possible, with little if any difference in sense, although *zhèng* and -*.zhe* do give more emphasis:

> *Tā zhèng .zài .nàr zǒu.zhe .ne.*
> *Tā .zài .nàr zǒu.zhe .ne.*
> *Tā zhèng .zài .nàr zǒu .ne.*
> *Tā .zài .nàr zǒu .ne.*
> *Tā zhèng .zài zǒu.zhe .ne.*
> *Tā zhèng .zài zǒu .ne.*
> *Tā zài zǒu.zhe .ne.*
> *Tā zài zǒu .ne.*

One important difference among the above usages is that any example including *.nàr* still has some of the original sense of "over there, away from the speaker". Therefore you would not use it with *wǒ* or *wǒ.mén* or *zá.mén*, unless you were referring to a different time, when you were located somewhere else. You can use *zhèr* to indicate progressive action for *wǒ*, *wǒ.mén* or *zá.mén* in the present, e.g., *Wǒ .zài .zhèr xiě tiáo.zí .ne.*

Culture Note 13:   The Terms "Zhōng.guó" and "Wài.guó"

A basic textbook on East Asian civilization explains the term *Zhōng.guó* this way:

> The Chinese early developed a strong sense of history and the ideal of
> political unity. Unaware of the great civilizations to the west, they
> considered China the unique land of civilization, surrounded on all sides by
> the "four barbarians." They therefore called it the "Central Country," or
> *Chung-kuo* [*Zhōng.guó*].[8]

The term *wài.guó*, which refers to all countries outside of *Zhōng.guó*, is conceptually
different from the term "foreign" in English. In English, "foreigner" generally refers
to a person who is not in his or her own country. Thus an American in China is a
foreigner; a Chinese in America is also a foreigner. But the Chinese term *wài.guórén*
refers to all people who are not *Zhōng.guórén*, regardless of where anybody is located.
Thus a Chinese in America is still a *Zhōng.guórén*, not a *wài.guórén*. And the Americans
whom a Chinese meets in America are still *wài.guórén*, who are living in a *wài.guó* and
speaking a *wài.guó-huà*.

Some people criticize the Chinese for coming to other countries and calling the local
people "foreigners". This criticism reflects a misunderstanding of the term *wài.guó*.
In using it, Chinese are not expatriating their hosts, but simply observing that they
are not Chinese people.

Exercises

In-class exercises:

1.   Fill in the missing elements for the following sentences.

    A.   Nǐ lèi ... .ma?   Are you tired?
    B.   Nǐ xiē ... .   Rest for a while.
    C.   Hē ... shuǐ.   Drink some water.
    D.   Nǐ zhàn ... .   Stand up.
    E.   Zuò ... .   Sit down.
    F.   Bié ... zhèr zǒu.   Don't walk around here.
    G.   Dào fáng.zi pángbiānr ... zǒu.   Go beside the house and walk around.
    H.   Xiànzài tā zhèng ... fáng.zi pángbiānr zǒu .ne.   Right now he's walking
        around beside the house.

2.   V.V *.kàn*

    A.   Zhè.shi wǒ zuò .de cài, qǐng .nǐ ... .   (zuò-cài: to prepare dishes)
    B.   Zhèi-jiàn yī.fú shi wǒ gāng mǎi (buy) .de, wǒ yào ... .
    C.   Xié héshì .bù.hé.shì, děi ... cái zhīdào.
    D.   Bǐ (pen) dào.dǐ hǎo .bú.hǎo xiě, nǐ zìjǐ ... .ba.

---

[8] John K. Fairbank and Edwin O. Reischauer, **East Asia: The Great Tradition** (Houghton
Mifflin, 1958), p. 37.

    E.   Mén hǎo.xiàng huài .le (out of order), wǒ kāi.le bàn.ge zhōngtóu hái.shi
             kāi.bù-kāi, nǐ lái ... .ba.

    F.   Chē.zi (car) zuò.de.xià .zuò.bú.xià wǔ.ge rén, wǒ.mén ... jiù zhīdào .le.

    G.   Zhèi-jǐ.ge zì wǒ kàn.bù-qīng.chǔ, nǐ.de yǎn.jīng hǎo, nǐ lái ... .

3.   *Zhèng .zài (.nàr)* V *.ne*

    A.   Zuó.tiān nǐ lái kàn .wǒ .de shí.hòur, wǒ ... kàn-shū .ne.

    B.   Nǐ shàng-kè .de shí.hòur, wǒ ... . (eating lunch)

    C.   Tā qǐ.lái .de shí.hòur, wǒ ... . (writing a letter to my friend)

    D.   *Lǐ* lǎoshī jiǎng-kè .de shí.hòur, tā ... xiǎng bié.de shì.qíng .ne.

    E.   Nǐ jìn.lái .de shí.hòur, wǒ ... . (cleaning the room)

4.   V-*lái* V-*qù*

    A.   Nèi.ge *xiǎo* gǒu zài wū.zi.lǐ ... . (run about)

    B.   Xiǎo hóu.zi (monkey) zài fángdǐng.shàng ... . (jump around)

    C.   Lǎo Huáng zài gǒu fáng.zi pángbiānr ... . (walk back and forth)

5.   Extended use of V-*lái* V-*qù*

    A.   Wǒ chī ... hái.shi jué.de Zhōng.guó-cài zuì hǎochī.

    B.   Lǎo Zhāng ... dōu xiǎng.bù-chūlái yǒu shém gèng hǎo .de fá.zi.

    C.   Zhèi.ge zì zhēn nán xiě, *wǒ* ... hái.shi xiě .de bùhǎokàn.

    D.   Tā shuō-huà shuō .de tài kuài, wǒ ... dōu tīng.bù-dǒng.

Homework:

1.   Translate the following sentences into Chinese.

    A.   He has now walked into that house. I can no longer see (him).

    B.   Now I want you first to run to the left side of the table, and next to the
             right side, and then come back and lie on the bed in front of me. After you
             rest enough, you should lie (on your stomach) on the floor.

    C.   I told him not to walk back and forth in front of me, so he has gone beside
             the dog house and is walking around there.

    D.   Please try to eat it; see if it tastes good.

    E.   I feel that standing in the street is more comfortable than sitting in his
             room.

    F.   That mountain (shān) is too high. I am too tired; I can't climb up. I
             don't know if he can climb up. You better ask him yourself.

2.   *Xiān* V$_1$ (*zài* V$_2$)... *ránhòu zài* V$_3$

    Write sentences according to the order of the activities.

    A.   pǎo .dào zhuō.zi zuǒ.biānr; pǎo .dào zhuō.zi yòu.biānr; dào yǐ.zi hòu.tou
             zhàn.zhe

    B.   yòng yòu.shǒu ná dāo.zi qiē; fàng.xià dāo.zi; yòng yòu.shǒu ná chā.zi
             yí-kuài yí-kuài .de chī

    C.   *zhěng*.lǐ wū.zi; kàn yì-běn shū; xiě yì-fēng xìn

    D.   shàng túshūguǎn; qù kàn yáyī; huí sùshè gēn Dīng Xīn tán.x

    E.   hē yì-bēi kāfēi; chī jǐ-kuài bǐnggān; kàn-shū

Classroom/Homework exercises:

1.   Use the potential complement to finish the following sentences.

    A.   Yǐ.zi tài xiǎo .le, liǎng.ge rén ... .
    B.   Sān-wǎn fàn wǒ yí.ge rén ... .
    C.   Qiáng tài gāo .le, wǒ ... .   (climb)
    D.   Yīn.wèi mén kāi.bù-kāi, *suǒ*.yi wǒ ... .
    E.   Wū.zi.li búgòu liàng, wǒ ... .
    F.   Tā lí wǒ tài yuǎn (far), tā shuō-huà wǒ ... .

2.   Answer the following questions.

    A.   Nèi-zhāng dèng.zi wèishém Lǎo Huáng pá.bú-shàngqù?
    B.   Nèi-*bǎ* yǐ.zi wèishém Lǎo Huáng zuò.bú-xiàqù?
    C.   Lǎo Huáng wèishém bù xi.huān zuò .zài lǎoshī shēn.shàng?
    D.   Tǎng.zhe gēn pā.zhe yǒu shém bùtóng?
    E.   Lǎoshī wèishém méi fá.zi zuò shì.qíng?

LESSON 4

Vocabulary

lǐ.tou	裏頭	inside	gāoxìng	高興	happy
wài.tou	外頭	outside	ménkǒur	門口ㄦ	doorway
dāi	待	to stay	jiào	叫	call (to someone)
wánr	玩ㄦ	to play	shānshuǐ-huàr	山水畫ㄦ	'mountain-water-painting', landscape painting
kōngqì	空氣	air			
dì.fāng	地方	space	shàng.tou	上頭	above, top
cǎodì	草地	lawn	kàn.chū.lái	看出來	make out by looking at
huār	花ㄦ	flower			
shù	樹	tree	niàn	念	to read aloud
gào.sù	告訴	to tell	suǒ yǒu .de	所有的	all
bùxǔ	不許	not permit, not allow	lián	連	including (see Grammar Notes)
.l'a	啦	contraction of .le and .a	nándào	難道	do you mean to say?
yáo	搖	to shake	cāi	猜	to guess
yáo-tóu	搖頭	shake head	cōng.míng	聰明	intelligent, smart
bùgǎn	不敢	dare not	bèn	笨	stupid

Vocabulary Classified by Type

Nouns	Verbs	First Position Verbs
kōngqì	wánr	lián
dì.fāng	gào.sù	
cǎodì	yáo	**Adjectives**
huār	jiào	gāoxìng
shù	niàn	suǒ yǒu .de
shānshuǐ-huàr	cāi	cōng.míng
		bèn
Verbs	**Auxiliary Verbs**	
dāi	bùxǔ	
	bùgǎn	

Sentential Adverbs (Moveable Adverbs)	Verb-Complements	Place Words
nándào	kàn.chū.lái	ménkǒur

V-Os	Localizers	Particles
yáo-tóu	lǐ.tou wài.tou shàng.tou	.l'a

Grammar Notes

1. *Yòu...yòu...* (literally "again... and again...") means "both...and...". But unlike "both" and "and" in English, *yòu* is an adverb and therefore must **always** precede a verb or adjective, never a noun. Thus, to say "there were both flowers and trees", you cannot say *yǒu yòu huār yòu shù*; you have to say *yòu yǒu huār yòu yǒu shù*. Note that in the example in the text, there are actually three *yòu* in series (*yòu yǒu cǎodì, yòu yǒu huār, yòu yǒu shù*). This is fine; there can also be four, five, or even more.

"Nǐ yòu chī huār .le. Wǒ gào.sù .nǐ bùxǔ chī huār .ma"

2. *Yòu* in this line and *zài* in the next both are adverbs meaning "again", but they have different uses and are not interchangeable. *Yòu* is used with verbs for actual, and therefore unchangeable, events. *Nǐ yòu chī huār .le* means that the eating of flowers has actually happened, or at least has definitely begun. *Zài*, on the other hand, is used with verbs for actions that are not actual but only projected or under consideration. *Nǐ yào.shi zài chī huār...* would refer to an eating of flowers that has not yet happened but is imagined.

Usually, but not quite always, you can use the rule of thumb that *you* refers to past or present events, while *zài* refers to future events. Exceptions to this general rule are examples like *Míng.tiān yòu.shi lǐbàiwǔ .le* "Tomorrow it's Friday again". Although referring to the future, the fact cannot be changed, and therefore *yòu* is used. *Zài* can refer to the past in examples like *Zuó.tiān tā shuō tā xiǎng zài lái, jīn.tiān tā zhēn.de lái.le* "Yesterday she said she would like to come again, and today she really did".

3. *.Ma* (sometimes *.me*), as a final particle indicating impatience in the speaker, has the force of "Can't you see?".

4. *.L'a* is a fusion of *.le* and *.a*, and is usually represented by the character 啦.

5. *Yì.sī shi shuō* "meaning is to say—meaning that". The phrase can also be preceded by a noun or pronoun plus *.de*:

> Wǒ.de yì.sī shi shuō...   What I meant was ...
> Lǎoshī .de yì.sī shi shuō ...   What the teacher means is ...

By itself, *yì.sī* "meaning" can also be used in the following very handy sentences:

> "X" shi shém yì.sī?   What does "X" mean?
> "X" shi (or jiù.shi) "Y".de yì.sī.   "X" means "Y".

You can use these sentences to ask for explanations in Chinese, as in: *"Xīngqī" shi shém yì.sī?* —*.Oh, "xīngqī" jiù.shi "lǐbài" .de yì.sī.* You can, as well, use the same patterns to ask for meanings between Chinese and English: *"Lóngxiā" shi shém yì.sī?* —*"Lóngxiā" shi "lobster" .de yì.sī.*

6. *Shānshuǐ-huàr*, literally "mountain water painting", means a Chinese landscape painting. *Huà* "paint(ing)" can be a noun or a verb, but only as a noun can it be pronounced *huàr*. Thus *huà-huà* (or *huà-huàr*) "paint a painting"; *huà shānshuǐ huà* (or *huàr*) "paint a landscape painting".

7. The complement *chū.lái* "come out" can be a regular directional complement: *zǒu.chū.lái* "walk out (from somewhere)" (see IV.2.8). But *chū.lái* can also have an extended meaning. As a complement to the verb *kàn*, *chū.lái* means "look at with the result of 'out'—make out (by looking at)". Similarly, *tīng.chū.lái* "make out by listening to", *xiǎng.chū.lái* "make out by thinking—figure out". In a related sense, *xiě.chū.lái* means "write out" and *shuō.chū.lái* "come out with (in speech)".

The example in the text, *kàn.bù-chūlái*, is a negative potential complement meaning "cannot make out (by looking at)". All of the *chū.lái* complements in the preceding paragraph can be potential as well.

Note that what follows *kàn.bù-chūlái* is, by itself, a grammatical question: *Shì shém zì?* "What character is it?". But the sentence as a whole is not a question: *Wǒ kàn.bù-chūlái shi shém zì* "I can't make out (by looking) what character it is". Similarly, *tīng.de-chūlái shi shéi* "can make out (by ear) who it is", *xiǎng.bù-chūlái zěm xiě* "can't figure out how to write it", etc.

8. *Kàn.bù-chū shi shém zì .lái* is called a "split" complement. It is entirely equivalent to the unsplit form *kàn.bù-chūlái shi shém zì*. Other split forms

(using the examples of the previous note) are: *tīng.de-chū shi shéi .lái*, *xiǎng.bù-chū zěm xiě .lái*. As well as being split by a grammatical question, as in the examples just given, *chū.lái* can be split by a regular noun object: *shuō.bù-chū huà .lái* "can't come out with any words", *tīng.de-chū yi.sī .lái* "can make out the meaning by listening". Note that the final *.lái* in the split form is almost always neutral tone.

9. *Suǒ yǒu .de zì* "all of the characters". On *suǒ yǒu .de*, review IV.1.8.

10. *Lián* "include" can be paired with *dōu* to mean "even":

> Lián Lǎo Huáng dōu dǒng.le.   Even Old Yaller has understood.
> Lián lǎoshī dōu méi xiě-duì.   Even the teacher did not write it
>   correctly.

When the verb is negative, *yě* can replace *dōu*:

> Lián lǎoshī yě méi xiě-duì.   Even the teacher did not write it
>   correctly.
>
> Tā.de Zhōng.guó-huà, lián   Not even Chinese can understand his
>   Zhōng.guórén yě tīng.bù-dǒng.   Chinese.

All of the above examples follow the pattern:

> *lián* Subject *dōu/yě* Verb

Another variant of the pattern is:

> Subject *lián* Object *dōu/yě* Verb

For example:

> Tā lián yí.ge "dà" .zì dōu búhuì   He can't even write the character
>   xiě.   "dà".
> Wǒ gāng lái, lián sùshè zài   I just arrived, and don't even know
>   nǎr yě bùzhīdào.   where the dorm is.

11. *Nándào*, literally "hard to say", means "do you mean to say that?". It is accompanied by *.ma* at the end of the sentence. What comes between *nándào* and *.ma* can itself be a grammatical sentence:

> Nándào ni bù xi.huān hē   Do you mean to say you don't like
>   Zhōng.guó-chá .ma?   Chinese tea?
> Nándào tā méi pǎo.guò mǎ.lāsōng   You mean she's never run the marathon?
>   .ma?

Alternatively, *nándào* can come between subject and verb, with *.ma* still at the end:

> Tā nándào méi pǎo.guò mǎ.lāsōng   You mean she's never run the marathon?
>   .ma?
>
> Ni nándào lián zèm jiǎndān .de   Do you mean to say you can't
>   wèntí dōu kàn.bù-dǒng .ma?   understand (from reading)

even a simple question like
this?

WARNING: *Nándào* means **the whole phrase** "Do you mean to say that...?". Thus when you want to translate this phrase from the English, just say *nándào*, not *nándào nǐ shuō*. "Do you mean to say you don't understand?" is *Nándào nǐ bù dǒng .ma?*. (Don't say *Nándào nǐ shuō nǐ bù dǒng .ma?*.)

12. *Cāi* "guess" is used only in the literal English sense of guessing, as in "guess what I have in my hand" or "guess heads or tails". But "guess" in English can also mean "tentatively think". For this meaning you cannot use *cāi* but must use a word like *xiǎng*:

　　　　　Wǒ xiǎng wǒ jīn.tiān huì qù.　　　　I guess I'll go today.

WARNING: The tentative expression "I guess so" in English **cannot** be translated using *cāi*. For this meaning say *(wǒ xiǎng) dàgài shi zhèi-yàngr .ba*; **don't** say *wǒ cāi zhèi-yàngr .ba*.

Exercises

In-class exercises:

1. Oral Substitution

    Given: Suírán tā xué.le liǎng-nián .de Zhōngwén, kě.shi tā búhuì xiě "shàng," "xià" zhèi-liǎng.ge zì.

    Response: Nándào tā lián zhèi-liǎng.ge zì yě búhuì xiě .ma?

    A.　Suírán tā shi wǒ mèi.x, kě.shi wǒ kàn.bù-chūlái zhè shi .bú.shi wǒ mèi.x xiě .de zì.
    B.　Suírán wǒ shi Zhōng.guórén, dàn.shi wǒ chī.bù-chūlái zhè shi .bú.shi Zhōng.guó-cài.
    C.　Suírán *wǒ bǐ* Lǎo Huáng cōng.míng, kě.shi wǒ tīng.bù-chūlái mén wài.tou shi shéi.
    D.　Suírán *wǒ* xiǎng bāng nǐ.de máng, kě.shi *wǒ* xiǎng.bù-chū .ge hǎo fá.zi .lái.
    E.　Jīn.tiān .de kǎoshì nán shi bù nán, kě.shi wǒ búhuì xiě "rén" .zhèi.ge zì.

2. True or False. (If the statement is false then provide the correct answer orally.)

    A.　Lǎo Huáng xǐ.huān zài wū.zi wài.tou wánr, yīn.wèi wū.zi lǐ.tou tài luàn.
    B.　Wū.zi wài.tou .de kōng.qì bǐ wū.zi lǐ.tou hǎo.
    C.　Lǎo Huáng .de zhǔrén (master) bù xǐ.huān Lǎo Huáng chī-huā.
    D.　Lǎo Huáng yǐhòu bùgǎn zài chī huā .le.
    E.　Lǎo Huáng kàn.bù-chū mén.shàng shi shém zì, yīn.wèi tā .hěn bèn.
    F.　Dì-bā kè *suǒ* yǒu .de zì xué.shēng dōu dǒng .le.
    G.　Xué.shēng shuō tā.mén *bǐ* Lǎo Huáng cōng.míng .yì.diǎnr.

Homework:

1.   Translate the following sentences into Chinese.

A.   What's on the window? There is a note on the window. What's above the
      window? There is a lamp above the window.

B.   You have tricked me again. I told you that you shouldn't trick people. In
      the future if you trick me again, I will definitely beat you to death.

C.   He is the most intelligent student in our school. Even he can't make out
      (by looking) what tree this is. Do you mean to say that you want us to tell
      you what tree this is?

D.   Although he is very happy visiting (playing in) America, he has to go back
      to Běijīng now.

E.   Tomorrow morning I want to jog in the street because all day long I work
      inside the house. The air in the room is very bad; I feel very
      uncomfortable.

F.   The house caught fire (zháo-huǒ.le). Everyone had to jump down. I asked
      him if he dared to jump. He shook his head, meaning that he didn't dare.
      Fortunately we don't have to jump now because they (the firemen) let us walk
      down.

G.   The restaurant behind the library is much better than the one in front of
      the dormitory because it has both lobster and beef.

H.   I said to Lǎo Huáng, "I guess that you must enjoy (like) lying (on stomach)
      on the lawn." He said, "Your guess is definitely wrong. I really don't
      enjoy playing outside. I like to lie (on back) on your bed."

I.   Please put all the red flowers that are under the stool into that big box.

J.   "Láixi" is an excellent name. Why don't you use this name? Why do you
      always call him Lǎo Huáng?

Classroom/Homework exercises:

1.   More practice on directional complements and localizers

A.   Zhāng Rúsī is standing on the top of a small hill. Translate into Chinese
      what he says.

      Zhāng (to his friends below): Come up, all of you. It's beautiful here.

      (His friends come up. Then Zhāng receives two phone calls.)

      Zhāng to A: You better return home immediately. Your sister is not feeling
      well.

      Zhāng to B: Your guests have come. They are standing outside your room
      because your roommate (tóngwūr) doesn't have a key (yào.shi). He also wants
      you to come back right away to help entertain the guests.

B.   A teacher, a dentist, a college student, an elementary school student, and
      Old Yaller are in a room.

      Exercise 1:   Assign each one a position, then describe the situation in
      Chinese.

      Example 1:

                  Person and position: The dentist is standing between the
                     two windows.
                  Chinese: Yáyī zhàn .zài liǎng.ge chuāng.hù .de zhōngjiànr.

      Exercise 2:   Assign each one a position and an action, then describe the
      situation in Chinese.

      Example 2:

                  Person, position and action: The dentist is sitting near
                     the table painting a landscape painting.
                  Chinese: Yáyī zuò .zài zhuō.zi pángbiānr huà shānshui-
                     huàr.

      As a classroom exercise, the teacher can call on several students to
      participate in the creation of a sentence. The last student of the group
      will make a complete sentence using the selections made by his/her
      classmates.

      Example 1:

                  Student A: Yáyī
                  Student B: zhàn
                  Student C: liǎng.ge chuāng.hù .de zhōngjiànr
                  Student D: Yáyī zhàn .zài liǎng.ge chuāng.hù .de zhōngjiànr.

      Example 2:

                  Student A: Yáyī
                  Student B: zuò
                  Student C: zhuō.zi pángbiānr
                  Student D: huà shānshui-huàr
                  Student E: Yáyī zuò .zài zhuō.zi pángbiānr huà shānshui-
                     huàr.

      From the following list you can make free combinations as long as they are
      logical. You can also create your own combinations from the vocabulary you
      have learned.

      stand   between two windows   reading a book
      sit   on the bed   reading a newspaper
      lie (on one's back)   near the table   eating flowers
      lie (on one's stomach)   under the chair   shining (wiping) shoes
                               on the stool   painting landscape paintings
                               in front of the wall   cutting the cherry tomato
                               behind the door   eating cookies
                               inside a big box
                               on the floor

UNIT V

LESSON 1

Vocabulary

huà	畫	to paint	shì.jiè	世界	world	
kùn	睏	sleepy	mào.yì	貿易	trade	
shàng-chuáng	上牀	go to bed	zhōngxīn	中心	center	
qián.tiān	前天	day before yesterday	Shì.jiè Mào.yì Zhōngxīn	世界貿易中心	World Trade Center	
Niŭyuē	紐約	New York City	Zìyóushénxiàng	自由神像	Statue of Liberty	
dă-diànhuà	打電話	make a telephone call	guăn.zi	館子	restaurant	
diànhuà	電話	telephone call; telephone (machine)	dùn	頓	AN for meal	
			.lo	咯	final particle for obviousness; of course	
gē.x	哥哥	elder brother				
jiě.x	姐姐	elder sister	dàgài	大概	probably, perhaps	
dì.x	弟弟	younger brother				
cóng	從	from	shuì-jiào	睡覺	to sleep	
Bōshìdùn	波士頓	Boston	kèwén	課文	text of a lesson	
Fèichéng	費城	Philadelphia	...yĭqián	以前	before...	
-xiē	些	some	Wŭ-sì	五四	the May Fourth Movement (see Grammar Notes)	
dì.fāng	地方	place				
fù-mŭ	父母	parents	shídài	時代	era, period	
Liánhéguó	聯合國	United Nations	shèhuì	社會	society	

Vocabulary Classified by Type

Nouns	Bōshìdùn	ANs
gē.x	Fèichéng	-xiē
jiě.x	Liánhéguó	dùn
dì.x	Shì.jiè Mào.yì Zhōngxīn	
dì.fāng	Zìyóushén-xiàng	**V-Os**
fù-mǔ	Wǔsì	shàng-chuáng
shì.jiè		dǎ-diànhuà
mào.yì	**Verbs**	shuì-jiào
zhōngxīn	huà	
guǎn.zi		**Particles**
kèwén	**First Position Verbs**	.lo
shídài	cóng	
shèhuì		**Time Words**
	Adjectives	qián.tiān
Proper Nouns	kùn	...yǐqián
Niǔyuē		

Grammar Notes

1. *Wǎn.shàng* can mean either "evening" or "night"; *yè.lǐ* means "(late) night" only.

2. This is the "new situation" *.le*, whose use is appropriate not only after statements that describe new situations but after questions that *respond* to new or unusual situations. (Staying out until 2 a.m. is new in that it departs from the normal pattern.) If one of your classmates suddenly stands up in the middle of class and walks out crying loudly, you could ask *tā zěm.me .le?*, where *.le* would be appropriate because the question responds to an unusual situation.

3. *Fù-mǔ* "parents" is a contraction of *fù.qīn* and *mǔ.qīn*. Note that *fù.qīn*, *mǔ.qīn*, and *fù-mǔ* cannot be used in the direct address of parents. For that purpose you must use *bà.x* and *mā.x*.

4. *Qián.tiān* is "the day before yesterday". *Hòu.tiān*, correspondingly, is "the day after tomorrow". "The day before the day before yesterday" is *dà qián.tiān*; *dà hòu.tiān* is "the day after the day after tomorrow". The same phrases apply to years, if you substitute *nián* for *tiān*.

5. You have learned two major uses of *.le*: (1) Completed action *.le*, also known as suffix *.le* because it is a verb suffix and (2) New Situation *.le*, also known as sentence *.le* because it occurs at the end of a sentence.

    Here another usage of *.le* will be introduced, i.e., *.le* for isolated events in the past, used at the ends of sentences in narrating past events when no perfective aspect or new situation is involved. An example occurs in the sentence: *Wǒ fù-mǔ qián.tiān dào Niǔyuē lái .le* "My parents came to New York the day before yesterday". This *.le* is not, of course, required of all sentences that refer to the past.

6. *Dǎ-diànhuà*, literally "strike telephone", means "make a telephone call". *Dǎ* "strike, beat" has a broad range of uses (cf. German *schlagen*): *dǎ wǎngqiú* "play tennis"; *dǎ máoyī* "knit a sweater"; *dǎ guān.sī* "bring a lawsuit"; etc.

7. The full name for Philadelphia is *Fèilèdá'ěrfēiyǎ*. But when transliterated names become as unwieldy as this, happily they are shortened. Philadelphia becomes *Fèichéng*, literally "*Fèi*-city". San Francisco becomes *Sānfánshì*, where *shì*, like *chéng*, means "city".

8. *Xiē*, an AN for an indefinite number or quantity, means "some, few". It combines with *yī* "one" to form *yi-xiē* "a few", or with *zhèi, nèi*, or *něi*: *zhèi.xiē* "these", *nèi.xiē* "those", *něi.xiē*? "which ones?". Note that it is not *required* to use *xiē* when referring to more than one thing. *Zhè.shi bǐ* can mean "this is a pen" or "these are pens". But if you choose to make it clear that more than one pen is involved, you can say *Zhèi.xiē shi bǐ*.

    In the example in the text, *.xiē* is short for *yi-xiē*. The *yī* can drop out, just as it does for the other ANs. (See II.3.3.)

9. *Zìyóu* "freedom, liberty"; *shén* "god, goddess"; *xiàng* "portrait, statue".

10. *Guǎn.zi* "restaurant" is interchangeable with *fàn.guǎnr* (I.5).

11. *Dà* "big" here is an adverb meaning "greatly". *Dà chī.le yí-dùn* "greatly ate one instance of eating—ate a big meal". Similarly: *dà wánr.le yi-tiān* "had a great time for a day", *dà shuì.le èr.shí-nián* "had a big sleep for twenty years". WARNING: Not all verbs can be preceded by *dà* in this way. Learn examples on a case-by-case basis.

12. *.Lo* as a final particle indicates obviousness.

13. Review IV.4.2, where we said that "usually" *zài* refers to future actions and *yòu* to past ones. Here, *yòu yào shuì jiào* "will fall asleep again" is one of the exceptional cases where *yòu* refers to a future action "bound to happen". (Cf. *Míng.tiān yòu.shi lǐbàiwǔ .le* "Tomorrow it's Friday again".)

14. *Zài méi.yǒu jiǎng kèwén yǐqián,...* "Before discussing the text,...". There are two ways in Chinese to say "before doing something":

    1. Verb *yǐqián*

       jiǎng kèwén yǐqián   before discussing the text
       xué Zhōngwén yǐqián   before studying Chinese

    2. *(Zài) méi(.yǒu)* Verb *yǐqián*

       zài méi.yǒu jiǎng kèwén yǐqián before discussing the text
       méi lái yǐqián   before coming

The two usages mean exactly the same thing. Since the first is closer to English usage, you will naturally find it easier to adopt it in your own speech. This is fine. But study the second usage enough that you can recognize it when you hear it, because Chinese use the second very often.

15.   *Wǔ-sì*, literally "five-four", is a shorthand way of referring to *wǔ-yuè sì-hào*, or May 4. See Culture Note 14 below.

Culture Note 14:   The May Fourth Movement

On May 4, 1919, there was a large student demonstration at *Tiānānmén* Square, in the heart of Peking, to protest the Chinese government's readiness to grant to Japan special rights in Shantung (*Shāndōng*) after World War I. The famous demonstration eventually became a label for the intellectual ferment of the times in a larger sense. The "May Fourth Period" (*Wǔsì shídài* as it appears in the text) refers to years from about 1917 through the mid-1920s, which saw the advocacy of modern vernacular language (*báihuà*) to replace classical Chinese, the introduction and study of Western literary forms, and radical critiques of traditional Chinese society and thought. For more, see Tse-tsung Chow, **The May Fourth Movement: Intellectual Revolution in Modern China** (Harvard University Press, 1960).

The use of numbers for shorthand reference to dates of famous events has many examples in twentieth-century China. *Jiǔ-yī-bā* "September 18" refers to the famous Mukden Incident in 1931, which marked the onset of Japan's invasion of China's northeastern provinces. On April 5, 1976 there was a large demonstration in Peking to commemorate the former Chinese Prime Minister Chou En-lai (*Zhōu Enlái*) and to protest the harsh rule of Mao Tse-tung (*Máo Zédōng*), his wife Chiang Ch'ing (*Jiāng Qīng*) and others. This event became known as *Sìwǔ*. On June 4, 1989, Chinese troops opened fire on peaceful protesters, killing hundreds and perhaps thousands. This day is remembered as *Liùsì*. *Wǔsì*, *Sìwǔ*, and *Liùsì* were all centered at Peking's Tiananmen Square.

Exercises

In-class exercises:

1.   Fill in the blanks in the following sentences with "*zài*", "*cái*" or "*jiù*".

   A.   Yào.shi nǐ.mén hái.bù dǒng, wǒ kě.yǐ ... shuō yí-cì.
   B.   Tā lái .de shí.hòur wǒ bú zài-jiā, tā liú.le .ge tiáo.zi shuō xià.wǔ sān-diǎn zhōng ... lái.
   C.   Tā běnlái shūo lǐbàiwǔ lái, hòulái yīn.wèi yào dào zhèr lái kàn yáyī, lǐbàisì ... lái .le.
   D.   Wǒ zuó.tiān huí.lái .de hěn wǎn, bā-diǎn zhōng ... chī wǎnfàn.
   E.   Wǒ míng.tiān yǒu .ge kǎoshì, hòu.tiān ... néng qù kàn .nǐ.
   F.   Nǐ.de yáyī bùxǔ nǐ chī táng (candy). Yào.shi nǐ ... chī táng, wǒ jiù yào qù gào.sù tā .le.
   G.   Nèi.ge xué.shēng zhēn cōng.míng. Wǒ gěi .tā jiǎng .le yí-cì tā ... dǒng .le.
   H.   Wǒ jiào.le Lǎo Huáng sān-cì, tā ... zǒu.guò.lái.
   I.   Wǒ.mén.de shíyàn shi sì-diǎn zhōng, tā zěm liǎng-diǎn ... qù .le.

2.   Complete the following sentences with an appropriate complement.

A.   Zuó.tiān wǒ.mén wánr .de hěn ... .
B.   Wǒ zhēn kùn, kùn .de ... .
C.   Wǒ hěn lèi, lèi ... .
D.   Wǒ dāngrán hē.de ... qīngchá, wǒ zài Zhōng.guó .de shí.hòur tiānx hē qīngchá.
E.   Tā.de wū.zi luàn .de ... .
F.   .He, zhēn gān.jìng, gān.jìng ... .
G.   Wǒ děng .nǐ děng .de ... , nǐ zěm xiànzài cái lái?

3.   Answer the following questions orally.

A.   Cóng lǐbàiyī dào lǐbàiwǔ yǒu jǐ-tiān?
B.   Nǐ jīn.tiān .de Zhōngwén-kè shi cóng shém shí.hòur dào shém shí.hòur?
C.   Cóng dìyī dānyuán dào dìsì dānyuán suǒ jiǎng .de nǐ dōu dǒng.le ma?
D.   Cóng Bōshìdùn dào Fèichéng yǒu jǐ-lǐ?
E.   Cóng Měi.guó kě.yǐ .bù.kě.yǐ dǎ-diànhuà dào Zhōng.guó .qù?

4.   *Xīe* some

A: Zuó.tiān wǒ kàn-shū .le.
   B: Nǐ kàn.le .xiē shém shū?
A: Wǒ kàn.le ... jiǎng Wǔ-sì shídài Zhōng.guó shè.huì .de shū, .ne.me nǐ .ne?
B: Wǒ zuó.tiān shàng Niǔyuē .qù.le.
A: Hǎo-jí.le. Nǐ dōu wánr.le ... shém dì.fāng?
B: Wǒ kàn.le Liánhéguó, hái.yǒu Shì.jiè Mào.yì Zhōngxīn.
A: Zài Niǔyuē nǐ chī.le ... shém dōng.xī?
B: Wǒ chī.le "Pizza".
A: Nǐ yì shūo "Pizza" wǒ ... è .le.
B: Wǒ .zhèr yǒu ... bǐnggān, hái.yǒu ... niúròu tāng, nǐ yào .bú.yào?
A: Niúròu tāng nǐ zìjǐ hē .ba; Wǒ zhǐ xiǎng chī jǐ-kuài bǐnggān.

5.   *Kàn* think, believe, figure

A.   Yǐ.jīng jiǔ-diǎn .le, tā hái méi qǐ.lái, wǒ ... tā jīn.tiān shàng-kè yòu yào chídào.
B.   Zhèi liǎng-jiàn yī.fú nǐ ... něi-yí-jiàn héshì?
C.   Nǐ bié děng tā .le. Wǒ ... tā shi búhuì lái .de.
D.   ... zhèi-zhī gǒu yídìng tīng.bù-dǒng nǐ shūo .de huà. Nǐ jiào tā zuò.xià tā dào zhàn .qǐ.lái .le.
E.   A: Nǐ zěm .l'a?
     B: Wǒ yīn.wèi qìshuǐ hē .de tài duō, dù.zi bùshū.fú.
     A: Huógāi! (You deserved it!) Wǒ ... nǐ yǐhòu hái gǎn .bù.gǎn hē nèm duō qìshuǐ?

Homework:

1.   Translate the following two dialogues into Chinese.

A: Why are you so sleepy?
B: I didn't go to bed till 3:00 A.M. in the morning.
A: Why did you go to bed so late? Were you studying for an exam or doing homework?

B: No, I wasn't studying. I went to New York yesterday afternoon and got back
    very late. I was exhausted.
A: I imagine you'll be nodding off again in class today.

A: Your younger sister just called me. She asked (wanted) me to tell you that
    your parents have already come.
B: Where are they?
A: They are waiting for you at the Student Center.
B: How about my elder brother and sister, and my younger brother? Have they come
    too?
A: That I don't know, because your younger sister didn't say.

Classroom/Homework exercises:

1.   Oral Substitution

      Given: Wǒ xiǎo .de shí.hòur búhuì yòng zuǒ.shǒu ná dōng.xī.

      Response: Oh, ne.me nǐ shi dà.le yǐhòu cái xué-huì yòng zuǒ.shǒu ná dōng.xī
      .de'a.

      A.   Wǒ méi dào Měi.guó .lái yǐqián bù chī niúròu.
      B.   Méi kàn yáyī yǐqián wǒ bùzhīdào zài Měi.guó kàn yáyī zèm guì.
      C.   Méi xué Rìwén (Japanese) yǐqián wǒ yǐwéi Zhōngwén bǐ Rìwén nán.
      D.   Méi dào Niǔyuē .qù yǐqián wǒ bùzhīdào Niǔyuē .de rén zèm duō.

      Given: Xǐ (wash) .le shǒu yǐhòu cái néng chī-fàn.

      Response: Chī-fàn yǐqián děi xiān xǐ-shǒu.

      A.   Gěi wǒ dǎ.le diànhuà yǐhòu cái néng lái kàn .wǒ.
      B.   Xué shuō-huà yǐhòu cái néng xué xiě-zì.
      C.   Niàn.le shū yǐhòu cái néng chū.qù wánr.
      D.   Xǐ.le shǒu yǐhòu cái néng chī dōng.xī.
      E.   Cā.le zhuō.zi yǐhòu cái néng sǎo-dì.

LESSON 2

Vocabulary

shuì-zháo	睡着	to fall asleep	lùyīndài	錄音帶	'record-sound-belt', audio-tape
gè	各	each; various			
yán.sè	顏色	color	jiào-xǐng	叫醒	wake up (some-one)
bǐ	筆	writing instru-ment	huí	回	time (same as cì)
dài	戴	to wear (see Grammar Notes)	shuì	睡	to sleep
biǎo	錶	watch, wrist-watch	hǎo	好	how, really
jǐ-diǎn	幾點	what time	rèn.de,	認得	to know, recog-nize (a person,
-fēn	分	minute	rèn.shì	認識	word, character)
kuài....le	快…了	about to...	dàjiā	大家	everyone
xià-kè	下課	get out of class	bú.shi... jiù.shi...	不是…就是…	if not...then...
xià.cì	下次	next time	dàshēng	大聲	loudly
chú.le... yǐwài	除了…以外	except for...	gēr	歌儿	song
yù.bèi	預備	to prepare	chàng-gēr	唱歌儿	to sing (song)
liànxí	練習	exercise, prac-tice	diànchàngjī	電唱機	phonograph
yǔyán shíxíshì	語言實習室	language lab	xiǎng	響	loud(ly)
			tǎoyàn	討厭	to find disgust-ing

Vocabulary Classified by Type

Nouns		Verbs
yán.sè	dàjiā	dài
bǐ	gēr	yù.bèi
biǎo	diànchàngjī	shuì
liànxí		rèn.shì
yǔyán shíxíshì	**Pronouns**	rèn.de
lùyīndài	dàjiā	tǎoyàn

V-Os	Adverbs	Time Words
xià-kè	hǎo	jǐ-diǎn
chàng-gēr	dàshēng	xià.cì

Verb-RCs	Conjunctions	Idiomatic Expressions
shuì-zháo	bú.shi...jiù.shi...	kuài....le
jiào-xǐng		chú.le...yǐwài

	ANs	
Adjectives	-fēn	**Determinatives**
xiǎng	huí	gè

Grammar Notes

1. *Zháo* is a complement indicating that the preceding verb "actually is realized" or "takes effect". *Shuì-zháo*, "go to sleep and the sleeping takes effect", means "fall asleep"; *zhǎo-zháo*, "search for and the search is realized", means "find", etc.

    Be careful to distinguish *shuì-zháo* "to fall asleep" from *shuì-jiào* "to sleep". *Shuì-zháo* is a Verb-Complement, which means you can say things like *shuì.bù-zháo* "cannot fall asleep"; *shuì-jiào* is a Verb-Object, allowing you to say things like *shuì.le yí dà jiào* "had a big sleep". Strictly speaking, *shuì-zháo* happens at an instant—the instant at which consciousness is lost. When you add the *.le* to make *shuì-zháo.le*, the time referred to is not instantaneous but extended to "is (are) asleep". But *shuì-zháo.le* is not quite the same as *shuì-jiào*, either. *Shuì-zháo.le* definitely implies loss of consciousness, while *shuì-jiào* refers to the whole process of retiring for sleep, whether or not one actually sleeps. For example, *mèi.x shuì-jiào.le* means that younger sister has gone to bed, and may well be asleep (*shuì-zháo.le*), but on the other hand perhaps cannot fall asleep (*shuì.bù-zháo*).

    To ask "what time do you go to bed every day?" most people would say *nǐ měi-tiān jǐ-diǎn zhōng shuì-jiào?* instead of *nǐ měi-tiān jǐ-diǎn zhōng shàng-chuáng?*.

2. *Gè* "various" or "the various" or sometimes "each". *Gè-zhǒng* "various kinds", *gè-chù* "various places". This *gè* is a determinative (like *zhèi, nèi*) and is different from the AN *gè* that we often abbreviate as *.ge*.

3. *Bǐ* is a general word for "writing instrument". It can be used alone or with modifiers that specify the kind of writing instrument: *qiānbǐ* "lead-*bǐ*—pencil", *máobǐ* "hair-*bǐ*—brush", *fénbǐ* "powder-*bǐ*—chalk", *gāngbǐ* "steel-*bǐ*—fountain pen", etc.

4. There are two verbs meaning "wear" in Chinese, *dài* and *chuān*. (*Chuān* appeared in IV.1.) *Chuān* literally means "penetrate, pierce" and is used for articles that part of the body goes through, like shirts or pants. *Chuān* is also used for shoes (*chuān-xié*) and socks (*chuān wà.zi*), even though the foot does not go entirely through. *Dài* literally means "put on top" and is used for hats (*dài mào.zi*) and glasses (*dài yǎnjìng*). With only a few exceptions, *dài* is used for things that

are worn as accessories (glasses, watches, earrings, false teeth, etc.) while *chuān* is used for more necessary basic clothing.

5.   *Kuài* "fast" here indicates imminent action: "fast (becoming)" or "on the point of". In this use it precedes a predicate and is followed by *.le*:

> Kuài xià-kè .le.   Class is about to end.
> Lóngxiā kuài méi.yǒu .le.   The lobster is almost gone.

(The final *.le* in this usage is a "new situation *.le*" indicating that a new situation is about to arrive, or that the situation of imminence is itself new.) *Yào*, which can mean "will" (see III.3.1), often follows *kuài* in this pattern, and can also replace it:

> kè.rén $\begin{cases} \text{kuài} \\ \text{yào} \\ \text{kuài yào} \end{cases}$ lái .le.   The guests are about to arrive.

6.   Review II.3.35 on *.dào* plus Place Word in the complement position. Here, *.dào* has the sense of "up to" or "as far as" a certain place. *Jiǎng .dào zhèr* "lecture up to this point"; *kàn .dào dì'èr.shíwǔ yè* "read as far as page 25"; etc.

7.   *Chú.le...yǐwài* "besides, except for, outside of". To a Chinese mind, *chú.le...yǐwài* has a single meaning; but in terms of English it corresponds to (1) "besides, in addition to" if a positive statement follows and (2) "except for" if a negative statement follows:

> (1) Chú.le qiānbǐ yǐwài, wǒ hái   Besides pencils, I also have
>   yǒu máobǐ, fěnbǐ, gāngbǐ.   brushes, chalk, and pens.

> (2) Chú.le qiānbǐ gēn gāngbǐ   Except for pencils and pens, I have
>   yǐwài, wǒ méi.yǒu bié.de bǐ.   no (other) writing instruments.

When the exception or addition that falls between *chú.le* and *yǐwài* is brief, it is common to drop *yǐwài*:

> Chú.le máobǐ, tā méi.yǒu bié-   She has no writing instruments
>   zhǒng bǐ.   except brushes.

But when the exception or addition is lengthy, it is good to keep both *chú.le* at the beginning and *yǐwài* at the end, because, to the listener, they signal "beginning" and "end" of exception or addition:

> Chú.le gēn .tā yíkuàir zuò-chē   He has no friends other than that
>   lái .de nèi.ge tóngxué yǐwài,   one who came in the same car with
>   tā méi.yǒu bié.de péng.yǒu.   him.

Although the addition or exception that is framed by *chú.le...yǐwài* is often a grammatical noun (as in all the above examples), it can also be a verb:

> Chú.le chī Zhōng.guó-fàn, hē   Besides eating Chinese food and
>   Zhōng.guó-chá yǐwài, tā hái   drinking Chinese tea, she can
>   huì shuō Zhōng.guó-huà.   also speak Chinese.

8. *Hǎo* "good" can precede an adjective to mean "how, what a...". *Hǎo lěng .a!* "how cold it is!"; *hǎo dà .de fángjiān!* "what a big room it is!". In this usage *hǎo* is very similar to *zhēn* "really". *Hǎo qíguài* "how strange!" and *zhēn qíguài* "really strange!" are quite similar.

9. *Yě* here is used in a way that "also" cannot be used in English. *Yě kě.yi shuō rèn.de* means "you could say that I know him, (but actually....)" When *yě kě.yi shuō* precedes a statement, it indicates that the speaker has some reservation about that statement. Use the set phrase *yě kě.yi shuō X* to mean "you could say X" when you want to cushion your statement with some tentativeness.

10. *Rèn.de* (in this line) and *rèn.shì* (in the previous line) both mean "know", but they are different from *zhī.dào* "know". *Zhī.dào* is to know a fact: *Wǒ zhī.dào tā búhuì lái* "I know he's not likely to come"; *wǒ bùzhīdào tā shi shéi* "I don't know who she is." *Rèn.de* and *rèn.shì*, which sometimes can be translated "recognize" as well as "know", apply to people (*wǒ rèn.de tā jiě.x* "I know his older sister") or to words and characters (*tā bú rèn.shì nèi.ge zì* "she doesn't recognize that character"). Avoid the common mistake of saying *wǒ zhī.dào nèi.ge rén* to mean "I know that person". This sentence is possible, but it means "I know *of* (or about) that person".

    The *.de* (得) in *rèn.de* is an integral part of the word, and remains in a sentence even when followed by a *.de* (的) particle. *Wǒ rèn.de .de rén...* "the people I know...".

    Rèn.shì (but not *rèn.de*) can also mean "know, understand, be familiar with" a question, topic or field. *Zhèi.ge wèntí tā rèn.shì .de búgòu qīng.chǔ* "He doesn't understand this question clearly enough". Other examples of tricky cases:

Wǒ búrèn.shì (**not** bùzhīdào!) zhèi.ge zì.	I don't know this character.
Nǐ zhī.dào .bù.zhī.dào (**not** rèn.shì .bú.rèn.shì) zhèi-jiàn shì?	Do you know about this matter?

11. *Zěm jiào 'X'?* and *shém jiào 'X'?* both mean "what does 'X' mean?". For example: *Zěm jiào 'shuō.qǐ.lái róng.yì, zuò.qǐ.lái nán'?* "What does 'easier said than done' mean?".

12. *Yí.ge* here means "the same". *Wǒ.mén zhù .zài yí.ge sùshè.lǐ* "we lived in the same dorm". True, the sentence could also simply mean "we lived in a dorm". But when "the same dorm" is implied, there is more stress on *yí.ge*, and it cannot be shortened to *.ge*. To make the meaning of "the same" unambiguously clear, you can also add *tóng* "same" before *yí.ge*: *wǒ.mén zhù .zài tóng yí.ge sùshè.lǐ* "we lived in the same dorm".

13. *Bú.shì...jiù.shì...* "if not...then..." is used to assert that one or another alternative is bound to be the case. The basic pattern is:

    Subject *bú.shì* Verb$_1$ *jiù.shì* Verb$_2$

Tā bú.shì chàng-gēr jiù.shì tīng diànchàngjī.	If he's not singing he's (sure to be) listening to the phonograph.

It is often very natural to translate *bú.shi...jiù.shi...* using "either...or...":

Jīdàn bú.shi tài shēng jiù.shi tài   The eggs are either too raw or
lǎo.   over-cooked.

14. *Dàshēng* "in a loud voice". In Běijīng Mandarin, *dàshēngr*.

15. *Gē* "song". Note that with the Mandarin -*r* ending the spelling is *gēr* and is pronounced differently from *gēnr*.

16. *Kāi* "open" is used to mean "turn on" or "operate" for electrical devices and machines. *Kāi-dēng* "turn on the light (or lamp)"; *kāi diànchàngjī* "turn on the phonograph"; *kāi-chē* "drive a car"; *kāi-fēijī* "pilot an airplane". Similarly, *guān* "close" is used for "turn off": *guān-dēng* "turn off the light (lamp)"; *guān diànchàngjī* "turn off the phonograph".

17. *Xiǎng* "loud" is an adjective. But the same word and character can be a verb meaning "sound" or "make noise": *shém.me xiǎng* "what sounds—what's making the noise?"

18. *Tǎoyàn* can be:

(a) a transitive verb meaning "despise, can't stand; find (someone or something) disgusting or highly annoying":

Tā tǎoyàn .wǒ.   She finds me disgusting.
Wǒ zuì tǎoyàn zhěng.lǐ   I can't stand cleaning up the room.
  fángjiān.

(b) an adjective "disgusting, annoying":

Nèi-tiáo gǒu hǎo tǎoyàn.   That dog is most annoying.

(c) an expletive "disgusting!", commonly used with *zhēn* "really":

Zhēn tǎoyàn! Yòu xià-yǔ .le!   Oh no! It's raining again!

Exercises

In-class exercises:

1. *Zǒng.shi* always

A. Wǒ ... zǎo.shàng liù-diǎn zhōng qǐ.lái.
B. Wǒ mǔ.qīn ... bùxǔ wǒ chū.qù wánr, tā ... yào wǒ dài .zài jiā.lǐ.
C. Nèi.ge xué.shēng shàng-kè ... chídào.
D. Tā měi-yí-cì dào Niǔyuē .lái, ... dào Shì.jiè Mào.yì Zhōngxīn .qù wánr.
E. Wǒ ... zuò .zài nèi-zhāng zhuō.zi pángbiānr chī-fàn.

2. *Kuài* V *.le*

A. Kuài ... , zá.mén děi kàn-shū .le. (take exam)

B.   Wǒ ... , nǐ kě.yǐ .bù.kě.yǐ zài děng yì-huǐr. (finish writing)
C.   Wǒ kàn nèi-zhī gǒu ... yīn.wèi lǎoshī jiào .tā pǎo-lái pǎo-qù. (tired to
     death)
D.   Qìshuǐr ... , zài qù mǎi yìdiǎnr .ba. (finish drinking)
E.   Yǐ.jīng wǔ-diǎn .le, tā yěxǔ ... . (come back)

3.   Complete the following dialogues according to the example given.

     Example:
               A: Nǐ xǐ.huān .bù.xǐ.huān chī bǐnggān?
               B: Yě kě.yǐ shuō xǐ.huān.
               A: Zěm jiào "yě kě.yǐ shuō xǐ.huān"?
               B: Yīn.wèi wǒ zhǐ xǐ.huān chī wǒ mǔ.qīn zuò .de bǐnggān, bié .de
                   bǐnggān wǒ dōu bù xǐ.huān chī.

     A: Nǐ zài Niǔyuē zhù.guò .ma?
     B:
     A:
     B: Yīn.wèi wǒ zhǐ zài Niǔyuē zhù.le yì-tiān.

     A: Nǐ kàn.guò nèi-běn shū .ma?
     B:
     A:
     B: Yīn.wèi wǒ zhǐ kàn.le yì.diǎnr.

     A: Nǐ zuó.tiān shuì-jiào .le .méi.yǒu?
     B:
     A:
     B: Yīn.wèi wǒ shuì shi shuì.le, kě.shi méi shuì-zháo.

     A: Nǐ rèn .bú.rèn.shì .tā?
     B:
     A:
     B:

Homework:

1.   Translate the following sentences into Chinese.

     A.   Yesterday I dined at a Chinese restaurant in New York. The food there was
          far better than what we have at school.
     B.   Though I had a wonderful (good) time in New York, I was totally exhausted by
          the evening.
     C.   Philadelphia is close to New York. From Philadelphia to New York is only
          (only needs) two hours.
     D.   I forgot to wear my watch today. What time is it now?
     E.   It's almost three. Do you have other classes today?
     F.   No, I have no more classes. Except for going to the Third World Center to
          see a friend, I don't have anything (to do) this afternoon.
     G.   I'm going to the language lab to listen to the tapes. How about you?
     H.   I am going back to the dorm to rest for a while. Then I have to go to the
          library to study for tomorrow's exam.

I.   I have an idea. We can both go to the language lab first, and then I'll go
      to the library with you after dinner.

J.   Okay, let's do that.

K.   Before going to the classroom to attend Chinese class, I want to go first to
      the Student Center to have some soda.

L.   My roommate is really lazy. If he is not sleeping, he is listening to his
      phonograph (stereo). He doesn't study at all.

Classroom/Homework exercises:

1.   Describe in Chinese how the student in this lesson got his nose painted.

2.   Oral Substitution

Given: Měi-tiān tā chú.le gěi nánpéng.yǒu xiě-xìn yǐwài, jiù.shi dāi .zài jiā.li
kàn-shū.

Response: Měi-tiān tā bú.shi gěi nánpéng.yǒu xiě-xìn jiù.shi dāi .zài jiā.li
kàn-shū, shém bié.de shì dōu bú zuò.

A.   Wǒ zài sùshè.li chú.le niàn-shū yǐwài, jiù.shi shuì-jiào.

B.   Wǒ.de péng.yǒu, chú.le Zhōng.guórén yǐwài, jiù.shi huì shuō Zhōngwén .de
      Měi.guórén.

C.   Tā hěn xǐ.huān hóng yán.sè gēn huáng yán.sè, suǒ.yǐ tā.de yī.fú chú.le hóng
      .de yǐwài jiù.shi huáng .de.

D.   Wǒ.mén jiā .de gǒu zuì xǐ.huān chī, tā yì-tiān-dào-wǎn chú.le chī huār yǐwài
      jiù.shi chī bǐnggān.

Given: Wǒm búdàn xué shuō Zhōng.guó-huà, yě xué xiě Zhōng.guó-zì.

Response: Wǒ.mén chú.le xué shuō Zhōng.guó-huà yǐwài hái xué xiě Zhōng.guó-zì.

A.   Shàng-kè yǐqián wǒm búdàn děi yù.bèi kèwén, zuò liànxí, hái děi dào yǔyán
      shíxíshì .qù tīng lùyīndài.

B.   Shàng-kè .de shí.hòur lǎoshī búdàn gěi wǒ.mén jiǎng Zhōng.guó yǔyán
      (language) wèntí, hái gěi wǒ.mén jiǎng Zhōng.guó .de shè.huì wèntí.

C.   Wǒ.mén zài Niǔyuē .de shí.hòur búdàn kàn.le Shì.jiè Mào.yì Zhōngxīn gēn
      Liánhéguó, yě zài Zhōng.guó guǎn.zi.li dà chī.le yí-dùn.

D.   Jīn.tiān wǒ búdàn yǒu yì-táng shíyàn, hái.yǒu kǎoshì, suǒ.yǐ máng .de
      bùdéliǎo.

LESSON 3

Vocabulary

dǎ-hū.lu	打呼嚕	to snore	xǐng	醒	to wake up
dǎ-hū	打呼	to snore	diànzǐ-jìsuànjī	電子計算機	computer
zěm bàn	怎麼辦	what should (one) do?	bān	班	class
bàn	辦	to do	cèsuǒ	廁所	toilet
lán	藍	blue	jìng.zi	鏡子	mirror
bái	白	white	zhào-jìng.zi	照鏡子	to look into the mirror
.hei	嘿	interjection for calling attention	xǐ	洗	to wash
			gàn	幹	to do

Vocabulary Classified by Type

Nouns		V-Os
diànzǐ-jìsuànjī	xǐng	dǎ-hū.lu
bān	xǐ	dǎ-hū
cèsuǒ	gàn	zhào-jìng.zi
jìng.zi		

Adjectives
lán
bái

Interjections
.hei

Verbs
bàn

Grammar Notes

1. *Hū.lu* "snoring", a noun, is derived from the sound of snoring. *Dǎ-hū.lu* (or *dǎ-hū*, for short) is a verb-object compound meaning "to snore". (Review V.1.6 on the many uses of *dǎ*.)

2. *Bàn* "manage, handle" is sometimes interchangeable with *zuò* "do". But sometimes, especially when the sense is "do (about it)", *bàn* should be used instead of *zuò*. Here, for example, the question is "What is the teacher going to do about it?", and thus *bàn* is used. To say "What should I do?", say *Zěm bàn?* (not *Zěm zuò?*).

   WARNING: The Chinese word *zuò* has a much more limited use than the English word "do", because it only means "to do" and cannot stand for other verbs. In English, to answer the question "Do you know him?", you can say "I do." But in Chinese you have to say *wǒ rèn.de*, never *wǒ zuò*. Similarly, to compliment a calligrapher who has just given a demonstration, you must say *Nín xiě .de zhēn hǎo*. You cannot, following the English usage "You did extremely well", say *Nín zuò .de zhēn hǎo*. In Chinese, specific actions are represented by specific verbs that cannot be replaced.

3. *Tóngxué* means "schoolmate"--someone who went with one to the same school at the same time. More narrowly, it can also mean "classmate"--someone in the same class at school. (To be unambiguous about "classmate" in the narrow sense, you can say *tóngbān tóngxué*, literally "same class schoolmate".) *Tóngxué* can also be a verb: *tā gēn .wǒ tóngxué* "he same-studied with me--he was my schoolmate".

    Unlike the English word "classmate", *tóngxué* can also be used by superiors like teachers, principals, and guest speakers at a school to address students. For example, a principal or guest speaker can address a group of students with *gè-wèi tóngxué*--"dear assembled students". In writing to a student, a teacher might begin *Rúsī tóngxué*--"Dear student *Rúsī*".

"Zěm hái méi.yǒu kāishǐ shàng-kè jiù dǎ.qǐ hū .lái.le?"

4. *Hóng, huáng, lán, bái, hēi* are "the five basic colors" in Chinese, and they are customarily listed in exactly this order. In any language, things that are logically parallel tend to take on customary orders in set phrases, and you should note what these are for Chinese. For example, right and left are *zuǒyòu* instead of the other way around; inside and outside are *lǐwài*; male and female are *nán-nǚ*; the four directions are usually *dōng-nán-xī-běi* and sometimes *dōng-xī-nán-běi*, but not other combinations.

5. As well as indicating new situations, *.le* can be used with commands that are in response to new situations. *Xǐng.le!* "Wake up (now)!" If your roof suddenly caves in, you might say *zǒu.le!* "let's leave!".

6.   *Diànzǐ-jìsuànjī*, literally "electronic calculating machine", means "computer". A less formal term, common in Taiwan and overseas Chinese communities, is *diànnǎo* "electric brain". (Chinese uses *diàn* "electric" in many words for electric gadgets that came with modernization: *diànhuà* "electric words—telephone", *diànbào* "electric report—telegram", *diànchē* "electric cart—trolley", etc.)

7.   On *zuì hǎo*, review III.2.25.

8.   Review IV.1.7 on the use of *zhào* "shine, illuminate" to mean "according to". Here, it means "reflect". *Zhào-jìng.zi*, literally "reflect mirror", means "look into the mirror". Use only *zhào*, not *kàn* or other verbs, for looking into mirrors.

9.   In III.2.26 we introduced the basic pattern for *bǎ* sentences as:

Subject + *bǎ* + Object + Verb + other elements

We also noted that in most cases the "other elements" are complements. Now we have an example of what else the "other elements" can be. *Bǎ liǎn xǐ .yi.xǐ* "take the face and wash it a washing—wash the face" shows that reduplicated verbs such as *xǐ .yi.xǐ* can replace the complement. Similarly: *bǎ zhūo.zi cā .yi.cā* "wipe the table"; *bǎ ròu qiē .yi.qiē* "slice the meat".

Review II.1.9 on the light, informal tone of the "Verb .*yi* (*yí*) Verb" pattern. If the verb is only one syllable, the .*yi* (*yí*) can drop out (*xǐ.xǐ liǎn*, *cā.cā zhūo.zi*, etc.) If the verb is **more than** one syllable, .*yi* (*yí*) **must** drop out: *zhěng.lǐ zhěng.lǐ fángjiān* (not *zhěng.lǐ .yi zhěng.lǐ*).

10.   "So-and-so *gàn .de hǎo shì*" is often used ironically: "the 'good deed' of so-and-so". Suppose your roommate leaves the faucet running. When you return to find water all over your floor, you might say *yòu.shi X X gàn .de hǎo shì—zhēn tǎoyàn!* When your roommate returns, you might say *kàn .nǐ gàn .de hǎo shì!* "Look what you've done!".

Culture Note 15: Chinese Words for "Chinese"

Zhōngwén is a broad term for both written and spoken "Chinese language". *Zhōng.guó-huà* refers only to the spoken language. In the PRC the term *Hànyǔ*, literally "language of the Han people", has been advocated by the government as a substitute for *Zhōngwén*. The rationale is that *Zhōngwén* theoretically should refer to all languages in China, including the national minority languages, while *Hànyǔ* refers specifically to the language of the Han majority (about 94% of the total population).

The term *Hànyǔ* has become standard in formal and official contexts in the PRC. In a university coursebook, for example, "modern Chinese" will be referred to as *xiàndài Hànyǔ* and "classical Chinese" as *gǔdài Hànyǔ*. Faculty at Chinese language training centers for foreigners will also standardly use the term *Hànyǔ*. But the term *Hànyǔ* has not caught on in the daily lives of average people, who still overwhelmingly use *Zhōngwén*, *Zhōng.guó-huà*, or other dialectal words. Hence we stick to the term *Zhōngwén* in this textbook.

The term *pǔtōnghuà* (literally "common language") refers to standard Mandarin, which is based on Běijīng Mandarin. Standard Mandarin is the language that speakers of all Chinese dialects are urged to learn as a Chinese lingua franca. Before 1949 the term for this language was *guóyǔ*, literally "national language". After 1949, *guóyǔ* has remained a standard term in Taiwan, Hong Kong, and overseas Chinese communities. In imperial times, standard Mandarin was called *guānhuà* "language of officials".

Although standard Mandarin has spread considerably in the 20th century, you will find, if you travel in China, great variation from place to place in the way it is pronounced. Depending on whom you are talking to, retroflex and palatal initials may not be distinguished; *-r* endings may or may not be used; the values of tones and vowels may vary; etc. As a first-year student you should not worry too much about all of this. Concentrate on the standard accent of your teacher and your tapes. When you do run into the problem later on, you should try to adjust your listening skills as necessary. But do not try to adjust your own pronunciation. If you try to adjust every time you encounter a new accent, you will never finish adjusting.

See Appendix in blue book for a more detailed account of the Chinese language.

Exercises

In-class exercises:

1.   V *qǐ* (O) *.lái*

    A.   Kǎoshì .de shí.hòur tā bùzhīdào wèishém.me ... . (started beating himself)
    B.   Shàng Zhōngwén-kè .de shí.hòur, tā ... . (started speaking English)
    C.   Tā zuó.tiān wǎn.shàng shuì-jiào .de shí.hòur ... . (started reciting the Chinese text; recite: bèi)
    D.   Yáyī kàn tā.de yá .de shí.hòur, tā ... . (started singing)

2.   Translate the following expressions into Chinese: last month; last year; next month; last time; next class; last week; next period of class; 9 a.m.; 3 p.m.; 10:18; half past five; quarter to twelve (eleven "and three quarters"); 8:15.

Homework

1.   Translate the following sentences into Chinese.

    A.   Hey! Wake up, wake up! Class is over.
    B.   Um. Who are you? Where am I? What's going on here? (Everyone else is laughing.)
    C.   I'm the computer science teacher. You are sitting in my classroom. You have been sleeping for quite a while, and snoring.
    D.   Look, you have a strange nose too! There are all sorts of colors on it. Where did they come from?
    E.   I don't know, sir. I have to look in the mirror first. Excuse me.
    F.   I find this guy disgusting because every day, while in the bathroom, he sings at the top of his lungs.

2.   Choose an appropriate word for each of the following sentences from among: *zhǐ
      hǎo*, *zuì hǎo*, *zhǐ yào*, *qíshí*, *yóuqí*, *dàodǐ*, *díquè*, *hébì*, *xìng.kuī* and *kǒngpà*.

      A.   Tā xǐ.huān shàng Zhōngwén-kè, tā ... xǐ.huān xiě Zhōng.guó-zì.
      B.   Jìrán nǐ nèm bù xǐ.huān .tā, nǐ ... gēn .tā yíkuàir zhù .ne?
      C.   Zhèi.ge zì wǒ yǐ.jīng jiǎng.le shí-cì .le, nǐ ... dǒng.le .méi.yǒu?
      D.   Kàn yáyī tài guì.le, ... wǒ.de yá hěn hǎo, búbì chángx qù kàn yáyī.
      E.   Hěn duō rén yǐwéi "lìkè" gēn "mǎshàng" bùyíyàng, ... lìkè jiù.shi mǎshàng
            .de yì.sī.
      F.   Wǒ xǐ.huān hē-chá kě.shi méi.yǒu cháyè, suǒ.yǐ jīn.tiān ... bù hē-chá .le.
      G.   Nǐ ... gēn .tā shuō "duì.bùqǐ," yào.bùrán (otherwise) tā yídìng huì dǎ-sǐ
            .nǐ.
      H.   Yào .tā bāng nǐ.de máng bìng bù nán, ... qǐng .tā chī yí-dùn fàn jiù xíng
            .le.
      I.   Xiànzài yǐ.jīng jiǔ.diǎn .le, tā ... búhuì lái .le .ba.
      J.   Zhèi.ge xué.shēng ... hěn tǎoyàn, zài sùshè.lǐ tā bú.shi dàshēng shuō-huà
            jiù.shi bǎ diànchàngjī kāi .de hěn xiǎng.

3.   Give in Chinese some situations where you can use the expression "Zhè.shi zěm huí
      shì?".

Classroom/Homework exercises:

1.   Complete the following sentences with a Verb plus Complement or Potential
      Complement.

      A.   Tā shuō Yīngwén shuō .de hěn bù qīng.chǔ, suǒ.yǐ wǒ cháng.x ... .
      B.   Zhèi.ge hé.zi tài xiǎo .le, shí-běn shū yídìng ... .
      C.   Wǒ zhàn .de lí mén hěn yuǎn, érqiě wǒ.de yǎn.jīng yě bùhǎo, suǒ.yǐ tiáo.zi
            shàng .de zì wǒ ... .
      D.   Wǒ.de píbāo zài lóuxià, qǐng .nǐ gěi .wǒ ... , .hǎo .bù.hǎo?
      E.   Zāogāo, mén kāi.bù-kāi .le, wǒ ... .le.
      F.   Tiān tài rè .le, suírán wǒ hěn zǎo jiù qù shuì-jiào .le, kě.shi wǒ ... .
      G.   Wǒ.mén.de shū yán.sè dōu yíyàng, suǒ.yǐ wǒ.mén cháng.x bǎ shū ... .
      H.   Tā bā-diǎn zhōng yǒu kǎoshì, xiànzài yǐ.jīng qī-diǎn bàn .le, tā hái méi
            qǐ.lái, wǒ.mén yào .bú.yào bǎ .tā ... .

2.   *Bǎ* O V (.yì(yí)) V

      A.   Nǐ.de liǎn.shàng yǒu fānqié zhī, nǐ kuài qù ... . (xǐ-liǎn)
      B.   Zhèi-jǐ.ge zì nǐ xiě .de bùhǎo, qǐng .nǐ bǎ zhèi-jǐ.ge zì zài ... .
      C.   Tāng jiàn .dào zhuō.zi.shàng .le, ... (cā-zhuō.zi)
      D.   Dì.shàng zhēn bù gān.jìng, nǐ néng .bù.néng bāng wǒ ... . (sǎo-dì)
      E.   Zhèi-jiān wū.zi tài luàn .le, jīn.tiān wǒ yào ... . (zhěng.lǐ wū.zi)

LESSON 4

Vocabulary

kěwù	可惡	abominable, detestable		diànyǐng (diànyǐngr)	電影 電影ㄦ	'electric-image' movie
zhèyàng	這樣	this way		zhōumò	週末	weekend
(zhèyàngr)	這樣ㄦ			jiānr	尖ㄦ	tip
kāi-wánxiào	開玩笑	to joke, to tease		pèng	碰	to bump
.ai.yo	哎喲	exclamation for pain		jiào	叫	tell...to, ask...to
				zhǎo	找	to look for
dào-qiàn	道歉	to apologize		chū-qián	出錢	give money, to pay

Vocabulary Classified by Type

Nouns
diànyǐng (diànyǐngr)
jiānr

Verbs
pèng
jiào

zhǎo

Adjectives
kěwù

V-Os
kāi-wánxiào

dào-qiàn
chū-qián

Time Words
zhōumò

Exclamations
.ai.yo

Grammar Notes

1.   *.Ai.yo* is used to express pain or suffering. Its closest English equivalent is probably "ouch", but its usage differs from "ouch" in several ways. First, *.ai.yo* is usually repeated one or more times in quick succession, whereas in English one seldom says "ouch, ouch, ouch, ouch...". Second, it is common in Chinese to utter one long, extended *A-a-a-i-i-i-y-y-y-o-o-o!*, whereas in English one very seldom says "Ou-u-u-u-ch-h!". Third, "ouch" in English is used for relatively short, sharp pains, like burning your finger. *.Ai.yo* can be used for burnt fingers, but is also appropriate for major constitutional illnesses, or even physical exhaustion. A patient lying in a hospital bed might use *.ai.yo!* in Chinese for a moan or groan, whereas an English-speaker would be thought very peculiar to use "ouch" in such a case. (Note that *.yo* of *.ai.yo* does not appear in the standard Table of Finals in the Foundation Work. Certain interjections in Mandarin fall outside this standard table.)

2.   *Zhōumò*, literally "week" plus "end", was invented to translate the English word
      "weekend". Although it has caught on in American Chinese communities well enough
      to be considered quite standard, it still is rather new in the PRC and in Taiwan,
      where the concept of "weekend" is itself not as strong as in the United States.
      (Most factories, offices, and schools are open at least half days on Saturdays in
      China.) While you should certainly learn and use words like *zhōumò* that are based
      on Western usages, you should also be cautious about their applicability when you
      cross the Pacific.

3.   **Shi....de emphasizing time, place, or manner of a past action.** In this and
      following sentences, the use of *shi....de* illustrates an important grammatical
      point. In sentences referring to past events, when we want to emphasize when,
      where, or how the action occurred, the *shi....de* construction is used.

          For a past event whose time, place, or manner does not require emphasis, there
      is no need to use *shi....de*. For "my parents arrived yesterday", you can simply
      say *Wǒ fù-mǔ zuó.tiān dào.le*. However, if you want to stress "yesterday" (the
      time they arrived), you will say *Wǒ fù-mǔ shi zuó.tiān dào .de* "my parents arrived
      yesterday", or, to overtranslate slightly, "it was yesterday that my parents
      arrived".

          If you want to recount the past event "we had our lunch at that restaurant
      yesterday", you can say *Wǒ.mén zuó.tiān zài nèi-jiā fànguǎnr chī zhōngfàn*. If,
      however, you develop serious stomach pain in the afternoon and want to trace the
      source of the trouble, you will likely say *Wǒ.mén shi zài nèi-jiā fànguǎnr chī
      zhōngfàn .de* (emphasizing **place**).

          For "he hit me with a shoe, not a book", you say *Tā shi yòng xié dǎ .wǒ .de,
      bú.shi yòng shū dǎ .de* (emphasizing **manner**). Similarly, for "How did you come?
      Did you run or walk?", say *Nǐ shi zěm lái .de? Nǐ shi pǎo-lái .de .hái.shi
      zǒu-lái .de?*. More examples:

Time:

Nǐ shi jǐ-diǎn zhōng xǐng .de?	What time did you wake up?
Wǒ shi shí-diǎn wǔ-fēn xǐng .de.	I woke up at 10:05.

Place:

Nǐ shi zài nǎr kāishǐ huà .de?	Where did you start painting? (Where was it that you started painting?)
Wǒ shi zài bí.zi jiānr.shàng kāishǐ huà.de.	I began painting from the tip of the nose. (It was from the tip of the nose that I began painting.)

Manner:

Nǐ shi zěm xǐng .de?	How did you awake? (How was it that you awoke?)
Shi yí.ge xué.shēng bǎ .wǒ jiào-xǐng .de.	A student woke me up.

4. When *shi....de* implying the past (with a time, place, or manner expression) is used with a verb that takes an object, two different forms are possible. To say "I ate lunch at 12 o'clock", you can say:

> A. *Wǒ (shi) shí'èr diǎn zhōng chī zhōngfàn .de.*
>
> (Time Word)   (V)   (O)

or:

> B. *Wǒ (shi) shí'èr diǎn zhōng chī .de zhōngfàn.*
>
> (Time Word)   (V)   (O)

Similarly, to ask "At what time did you paint my face?", you can say either *Nǐ shi shém.me shí.hòur gěi .wǒ huà liǎn .de?* or *Nǐ shi shém shí.hòur gěi .wǒ huà .de liǎn?*. Form B is more common.

Form B cannot be used with pronoun objects. To say "I saw her at school (It was at school that I saw her)" you have to use *Wǒ (shi) zài xuéxiào kàn.jiàn .tā .de.*

5. There is an implied *shi* in this sentence between *dàgài* and *jiǔ-diǎn*. The *shi* in the *shi....de* usage frequently drops out in this manner, but is implied by the final *.de*. There is no change in meaning. *Nǐ (shi) jǐ-diǎn kāishǐ .de? Wǒ (shi) jiǔ-diǎn yí-kè kāishǐ .de*, etc. Note that when the *shi....de* is negated by *bú*, the *shi* cannot drop out. *Wǒ bú.shi jiǔ-diǎn yì-kè kāishǐ .de; wǒ bú.shi zài xuéxiào kàn.jiàn .tā .de*; etc.

6. This sentence might appear to be an instance of *shi....de*, but it is not. *Bǐ* is understood at the end of the sentence, and it simply follows the "A *shi* B" pattern introduced in I.1.9. Unlike the *shi* in the *shi....de* pattern, the *shi* in this sentence cannot be omitted.

You should also note that *shi....de* can be used without a time, place, or manner expression: *tā shi bù dǒng Zhōngwén .de* "he (is one who) does not understand Chinese". In such cases *shi....de* does not imply the past, but is used (1) to emphasize the predicate ("he really *doesn't* understand Chinese"; see II.1.23) or (2) to make an explanation. (For example, if you continually say *nǐ hǎo .ma?* to someone who merely returns a blank stare to you, a third party might come along to explain: *tā shi bù dǒng Zhōngwén .de* "he (is one who) does not know Chinese".)

7. *Yǐngr*, the Běijīng Mandarin pronunciation of *yǐng*, is retroflex, nasalized, and considerably different from *yǐng*. Listen carefully to your teacher. Note also the Topic-Comment structure of this sentence: "As for movie-viewing (topic), he too should come up with money (comment)."

8. *Chū* is used here as a transitive verb meaning "produce, come up with". During World War II in China there was a patriotic slogan *yǒu qián chū-qián, yǒu lì chū-lì* "(those who) have money (should) contribute money, (and those who) have strength (should) contribute strength".

Exercises

Homework:

1. Translate the following sentences into Chinese:

    A. I find him disgusting because he often teases me and makes me feel extremely embarrassed.
    B. Her dog bit and injured my left hand. I wanted her to apologize. Not only did she not apologize, she herself bit my right hand, too.
    C. How come even before the movie started he had already fallen asleep?
    D. Listen, he is snoring. He's sleeping so well I don't know if we can wake him up.
    E. I don't like to look into the mirror because the color on my face is somewhat greenish and bluish. (It's) really ugly.
    F. Xiǎo Dīng is indeed abominable. Let's go find him. He has to pay (give money) for buying a new dress for me.
    G. (Before a murderer escapes, he stops at Lǎo Lǐ's place and makes a phone call. Later a police officer comes to ask Lǐ a few questions. Translate their dialogue into Chinese, making appropriate use of the "*shi ... .de*" pattern.)

        P (Police Officer): What time did he come?

        L (Lǎo Lǐ): He came at 3:00 p.m.

        P: Where did he make the phone call?

        L: He called from (in) my room.

        P: Which hand did he use to make the phone call?

        L: He used his left hand to make the call.

Classroom/Homework exercises:

1. With the information given, write questions and answers that use the "*shi ... .de*" construction to give emphasis to time, place or manner. For Verb-Objects, use "V .de O" form.

    Given: Tā zuó.tiān shàng.wǔ jiǔ-diǎn zhōng zuò-chē (car) dào xuéxiào .lái kàn Wáng lǎoshī.

    Response: Q. Tā shi shém shí.hòur lái .de?   (Time)
               A. Tā shi zuó tiān shàng.wǔ jiǔ-diǎn zhōng lái .de.

               Q. Tā shi zěm lái .de?   (Manner)
               A. Tā shi zuò-chē lái .de.

               Q. Tā shi zài nǎr kàn .de Wáng lǎoshī?   (Place)
               A. Tā shi zài xuéxiào kàn .de Wáng lǎoshī.

A. Xiǎo Lǐ zhù .zài Niǔyuē .de shí.hòur, yòng Yīngwén xiě .le yì-běn shū. Tā
    .de shū xiě-wán .de shí.hòur shi 1930 nián.

B. Jīn.tiān xià.wǔ Lǎo Wáng yòng Zhōng.guó fá.zi pào-chá. Tā zǒng.shi zài
    xuéxiào fùjìn .de nèi.ge pù.zi (shop) .lǐ mǎi cháyè.

C. Lǎo Zhāng qián.tiān zài Xiǎo Dīng jiā.lǐ chī wǎnfàn .de shí.hòur yòng yì-bǎ
    hěn dà .de dāo qiē yí.ge xiǎo fānqié.

D. Liǎng.ge lǐbài yǐqián wǒ gēn Dīng Xīn pǎo-bù .dào Liánhéguó fùjìn .de yì-jiā
    Zhōng.guó fànguǎnr .qù chī lóngxiā.

UNIT VI

LESSON 1

Vocabulary

shàng-xué	上學	go to school	qiúxié	球鞋	'ball shoe', sneakers	
mā	媽	mom	-máo	毛	dime (ten cents)	
(mā.x)	媽媽		-fēn	分	cent, penny	
dā	搭	to ride (car, plane, boat)	lìng	另	another	
dā X .de chē	搭X的車	get a ride with X	jià.qián	價錢	price	
chē	車	vehicle	zuò	坐	to ride (vehicle, ship, airplane, etc.)	
yí.gòng	一共	altogether	kāi-chē	開車	to drive a car	
hòu.tiān	後天	day after tomorrow	zúgòu	足夠	fully sufficient	
dòng-shēn	動身	'move body', set out (on a journey)	xiū-chē	修車	to repair a car	
			chángtú	長途	long distance	
			xīnshēng	新生	new student, freshman	
dài	帶	belt; carry with, bring	-niánjí	年級	grade, year	
mǎi	買	to buy	dàxué sānniánjí	大學三年級	third year in college	
xǐ-zǎo	洗澡	to take a bath	sānniánjí Zhōngwén	三年級中文	third year Chinese	
máojīn	毛巾	towel	míng.nián	明年	next year	
bǎihuò gōngsī	百貨公司	'hundred-goods-company', department store	bì-yè	畢業	to graduate	
gōngsī	公司	company	liàng	輛	AN for vehicle	
shuāng	雙	pair	wàn	萬	ten thousand	

qiān   千   one thousand | xiū.lǐ   修理   to repair |
sòng   送   send | |

Vocabulary Classified by Type

Nouns
mā (mā.x)
chángtú
chē
máojīn
bǎihuò gōngsī
gōngsī
qiúxié
jià.qián
xīnshēng

Verbs
dā
mǎi
zuò

sòng
xiū.lǐ

Adverbs
yí.gòng
lìng
zú

ANs
shuāng
-máo
-fēn
-niánjí
liàng

V-Os
shàng-xué
dòng-shēn
xǐ-zǎo
kāi-chē
xiū-chē
bì-yè

Time Words
hòu.tiān

Numerals
wàn
qiān

Grammar Notes

1. *Dào*, literally "arrive", is frequently used as a resultative complement signaling the attainment ("arrival") of the goal set by the verb. Thus *zhǎo.dào* "search for and the searching arrives at its goal--i.e., find". With some verbs *.dào* is equivalent to *zháo*: *zhǎo.dào* and *zhǎo-zháo* are interchangeable. (But be careful, because other verbs, like *shuì* "sleep", take *zháo* but not *.dào*.) With only slight differences in usage, *dào* can replace *jiàn* "perceive" in words like *kàn.jiàn* and *tīng.jiàn*. For example, *wǒ tīng.dào tā.de shēng.yīn, kě.shi wǒ kàn.bú-dào tā rén* "I can hear his voice but cannot see him (his person)". Other examples using *.dào*: *jiè.dào* "borrow (successfully)"; *mǎi.dào* "buy (and actually get)"; *chī.dào* "try to eat and actually get to eat". (For example, *wǒ.mén yào shàng guǎn.zi .qù chī lóngxiā, kě.shi qù wǎn .le, méi chī.dào* "We wanted to go to a restaurant for lobster, but we got there late and didn't get any.")

    From these examples you can see another reason why the word *shì* "try" (IV.3.1) is not used nearly as much as the word "try" in English. Often, Chinese verbs like *mǎi, jiè*, etc. do not mean "(actually) buy", "(actually) borrow", etc., but more nearly "(try to) buy", "(set about) borrowing", etc. In many contexts the idea of "try" is already there, and it is the complements like *dào, zháo, jiàn*, etc. that take the "try" notion out of them by specifying that the effort of the verb has been successful.

2. *Dā* "travel by means of" is a verb whose object is some kind of vehicle: *dā-chē* "ride in a car", *dā-chuán* "take a boat", *dā-fēijī* "take an airplane:, etc. *Dā* can also be translated "get a ride in" for phrases like *dā wǒ.de chē* that appears in the text.

3. The word *lián* was introduced in IV.4.10 as part of the *lián...dōu* construction meaning "even". By itself, *lián* means "join, include": *lián wǒ zìjǐ yígòng yǒu sì.ge rén* "including me, there are four people altogether".

4. *Hǎo* "good" here is used as a resultative complement for the verb *yù.bèi* "prepare". In this usage it is similar to *wán* "finish", except that *wán* is used in a more matter-of-fact sense and *hǎo* carries the ("good") notion of "all set, all done". *Yù.bèi-wán.le* "have finished preparing"; *yù.bèi-hǎo.le* "all set with the preparations". Similarly, *xiě-wán.le* "finished writing"; *xiě-hǎo.le* "finished writing (and all set to go)".

5. *Dài*, originally a noun meaning "belt", is also a verb meaning "bring or take (along with one)". It should be distinguished from *ná* "take (with the hand)". If your books are in your dorm room and you are in the dining hall, you might go to your room to get your books (*ná shū*), and then bring them with you to the classroom (*dài .dào kètáng .qù*). If you forget your books, you might say *Duì.bùqǐ lǎoshī, wǒ méi dài shū* ("I'm sorry, but I didn't bring my books, sir"). Don't say *Duì.bùqǐ lǎoshī, wǒ méi.yǒu shū*, because that implies you have no books at all. To ask someone to "take" you home, you can't use *ná*. Say: *qǐng .nǐ dài* (or *sòng*) *wǒ huí jiā .qù.*

6. **How to Count Money in Chinese.** In spoken Chinese, a dollar is *yí-kuài qián* ("one lump of money"); a dime is *yì-máo qián*, and a penny is *yì-fēn qián*. In formal written style (for use on invoices, checks, receipts, etc.) *yuán* 圓 is used for dollars and *jiǎo* 角 for dimes. Multi-unit amounts are expressed by stringing the appropriate units together:

	dollars	dimes	pennies
spoken:	kuài	máo	fēn
written:	yuán	jiǎo	fēn

$12.75	12	7	5	spoken: shí'èr-kuài qī-máo wǔ (fēn) written: shí'èr-yuán qī-jiǎo wǔ-fēn (qián)
$2.80	2	8	0	spoken: liǎng-kuài bā (máo) written: èr-yuán bā-jiǎo
$1.05	1	0	5	spoken: yí-kuài líng wǔ (fēn) written: yì-yuán wǔ fēn
$0.25	0	2	5	spoken: liǎng-máo wǔ written: èr-jiǎo wǔ-fēn

NOTES:

(a) The noun *qián*, which can appear at the end of a string, is usually omitted.

(b) In spoken style, *máo* or *fēn* is often omitted if it is the last item in a string.

(c)   *Fēn* cannot go higher than 9. You cannot say *sān.shíwǔ-fēn* as you would say "thirty-five cents" in English. You have to say *sān-máo wǔ*.

(d)   When a zero comes in the middle of a string, *líng* is used in the spoken style to replace the unit concerned.

(e)   "Two" is *liǎng* in spoken style, but *èr* in written style.

7.   The meaning of *lìng* or *lìngwài* "another" is similar to, but not exactly the same as, that of *bié.de* "other". *Lìng* and *lìngwài* generally refer to specific nouns and *bié.de* to non-specific nouns.

There are also clear grammatical differences between *bié.de* and *lìng(wài)*. *Bié.de* precedes a noun directly: *bié.de xué.shēng* "the other (indefinite) students"; *bié.de wèntí* "other problems". It cannot precede a number or AN (including quasi-ANs like *tiān* "day", *nián* "year", etc.). Thus you cannot say *bié.de yí.ge rén* "the other person" or *bié.de tiān* "the other day". *Lìng(wài)* is exactly the opposite of *bié.de* on these points. It *cannot* precede a noun directly. It precedes a number with attached AN (or quasi-AN): *lìngwài liǎng.ge rén* "the other two persons"; *lìngwài yì-tiān* "another day".

Lìng and *lìngwài* are exactly the same in meaning, but *lìng* can be followed only by the number *yì (yí)* "one": *lìng yí.ge wèntí* "another question"; *lìng.yi-jiā bǎihuò gōngsī* "another department store". (You cannot say *lìngliǎng* or *lìngsān*, etc.)

8.   *Yě...yě...* meaning "both...and..." is similar to *yòu...yòu...* "both...and..." as used in line 9 of the text. (See IV.4.1 on *yòu...yòu....*) Remember that both *yě* and *yòu* are adverbs and therefore must always precede verbs, whereas the English words "both" and "and" can precede nouns as well. In some cases *yě...yě...* and *yòu...yòu...* are interchangeable:

Tā yòu huì kāi-chē yòu huì xiū-chē.	She can repair cars as well as drive them.
Tā yě huì kāi-chē yě huì xiū-chē.	

But sometimes the two differ in usage. For example, when the words that follow are adjectives, you can use *yòu...yòu...* but not *yě...yě...*: *dōng.xī yòu* (not *yě!*) *pián.yí yòu hǎo* "the things are both inexpensive and good". Second, when the predicate is the same or similar, and you want to say that both of the two subjects can do the predicate, you can use *yě...yě...* but not *yòu...yòu....* For example:

Zhāng Sān yě (not *yòu!*) huì shuō Yīngwén, Lǐ Sì yě huì shuō Yīngwén.	Both Zhāng Sān and Lǐ Sì can speak English.

9.   A drawn-out and breathy *k-ā-i—* emphasizes the statement and reassures the listener: *"Of course* they have driven on long trips." Similarly:

Nǐ fàng-xīn .ba. Tā h-u-ì— lái .de.	Rest assured, she *will* come.

10.   When referring to age, *dà* and *xiǎo* can mean "old" and "young".

11.   **Nominal Predicates**. Review II.4.6 on topic-comment sentences. One important kind of topic-comment sentence uses a "nominal predicate", meaning a noun phrase that simply follows the noun subject and acts as the predicate, with an implied *shi* or other verb in between:

Zá.mén nèi-liàng jiù chē ji-wàn li .le?

noun subject   nominal predicate

Nominal predicates are common when numerals are involved:

> Liǎng.ge liǎng.ge sì.ge.   Two and two (are) four.
> Jīn.tiān lǐbàisān.   Today (is) Wednesday.
> Zhèi-běn shū èr.shíwǔ-kuài.   This book (sells for) 25 dollars.

Nominal predicates are also common when identifying where someone is from:

> Wǒ tài.x Měi.guórén.   My wife (is) American.

In all of the above cases, it is perfectly acceptable to re-insert the appropriate verb:

> Nèi-liàng jiù chē yǒu ji-wàn li?
> Liǎng.ge liǎng.ge shi sì.ge.
> Jīn.tiān shi lǐbàisān.
> Zhèi-běn shū mài èr.shíwǔ-kuài.
> Wǒ tài.x shi Měi.guórén.

When speaking of a person's age, the verb *shi* is *always* omitted:

> Nǐ mèi.x jīn.nián ji-suì?   How old is your little sister
>   (NOT: Nǐ mèi.x jīn.nián shi   this year?
>   ji-suì?)

Exercises

In-class exercises:

1.   Fill in the blanks with either *lìng (wài)* or *bié.de*.

A.   Zhūo.zi.shàng yǒu sān-běn shū, yǒu yì-běn shi hóng.de, ... dōu.shi lü.de.
B.   Xué Zhōngwén .de xué.shēng, zhǐ yǒu sān.shí.ge rén shi dàxué yì-niánjí .de xué.shēng, ... dōu shi sān-niánjí .de xué.shēng.
C.   Wǒ yǒu liǎng.ge hǎo péng.yǒu, yí.ge xìng Lǐ ... yí.ge xìng Wáng.
D.   Zhèi-ji-shuāng xié wǒ dōu bù xi.huān, wǒ kě .bù.kě.yǐ kàn.x ... .
E.   Wǒ.mén jiā.li yígòng yǒu liǎng-liàng chē, yí-liàng shi xīn .de, ... yí-liàng shi jiù .de. Wǒ.mén gāng bǎ nèi-liàng jiù chē sòng.qù xiū.li.

2.   Tell the amount of money in Chinese.

A.   2.45

B.   3.50
C.   101.00
D.   19.99
E.   3.09
F.   20.17

3.   Say the following numbers in Chinese: 2,300; 999; 45,600; 9,999; 210; 201; 10,050.

4.   Answer the following questions with the pattern: *"lián ... yígòng ..."*

Example:

> Nǐ yǒu jǐ-liàng chē?
> Lián zhèi-liàng hóng .de, yígòng yǒu sān-liàng.

A.   Nǐ.mén jiā yígòng yǒu jǐ.ge rén?
B.   Zhèi-liàng chē kě.yǐ zuò jǐ.ge rén?
C.   Zhūo.zi.shàng yǒu jǐ-běn shū?
D.   Jiàoshì.li yígòng yǒu jǐ.ge rén?
E.   Zuó.tiān yǒu jǐ.ge kè.rén zài nǐ jiā.li chī-fàn?
F.   Nǐ zuó.tiān zài nèi-jiā bǎihuò gōngsī mǎi.le jǐ-yàngr dōng.xī?

Homework:

1.   Translate the following sentences into Chinese.

A.   Have you gotten all your exercises done?
B.   I'll have them finished by dinner time.
C.   These exercises are quite easy. Why did you do them so slowly?
D.   For you they are easy; for me they are not simple at all.
E.   I'm going to New York on Saturday. May I drive your car?
F.   No. My car is out of order, it needs repair.
G.   Where is my wallet? May I ask you to help me to look for it?
H.   It's here. I found it. It's right behind the chair.
I.   Which department store is the biggest in New York?
J.   Do you know what the price is for this kind of bath towel?
K.   Four dollars and ninety-nine cents each. They are good, and inexpensive, too.
L.   I can wear any shoes but sneakers (Except for sneakers, I can wear any shoes). This is because there isn't enough air in sneakers. (They) are not suitable for my feet.
M.   Freshmen at that university are not allowed to have cars. The freshmen are demanding the freedom to drive.
N.   Those three female students (use polite form) are all older than I am. They are going to graduate next year.

Classroom/Homework exercises:

1.   Fill in the missing words in the following dialogue. Then rewrite the dialogue into a passage.

A: Míng.tiān jiù.shi zhōumò .le, nǐ xiǎng dào ... .qù wánr?

B: Wǒ yào qù Bōshìdùn, nǐ .ne?

A: Wǒ haí ... juédìng. Nǐ shém shí.hòur zǒu?

B: Wǒ xiǎng xīngqīwǔ dòng-shēn, xīngqītiān xià.wǔ huí.lái.

A: Bōshìdùn ... zhèr yuǎn (far) .bù.yuǎn?

B: Bù yuǎn, kāi-chē zhǐ yào sì-wǔ.ge zhōngtóu.

A: Sì-wǔ.ge zhōngtóu hái ... yuǎn .ma?

B: Dāngrán bù yuǎn. Shàng-yí-cì wǒ kāi-chē dào Huáshèngdùn (Washington) .qù,
    kāi.le liù.ge duō zhōngtóu ... dào .ne.

A: Nǐ xiǎng zhù ... péngyǒu jiā.lǐ, hái.shi zhù .zài lǚguǎn (hotel).lǐ?

B: Wǒ yǒu .ge péng.yǒu zhù .zài Bōshìdùn. Tā shuō tā huì zhāodài .wǒ, yào .wǒ
    fàng-xīn, zhǐ yào ... wǒ zìjǐ yào yòng .de dōng.xī yù.bèi-hǎo.le ... xíng .le.

A: Yǒu zhèyàngr .de péng.yǒu ... zhēn búcuò. (emphatic adverb)

B: Ḗ, nǐ hái méi gào.sù .wǒ nǐ yào shàng nǎr .qù wánr .ne.

A: .Oh, duì.bùqǐ, qíshí wǒ nǎr ... bú qù. Wǒ xiǎng dāi .zài sùshè.lǐ kàn-shū.
    Érqiě yīn.wèi wǒ búhuì kāi-chē, bié.rén dōu bù xǐ.huān ràng .wǒ dā tā.mén .de
    chē. Yóuqí shi dào yuǎn dì.fāng, děi kāi chángtú, yào.shi liǎng.ge rén dōu
    huì kāi-chē nà jiù hǎo .de duō .le.

B: Qíshí kāi-chē ... bù nán, zhǐ yào duō liàn.xí jǐ-cì jiù huì .le. Děng wǒ cóng
    Bōshìdùn huí.lái wǒ jiù jiāo .nǐ.

A: Tài hǎo .le, jiù zèm juédìng .le.

2. Nominal Predicate: Translate the following sentences into Chinese.

    A.   His sister is a sophomore (second year student).
    B.   What is the number of your room?
    C.   How many thousand miles are on that old car of ours?

LESSON 2

Vocabulary

Xiǎo Zhēn	小珍	a girl's name	yìbiānr V₁ -邊ㄦ -邊ㄦ V₂ while V₁	糖		
guì	貴	expensive	táng	糖	candy; sugar	
xì	系	department in a college	bànyè	半夜	'middle of the night', midnight	
quán	全	whole, complete	zhēng	睜	open (eyes)	
xīwàng	希望	hope; to hope	jīng.shén	精神	energy (spirit)	
hǎohāor.de	好好ㄦ地	properly, well	pén	盆	(flower) pot	
shēng.huó	生活	life	jīnyú	金魚	goldfish	
yì-fāngmiàn	一方面	on the one hand	guǎn	管	take care of	
yòng-gōng	用功	diligent(ly) (study)	yǎng	養	to raise (animals)	
dú-shū	讀書	'read book', to study	yú	魚	fish	
			má.fán	麻煩	troublesome, to trouble	
yàojǐn	要緊	important				
zuò-rén	作人	(how) to be a person	lí.kāi	離開	to leave, go away from	
xíguàn	習慣	habit	.ou	嘔	particle for mild warning: "mind you"	
gǎi	改	to change, modify				
			bà	爸	dad	
bǐ.fāng shuō	比方說	for example	(bà.x)	爸爸		

Vocabulary Classified by Type

Nouns		Verbs
xì	pén	xīwàng
xīwàng	jīnyú	gǎi
shēng.huó	bà (bà.x)	zhēng
xíguàn		guǎn
táng	**Proper Nouns**	yǎng
jīng.shén	Xiǎo Zhēn	má.fán

lí.kāi   **Sentential Adverbs**   **Time Words**
                                (Moveable Adverbs)   bànyè
          Adjectives   yì-fāngmiàn
quán   **Particles**
yàojǐn   **V-Os**   .ou
                                yòng-gōng
          Adverbs   dú-shū   **Idiomatic Expressions**
hǎohāor.de   zuò-rén   bǐ.fāng shuō
                                                              yìbiānr V_1 yìbiānr V_2

Grammar Notes

1. See Culture Note 6 (II.1) on the use of *xiǎo* "young" and *lǎo* "old" in familiar
    address. In those cases, *xiǎo* and *lǎo* preceded the family name or *xìng*. Here,
    xiǎo is used with the given name *Zhēn*. This is a common way in which parents
    address children.

    The usage of *Zhēn* (珍) "precious" for the girl's given name is also typical.
    Characters with the "jade radical" (玉 / 王) are frequently used in female given
    names: *zhū* (珠) "pearl", *líng* (玲) "tinkling (of jade pendants)", etc. Other
    characters commonly used in girls' names refer to flowers, fragrances, beautiful
    clouds, etc.

2. *Fāngmiàn* "side, aspect". If someone says to you *wǒ.de tóngwū jué.de hěn bù
    xíguàn*, you might ask *tā něi-fāngmiàn jué.de bù xíguàn?* "In what way does he feel
    unaccustomed?". *Fāngmiàn* is also used to mean "(academic) field or topic": *Nǐ
    yán.jiū* (research) *něi-fāngmiàn?* "What (aspect of reality) are you researching?"

    The present sentence uses a set pattern of:

    $$ \textit{yì-fāngmiàn} \; + \; V_1 \; + \; \textit{yì-fāngmiàn} \; + \; V_2 $$

    "On the one hand V_1, on the other hand V_2"

    Tā yì-fāngmiàn yònggòng dú-shū,   On the one hand, she studies
        yì-fāngmiàn zhī.dào zěm wánr.   diligently, and on the other,
                                              knows how to enjoy herself.

3. *Yònggōng*, "hard-working, diligent", is an adjective that often refers to one's
    performance in schoolwork: *nèi.ge xué.shēng hěn yònggōng* "that student is
    hard-working". *Yònggōng* can also be, as it is here, an adverb meaning
    "diligently".

4. *Dú-shū* "read books" is a synonym of *niàn-shū*. Both commonly mean "study".
    (Originally both *dú* and *niàn* meant "to read aloud", from the traditional practice
    of training children to memorize the classics by reading them aloud.) *Dú-shū* is
    slightly more formal than *niàn-shū*. To say "I was studying in the library
    yesterday" in natural speech, you would say *wǒ zuó.tiān zài túshūguǎn niàn-shū*
    (not *dú-shū*).

In a more abstract sense, *dú-shū* can also mean "receive an education": *Tā zài XX dàxué dú-shū* "She was educated at XX university". The common term *dúshūrén*, literally "people who have studied books", can be translated "educated people" or "literati".

5. *Zuò-rén*, literally "act as a person" or "play the role of a human being", has an important moral connotation that makes it translatable in all of the following ways, depending upon context: "to behave properly", "to get along with others", "to be pleasant in manner", "to be an upright person".

6. Review IV.2.2 on *diào* and *zhù* as complements.

7. The pattern:

$$\text{Subject} + \textit{yìbiānr} + V_1 + \textit{yìbiānr} + V_2$$

can be used to mean "do one thing while doing another":

Tā yìbiānr kàn-shū, yìbiānr chī-táng.	She eats candy while studying.
Lǎoshī yìbiānr hē-chá, yìbiānr kàn-bào.	The teacher drinks tea while reading the paper.

In Northern Mandarin, *yìtóur* can substitute for *yìbiānr*; in Southern Mandarin, both *yìbiānr* and *yí-miàn* are used. Compare this usage with *yì-fāngmiàn...yì-fāngmiàn...* as introduced in note 2 above. Although both can mean "do one thing while doing another", *yì-fāngmiàn* is used for more abstract and long-term things like *yònggōng dú-shū* "study diligently" and *xué zuò rén* "learn to be a (good) person", while *yìbiānr*, *yìtóur*, and *yí-miàn* are generally used for everyday acts like *chī-fàn*, *hē-chá*, *pǎo-bù*, etc.

Bǐ.fāng shuō nǐ zǒng.shi yìbiānr kàn-shū yìbiānr chī-táng.

8.   *Bànyè*, literally "half night", means "middle of the night"—not precisely "midnight", but in a more general sense covering all the hours of the "deep" of the night.

9.   *.De* showing extent or degree. This is a new use of *.de*. (Review others at II.2.35.) It occurs between an adjective and a phrase that tells the degree of the adjective or the extent that it reaches: *guì .de kěpà* "expensive to the extent of inducing fear—terribly expensive"; *nán .de bùdéliǎo* "difficult to an endless degree—extremely difficult". It is common, as in the example in the text, for the phrase that tells degree or extent to involve a *lián...dōu* meaning "even": *lèi .de (lián) yǎn.jīng dōu zhēng.bù-kāi* "tired to a degree where (one) can't even open (one's) eyes". The English phrase "so (Adj.) that..." is usually just right to translate this kind of *.de*: *nǐ.de wū.zi.li luàn .de lián zuò .de dì.fāng dōu méi.yǒu* "your room is so messy that there's not even a place to sit down"; *tā gāoxìng .de shuō.bù-chū huà .lái .le* "she was so happy she couldn't speak any more"; etc.

     This *.de* of "degree" or "extent" can easily appear in the same sentence as a "predicate *.de*" (see II.2.35(c)). The combination is worth special practice:

Tā shuō-huà shuō .de hěn kuài, kuài .de méi rén dǒng.	He speaks fast—so fast that no one understands him.
Wǒ zuó.tiān zuò shì.qíng zuò .de hěn lèi, lèi .de yǎn.jīng dōu zhēng.bù-kāi .le.	Yesterday I worked until I couldn't even open my eyes any more.

     This *.de* is the last major kind of *.de* in your introductory course. It is important that you be clear about all the uses of *.de* and distinguish them one from another. Review II.2.35 well.

     There are certain other, idiosyncratic uses of *.de* that are not, for now, worth your trying to analyze. The *.de* in *shì.de* "yes" or in *.de duō* "much more" (*hǎo .de duō*, *màn .de duō*, etc.) should simply be memorized as they are.

10. *Nǎr* (in Běijīng Mandarin) or *nǎ.li* (in Mandarin elsewhere) literally means "where?", but has two important extended meanings in:

     (a)   Rhetorical questions. As in the example in the text, *nǎr* or *nǎ.li* can be used in an ironic sense to **deny** what follows:

Wǒ nǎr hái yǒu jīng.shén shàng-kè?	*Where* would I still have energy for class? = *Of course* I don't have energy for class!

     Note that this ironic use is similar to "since when?" in English: "Since when do I have energy for class?". Similarly, *Tā nǎr huì shuō Zhōngwén?* could be translated "Since when can he speak Chinese? (The idea is ridiculous!)".

     (b)   Polite language. (See Culture Note 16, below.)

11. Review IV.2.5 on *guǎn* as a pretransitive (similar to *bǎ*) for the verb *jiào*. Here the same word *guǎn* is used without *jiào* in its normal meaning of "take care of, watch after".

12. *Lí.kāi* "depart" or "leave". *Lí* is the word you learned in III.3.3 for telling the distance from one place to another. *Kāi* "open" also means "away" or "free from involvement", as in *zǒu.de-kāi* "able to walk away".

13. Review III.3.13 on *lái-xìn* "cause a letter to come--write a letter". Similarly, *lái-diànhuà* "cause a phone call to come--call on the phone".

14. *.Ou* here indicates lively, but mild, urging or warning.

Culture Note 16:   Polite Language

It is a principle of polite language in China, especially in formal contexts, to elevate or honor your listener and to lower or disparage yourself. This has been especially important when speaking to superiors or elders. Traditionally, a polite request to visit someone was made by asking to *bàifǎng* "bow-visit--pay respects". When the guests arrived, a host might welcome them commenting that they *guānglín hánshè* "illustriously descend on (my) humble residence". Traditional polite words for "I" included *bǐrén* "rustic one" and *zài-xià* "the one below". "You" was *nín*, the honorific form of *nǐ*. "Your brother" was *lìngxiōng* "your respected brother", while "my brother" was *shèdì* "my humble brother". Etc.

By the late 20th century many of these traditional polite forms have fallen out of use. Terms like *guānglín hánshè* are now often used for humorous effect only. But, although you may not need such terms in your ordinary contacts, you should also avoid going to the other extreme, using language that is too blunt. For "your brother", *lìngxiōng* may be outmoded; but *nǐ.de bà.x* should also be avoided in any situation calling for politeness or formality--especially when talking to a person older than you. *Nín fù.chīn* would be a good compromise.

Nǎr and *nǎ.lǐ* (often a repeated *nǎ.lǐ nǎ.lǐ*) are short forms for *Nǎr (lái) .de hùa?* "Where did this talk come from?--How can you say that?". These are polite terms used in response to a compliment or an expression of the gratitude necessary. The terms function like the English phrases "Thank you", "You're welcome", or "Don't mention it", depending on context.

For example, if someone says *Nǐ.de Jōngwén shuō .de zhēn hǎo*, you should not say *xiè.x* "thank you", because this acknowledges the truth of the statement. It violates the principle that you should always be modest about yourself. Instead, you should say something like *Nǎ.lǐ, nǎ.lǐ, wǒ shuō .de bùhǎo*. Here *nǎ.lǐ* would be the functional equivalent of "thank you". But if you do a favor for someone and the person says *xiè.x*, you can also respond with *nǎ.lǐ*, which then would be equivalent to "you're welcome" or "don't mention it" in English.

Exercises

In-class exercises:

1.   Oral Substitution

      Given: Wǒ hěn è. Wǒ zhàn.bù-qǐ.lái.

      Response: Wǒ è .de zhàn.bù-qǐ.lái .le.

      A.   Tā hěn gāoxìng. Tā shuō.bù-chū huà .lái.
      B.   Tā shuō-huà shuō .de hěn kuài. Zhōng.guórén tīng.bù-dǒng tā shuō .de huà.
      C.   Tā.de wū.zi hěn luàn. Tā.de wū.zi méi.yǒu zuò .de dì.fāng.
      D.   Wǒ è.sǐ.le. Shí.ge hànbǎo (hamburger) wǒ yě chī.de-xià (.qù).

2.   Oral Substitution

      Given: Nǐ zǒng.shi bàn-yè liǎng-sān-diǎn cái shàng-chuáng, dì'èr-tiān yídìng méi.yǒu jīng.shén shàng-kè.

      Response: Nǐ zǒng.shi bàn-yè liǎng-sān-diǎn cái shàng-chuáng, dì'èr-tiān nǎr yǒu jīng.shén shàng-kè?

      A.   Nǐ pā.zhe xiě-zì, yídìng xiě.bù-hǎo.
      B.   Shàng-kè yǐqián bú yù.bèi kèwén, lǎoshī jiǎng .de nǐ yídìng tīng.bù-dǒng.
      C.   Shí-zhī dà lóngxiā, tā yí.ge rén yídìng chī.bù-wán.
      D.   Hē nèm duō kāfēi, wǎn.shàng yídìng shuì.bù-zháo.

Homework:

1.   Reorganize the following sentences into a meaningful passage.

      A.   Zhèyàng xué Zhōng.guó-zì jiù yīnggāi méi.yǒu wèntí .le.
      B.   Ránhòu měi-tiān bǎ bú rèn.shì .de zì duō kàn jǐ-cì.
      C.   Bú rèn.shì de .zì fàng .zài yòu.biān.
      D.   Bǎ rèn.shì .de zì fàng .zài zuǒ.biān.
      E.   Nǐ kě.yǐ měi-tiān bǎ yì-xiē zì yì-zhāng yì-zhāng .de kàn yí-cì.
      F.   Nà zěm bàn .ne?
      G.   Bù chángx kàn.jiàn jiù hěn róng.yì wàng.
      H.   Shi yīn.wèi bù chángx kàn.jiàn.
      I.   Kàn.jiàn yí.ge zì, wàng.le shi shém zì, zhè.shi wèishém.me?
      J.   Zhōng.guó-zì yòu nán xué yòu róng.yì wàng.

2.   Complete the following sentences. If a pattern is given, use that pattern in your sentence.

      A.   Xuéxiào .de sùshè suírán guì ... .
      B.   Wǒ běnlái xiǎng kāi tā.de chē qù kàn diànyǐng ... .
      C.   Wǒ zuì pà kǎoshì ... . (yì ... jiù)
      D.   Zhèi.ge rén tài bèn .le, ... (lián ... dōu)
      E.   Měi-tiān zǎo.shàng wǒ xǐ.huān ... . (yìbiānr ... yìbiānr)
      F.   ... , nà nǐ jiù bǎ zhèi.ge huài xíguàn gǎi-diào .ba. (jìrán)

G.   ... , suǒ.yǐ nèi.ge shí.hòur Zhōng.guó shèhuì yǒu hěn duō wèntí.
        (yì-fāngmiàn ... yì-fāngmiàn)

3.   Translate the following sentences into Chinese.

A.   I hope you make the best of your four years of college life. Study hard and
      also have fun.
B.   Don't stay up too late at night. Otherwise you won't be able to keep your
      eyes open in class.
C.   Since I can't take my flowers and my goldfish with me, I have to ask you to
      take care of them.
D.   But you know I'm terrible at keeping flowers, and I especially can't stand
      goldfish.
E.   Of course I do, but there's no way I can take them, so I have to trouble you
      to do it.
F.   The Ford Company is not only famous throughout the country, but also famous
      throughout the world.
G.   I am going to leave you. I have decided to go to California to live like a
      hippie (xīpí). I hope that from now on you will learn how to behave
      yourself and get rid of bad habits.

LESSON 3

Vocabulary

tóngwūr	同屋儿	roommate	gōng.kè	功課	schoolwork	
.wai	喂	hello (on tele-phone)	....de yàomìng	得要命	extremely...	
			yuán.gù	緣故	reason	
shēng.yīn	聲音	sound	chǎo-jià	吵架	to quarrel, to squabble	
tīng.chū.lái	聽出來	make out by lis-tening				
			bái.tiān	白天	daytime	
guà	掛	to hang	mèng	夢	dream	
cóng(chóng)	重	(to do some-thing) over again	shuō mènghuà	說夢話	to talk in one's sleep	
			yǎo-yá	咬牙	'bite teeth', to gnaw	
bān	搬	to move				
lù	路	road	nántīng	難聽	unpleasant to hear	
yí-lù	一路	all the way	nào	鬧	to disturb; noisy	
shùn.lì	順利	smooth, without difficulty				
			jiǎnzhí	簡直	simply	
tiān.qì	天氣	weather	búzhì.yú	不至於	not as (bad) as	
xià-yǔ	下雨	to rain	yuàn.yì	願意	willing, glad to	
qíng	晴	fine (for weath-er)	nánshòu	難受	feel bad	
jiàn-miàn	見面	'see face', to meet	xīn	心	heart	
			ài	愛	to love; to have a strong liking	
cóng (PW) lái	從...來	come from (PW)				
Jiāzhōu	加州	State of Cali-fornia	júhuā	菊花	chrysanthemum	
			lì.hài	利害	serious(ly)	
tán.de.lái	談得來	can talk (with someone)--find (someone) con-genial	qìchē	汽車	automobile	
			bèi...(gěi)	被 給	by	
xiāo.xí	消息	news	zǒu-lù	走路	to walk	

| bīng | 冰 | ice | | qīng | 輕 | light | |
| xiǎo.xīn | 小心 | careful | | méi.guìhuār | 玫瑰花儿 | rose | |

Vocabulary Classified by Type

Nouns

tóngwūr
shēng.yīn
lù
tiān.qì
xiāo.xí
gōng.kè
yuán.gù
mèng
xīn
júhuā
qìchē
méi.guìhuār

Proper Nouns

Jiāzhōu

Verbs

guà
bān
nào
ài

Auxiliary Verbs

yuàn.yì

Pretransitives

bèi...(gěi)

Adjectives

shùn.lì
qíng
nántīng
nào
nánshòu
lì.hài
xiǎo.xīn
qīng

Adverbs

cóng(chóng)
yí-lù
jiǎnzhí
búzhì.yú

V-Os

xià-yǔ

jiàn-miàn
chǎo-jià
shuō mènghuà
yǎo-yá
zǒu-lù

V-Directional Complements

tīng.chū.lái

V-Potential Complements

tán.de-lái

Complements

....de yàoming

Interjections

.wai

Idiomatic Expressions

cóng (PW) lái

Time Words

bái.tiān

Grammar Notes

1. *.Wai* or *.wei* (for some speakers, the sound is between *.wai* and *.wei*) is used for establishing contact on the telephone, or for hailing someone ("Hey! You there!"). It is not used for the greeting "hello".

2. *Nín nǎr?*, literally "what place are you?", is a polite way to ask in Peking Mandarin whom one is talking to. (It reflects the idea that telephone subscribers in China are often regarded as places, not persons.) You can respond by identifying yourself with the place or work unit you represent. See Culture Note 17 below.

3. *Cóng* is an adverb meaning "again, once more". It differs slightly from *zài* "again" because it suggests "start again from the beginning, do it all over". *Cóng dǎ yí.ge* "dial it over again (from the beginning)"; *cóng xiě yí-biàn* "write it (the whole thing) over again". *Cóng* has a more formal pronunciation, which is listed in most dictionaries, of *chóng*. It is also the same character (重) used for the adjective "heavy", which is pronounced *zhòng*.

4.   *Xià-yŭ* "it is raining" is an interesting example of a small number of verbs in Chinese that have no subjects at all. (This is different from having implied subjects, which is very common.) Many of these subject-less verbs have to do with the weather: *xià-yŭ* "downs rain—it is raining"; *xià-wù* "downs fog—there is a fog"; *xià-xuě* "downs snow—it is snowing"; *guā-fēng* "blows wind—the wind is blowing".

5.   *Jiù* here indicates "earlier than expected". (Review III.3.18 and III.3.21 on the uses of *cái* "later than expected" and *jiù....le* "earlier than expected".) Let's suppose Xiǎo Zhēn and her friends were expecting their trip to take eight hours. Because it took only six, she says *liù.ge zhōng.tóur jiù dào .le.* If it had taken ten, she might have said *shí.ge zhōng.tóur cái dào.*

6.   *Jiāzhōu* "California". The names of American states, when fully spelled out, can be cumbersome in Chinese: "California" is *Jiālifúníyǎ*, "Minnesota" is *Míngnísūdá*, etc. Such names are usually simplified by combining their first syllables with *zhōu* "state". Thus: *Jiāzhōu* "California", *Míngzhōu* "Minnesota", etc. (*Zhōu* refers to an administrative district in pre-modern China roughly the size of the modern provinces. The word for "province" today is *shěng*.)

     In certain cases, Chinese names for Western places have been created through a combination of translation and transliteration. For example: *Xīn* "New" + *Zéxī* "Jersey" = "New Jersey"; *Jiàn* (pronounced *kimm* in Cantonese, from which the name derives) + *qiáo* "bridge" = "*kimm*-bridge" = "Cambridge".

7.   "Dummy" complements. Normally, complements carry important meanings: *tīng-dŏng* tells you that *dŏng* "understand" is the result, *xĭ .de gān.jìng* that *gān.jìng* "clean" is a possible result, etc. But a small number of complements, such as *.de-lái* in *tán.de-lái*, carry no specific meaning. Called "dummy" complements, they simply indicate that the main verb is successful. *Gēn X tán.de-lái* simply means "can talk with X, find X congenial".

     NOTE: (1) Because very few verbs take dummy complements, you should learn them only on a case-by-case basis, starting with *tán.de-lái* and its opposite, *tán.bù-lái.*
            (2) The complements *tán.de-lái* and *tán.bù-lái* can be used only in potential form, not regular form. (You cannot say *tán-lái*, *tán-lái.le* or *méi tán-lái.*)

8.   Review III.1.25 on *zěmyàng*. This expression can also be used (but only with people one knows well) to mean "how are things?". *Nĭ zěmyàng?* is "How are things with you?".

9.   *Máng .de yàomìng*, literally "busy to-extent-of wants (a person's) life", means "terribly busy". The *.de* is the one analyzed in VI.2.9.

10. *Xiāo.xí* "news, information". The word is basically equivalent to *xīnwén* (III.2) when it refers to news items in newspapers or on television, radio, etc. But *xiāo.xí*, unlike *xīnwén*, can also be used for "news" of a friend or relative, rather like "tidings" in English. *Zěm méi.yŏu nĭ.de xiāo.xí?* "why haven't we heard from you?". (**Don't** say *zěm méi.yŏu nĭ.de xīnwén?*—unless, perchance, you are addressing a famous person who is often in the news, and wonder why you have seen no headlines recently.)

"Yǒu yí.ge bùhǎo .de xiāo.xí yào gào.sù .nǐ..."

11. *Yuán.gù* "reason, cause, reason why". There are two ways of using *yuán.gù* to say that one thing causes another:

> 1. A *.de yuán.gù shi yīn.wèi* B.

Wǒ shuì.bù-hǎo .de yuán.gù shi   The reason I can't sleep well is
  yīn.wèi wǒ tóngwūr dǎ-hū.   that my roommate snores.

> 2. A *shi yīn.wèi* B *.de yuán.gù*.

Wǒ shuì.bù-hǎo shi yīn.wèi wǒ   My not sleeping well is because of
  tóngwūr dǎ-hū .de yuán.gù.   (the reason of) my roommate's
                                             snoring.

(*.De yuán.gù* may seem redundant with *yīn.wèi* in these examples, but in Chinese grammar it is not.) WARNING: *Yuán.gù* means "reason" in the sense of "cause", not in the sense of "justification". To say you have a "good reason" for cutting class tomorrow, you have to use *lǐyóu*, not *yuán.gù*.

12. *Yǎo .de nántīng-jí.le*, literally "bites to-extent-of extremely unpleasant-sounding".

13. *Búzhì.yú*, literally "not reach to", is always used in a negative sense ("not reaching the bad extent of"). Thus it can be translated "not as bad as" or "not so bad that". For example:

Diànhuà shēng.yīn suírán bùhǎo,   The telephone connection is bad, but
  kě.shì hái búzhì.yú   not so bad that you can't make
  tīng.bù-chū.lái.   out (what's being said).

13. **S-P Predicates.** *Tā xīn hǎo* is not a short version of *Tā.de xīn hǎo*, although the two phrases mean about the same thing. *Tā* is the subject of *xīn hǎo* and *xīn* is the subject of *hǎo*: "As for him, the heart is good."

Forms like *xīn hǎo* are subject-predicate predicates or S-P predicates. In the following comparison, any one of the two Chinese constructions can be translated into any one of the three English constructions, but only the forms with *tā.de* and "his" correspond grammatically.

Tā xīn hǎo:	(No such form in English)
Tā.de xīn hǎo:	His heart is good.
(Not idiomatic in Chinese):	He has a good heart.
(No such form in Chinese):	He is good-hearted.

(From Y.R. Chao's **Mandarin Primer**, p. 186.)

14. *Lì.hài*, translatable as "fierce, fiercely" or "terrible, terribly" or "formidable, formidably", has a wide range of uses that should be learned case by case. For example, when you are very ill, you cannot say *wǒ hěn bìng*; but you can say *wǒ bìng .de lì.hài*.

15. Review II.3.9 on *méi-shìr* meaning "it doesn't matter, it's nothing".

16. **Passive voice markers.** To make a passive sentence like "my car *was taken out* for a drive *by* my roommate", you can use *bèi* in the following pattern:

Receiver of Action + *bèi* + Doer of Action + Verb + Other Elements

(This formula is adapted from **Modern Chinese Reader**, p. 609.)

Wǒ.de qìchē + bèi + wǒ.de tóngwūr + kāi + .chū.qù.le.

Other examples:

Nèi-kuài ròu bèi Lǎo Huáng chī.le.	That piece of meat has been eaten by Lǎo Huáng.
Wǒ dì.x bèi tā.mén dǎ-shāng.le.	My little brother was injured by them.

In place of *bèi* in this pattern, you can use *jiào* or *ràng*. *Bèi* is more formal and more common in written style; *jiào* and *ràng* are more informal and colloquial.

All adverbs come before *bèi* (or *ràng*, *jiào*), not immediately before the verb:

Wǒ.de qìchē yǐ.jīng bèi tóngwūr kāi.chū.qù.le.	My car has already been taken out for a drive by my roommate.
Nèi-jǐ-kuài ròu quán jiào Lǎo Huáng chī.le.	Those pieces of meat were all eaten by Lǎo Huáng.

Sometimes you will want to use the passive voice even when you do not know who the "doer" was. You can use *rén* to mean "somebody" in such cases:

Wǒ.de qìchē ràng rén kāi-zǒu.le.	My car was driven away by somebody.

Even more simply, you can omit *rén* (allowing "doers" to include animals, the wind, etc.):

> Nèi-xiē rén dōu bèi dǎ-sǐ.le.   Those people were all beaten to
>   death.

In this last usage, however, you can use only *bèi*, not *jiào* or *ràng*.

True to the notion that the receiver of action "suffers" the action in the passive sense, most (but not all) uses of *bèi*, *jiào*, and *ràng* suggest that the action of the verb is negative or unfortunate (a car driven away by a roommate, the meat eaten up by the dog, etc.).

It is important to bear in mind that you do not *have* to use *bèi* (or *ràng*, *jiào*) in order to communicate the "passive voice" in Chinese. (See III.1.18.) Many Chinese verbs are both "active" and "passive" depending on context. For example, *mén kāi.le* would naturally be understood as "the door has been opened" (passive voice), but *wǒ kāi.le* would be understood as "I have opened it" (active voice). A sentence like *wǒ jiào Zhāng Sān* can mean "I'm calling Zhāng Sān" (active) or "I am called Zhāng Sān" (passive).

Another way to express the "passive" idea uses a *shi....de* construction: *Jīnyú shi Mā.x yǎng .de* "The goldfish are Mom-raised ones—the goldfish were raised by Mom"; *xié shi wǒ mǎi .de* "the shoes were bought by me".

18. Optional *gěi*. *Gěi* "to give" also means "for, on behalf of". The "gěi" here is optional because without it the basic meaning of the sentence is not affected. However, with *gěi*, it carries the sense that the action is for the benefit of or to the harm of someone mentioned in the sentence. The word *gěi* can be added before verbs in two kinds of constructions:

(a)   Passive sentences using *bèi*, *ràng*, or *jiào*:

Receiver of Action + $\begin{Bmatrix} bèi \\ ràng \\ jiào \end{Bmatrix}$ + Doer of Action + (*gěi*) + Verb + Other Elements

All the examples using *bèi*, *ràng*, and *jiào* in the previous note could add *gěi*: *Nèi-kuài ròu bèi Lǎo Huáng gěi chī.le*; *wǒ dì.x bèi tā.mén gěi dǎ-shāng.le*, etc.

(b)   Sentences using *bǎ* (see III.2.26):

Subject + *bǎ* + Object + (*gěi*) + Verb + Other Elements

> Zám bǎ gōngzuò shíjiānbiǎo   Let's stick the work schedule up on
>   gěi tiē .zài qiáng.shàng,   the wall, okay?
>   .hǎo .bù.hǎo?

19. *Xiǎo.xīn* "careful" is normally an adjective (*Tā hěn xiǎo.xīn* "she is very careful") or an exclamation (*Xiǎo.xīn!* "Be careful!"). Here it is used as a noun in the phrase *yí.ge bù xiǎo.xīn* "with one carelessness—with one lapse in attention".

Culture Note 17: Telephone Talk

When you receive a telephone call, you can respond to the question *nín nǎr?* by identifying yourself with a place or unit. For example: *wǒ shì* XX *dàxué* "this is XX university".

The question *nín* (or *nǐ*) *něi-yí-wèi?* "Who is this?" asks specifically who (not where) you are. You can respond by saying "*wǒ* [full name]" or "*wǒ* [given name]" or "*shì* [given name]":

Wǒ Zhāng Rúsī.	It's Zhāng Rúsī.
Wǒ Rúsī.	It's Rúsī.
Shì Xiǎo Zhēn.	It's Xiǎo Zhēn.

WARNING: Do not say *Zhè.shì...* ("This is...") as you might based on English usage. Use only the forms introduced here.

Other phrases that are useful in making telephone contact are, from the calling end:

Nín něi-yí-wèi?	Who is this, please?
Qǐng wèn, XX zài .bú.zài jiā?	May I ask if XX is home?
Qǐng XX jiē diànhuà.	Please ask XX to come to the phone.
Wǒ xiǎng gēn XX shuō-huà.	I would like to speak with XX.
Má.fán nín gěi liú .ge huàr.	May I trouble you to leave a message?
Duì.bùqǐ, wǒ dǎ-cuò.le.	I'm sorry, I have the wrong number.

At the receiving end, some useful phrases are:

Nín yào něi-yí-wèi? or Nín zhǎo shéi?	With whom would you like to speak?
XX bú zài jiā; nín yào .bú.yào liú .ge huàr?	XX is not in; would you like to leave a message?
Qǐng .nín liú .ge hàomǎ, děng .huǐr tā gěi .nín dǎ.	Please leave your number and he/she will return your call shortly.
Nín dǎ-cuò.le; wǒ.mén zhèr méi.yǒu XX.	You have the wrong number; no XX lives (or works) here.

The verb "to dial" is *bō*, regardless of whether you actually dial or press buttons. To say "the line is busy", do not use *máng* "busy", but *zhàn-xiàn* "the line is occupied".

Exercises

In-class exercises:

1.   Fill in the blanks with either *zěm.me* or *zěmyàng*.

   A.   Nǐ yǐ.jīng bān.jìn sùshè .le .ba? Nǐ.de tóngwūr ... ?
   B.   Nǐ ... sān.ge xīngqī dōu méi lái diànhuà .ya?
   C.   Nǐ shuāi-shāng .de shǒu, xiànzài ... .le?
   D.   ... , nǐ gēn nǐ tóngwūr chǎo-jià .le .ma?

2.   Answer the following questions.

   A.   Xiǎo Zhēn kāi-chē dào xuéxiào .qù, shùn.lì .bú.shùn.lì?
   B.   Wèishém Xiǎo Zhēn shuì.bù-hǎo?
   C.   Xiǎo Zhēn wèishém bú yuàn.yì bān .dào bié.de wū.zi .qù?
   D.   Xiǎo Zhēn .de shǒu shi zěm shuāi-shāng .de?
   E.   Nǐ yǒu (.guò) tóngwūr .ma? Qǐng .nǐ shuō .yì.shuō nǐ.de tóngwūr. Yào.shi nǐ méi.yǒu tóngwūr jiù qǐng .nǐ shuō .yì.shuō nǐ.de yí.ge hǎo péng.yǒu. (at least 50 words)

3.   Oral Substitution

   Given: Tā.de tóngwūr dǎ-hū, suǒ.yǐ tā shuì.bù-hǎo.

   Response: Tā shuì.bù-hǎo shi yīn.wèi tā.de tóngwūr dǎ-hū .de yuán.gù.

   A.   Lǎo Wáng duì rén tài bú kè.qì, suǒ.yǐ tā.de péng.yǒu dōu tǎoyàn .tā.
   B.   Tā bǎ diànchàngjī kāi .de hěn xiǎng, suǒ.yǐ wǒ tīng.bú-jiàn nǐ shuō .de huà.
   C.   Tā.de liǎn zǒng.shi hóngx .de, suǒ.yǐ wǒ.mén dōu guǎn .tā jiào hóng píngguǒ (apple).
   D.   Yīn.wèi zhèi.ge dàxué quán shì.jiè dōu hěn yǒumíng, suǒ.yǐ xué.shēng dōu xiǎng zài zhèr niàn-shū.
   E.   Nèi-jiā bǎihuò gōngsī .de dōng.xī jià.qián hěn guì, suǒ.yǐ gùkè (customer) hěn shǎo.
   F.   Yīn.wèi xià-yǔ, suǒ.yǐ wǒ méi chū.qù wánr.

Homework:

1.   Translate the following sentences into Chinese.

   A.   When I was walking on the street yesterday, there was ice on the road. I wasn't paying attention, and slipped and hurt my arm.
   B.   We had a pleasant trip (Everything went well along the road). The weather was not very good at first; it was raining. But later it cleared up. It took us only six hours to get to school.
   C.   I have moved in already. My roommate is really a nice person. She is kind, cheerful and neat. I like her very much.

D.   Even though he is a rotten egg, he is not so bad that he would beat his (younger) sister to death.

E.   Chinese is a very difficult language, all right; but it is not so hard that no one can learn it.

F.   Although he is famous, he is not so famous that everyone in the world recognizes him.

Classroom/Homework exercises:

1.   Change the following sentences into the "*bèi (jiào, ràng)* + optional *.gěi*" construction.

Given: Zāogāo, tā bǎ wǒ.de jīnyú ná .dào túshūguǎn .qù .le.

Response: Zāogāo, wǒ.de jīnyú bèi tā .gěi ná .dào túshūguǎn .qù .le.

A.   Dì.x bǎ dàngāo (cake) chī-wán.le.
B.   Lǎo Wáng bǎ nèi-liàng jiù chē xiū.lǐ-hǎo.le.
C.   Tā bǎ .wǒ gāng mǎi .de máojīn ná qù yòng .le.
D.   Lǎoshī bǎ hé.zi.shàng .de bù ná-diào.le.

2.   Change the following sentences into the "*bǎ* + optional *.gěi*" construction.

A.   Tā.de chē bèi tā hǎo péng.yǒu .gěi kāi.chū.qù .le.
B.   Lǎo Wáng yòu bèi Xiǎo Lǐ gěi piàn .le.
C.   Nèi.ge huàidàn hòulái ràng nèi.ge cōngmíng rén .gěi dǎ.sǐ.le.
D.   Zhèi-jiān wū.zi bèi tā zhěng.lǐ .de hěn gān.jìng.
E.   Mèi.x .de tuǐ jiào Lǎo Huáng .gěi yǎo-shāng.le.

3.   Oral Substitution. Provide answer according to the clue given in parentheses.

Given: Tā měi-tiān wǎn.shàng shuō mènghuà, yǒu shí.hòur hái dǎ-hū. (can't sleep every night)

Response: Nà nǐ bú.shi měi-tiān wǎn.shàng dōu shuì.bù-zháo .le .ma?

A.   Wǒ.de nǚpéng.yǒu yào dào wài.guó .qù niàn-shū .qù .le. (can't see your girlfriend)
B.   Wǒ yǒu .ge xīn nánpéng.yǒu (nǚpéng.yǒu), tā yě xué Zhōngwén.   (practice conversation together)
C.   Wǒ zuó.tiān mǎi.le yí-liàng chē.   (drive us out to have fun)

4.   Change the following sentences into a S-P Predicate construction.

Example: Tā.de xīn (hěn) hǎo. Tā.de xìng.qíng yě hěn hǎo.
          Tā xīn hǎo, xìng.qíng yě hǎo.

A.   Zhèi.ge xuéxiào .de qiúchǎng hěn dà. Zhèi.ge xuéxiào .de jiàoshì hěn duō.
B.   Xiǎo Wáng .de yǎn.jīng yòu hēi yòu liàng. Xiǎo Wáng .de bí.zi hěn gāo.
C.   Zhèi-jiān wū.zi .de fángdǐng hěn gāo. Zhèi-jiān wū.zi .de chuāng.zi hěn dà.

LESSON 4

Vocabulary

dānxīn	担心	to worry	kěn	肯	be willing to
zuì hòu	最後	last, final	bàn.fǎ	辦法	method
yī.shēng	醫生	doctor	xiǎoháir	小孩儿	child
wǎnhuì	晚會	evening of entertainment; social evening	hǎotīng	好聽	pleasant to listen to
			fēng	風	wind
zuò	作	to make, to do	niǎor	鳥儿	bird
zuò-cài	作菜	to cook dishes	dāngshí	當時	at that time
bó.x*	伯伯	uncle (father's older brother)	nián.jì	年紀	age
shū.x*	叔叔	uncle (father's younger brother)	héchàng	合唱	to sing together, in chorus
Chén	陳	common surname	jì	寄	to mail
āyí*	阿姨	aunt (mother's sister)	yí	咦	interjection for surprise
lù	錄	to record	hú-shuō	胡說	nonsense
juǎn	卷	a reel, AN for tapes	...shém.me.de (.shém.de)	甚麽的	...and what not
lùyǐngdài	錄影帶	'record-image-tape', videotape	shēng-qì	生氣	to get mad; to be angry
(lùxiàngdài)	錄像帶		zàijiàn	再見	good-bye
huà-huàr	畫畫儿	to paint (a painting)			

---

* Also used as polite forms to address parents' friends.

Vocabulary Classified by Type

Nouns	lù	dān-xīn
yī.shēng	héchàng	huà-huàr
wǎnhuì	jì	shēng-qì
bó.x		
shū.x	**Auxiliary Verbs**	**Time Words**
āyí	kěn	zuì hòu
lùyǐngdài (lùxiàngdài)		dāngshí
bàn.fǎ	**Adjectives**	
xiǎoháir	hǎotīng	**Interjections**
fēng	shēng-qì	yí
niǎor		
nián.jì	**ANs**	**Idiomatic Expressions**
	juǎn	hú-shuō
Verbs		zàijiàn
dānxīn	**V-Os**	...shém.me.de
zuò	zuò-cài	(.shém.de)

Grammar Notes

1. *Dānxīn* "worry". *Xīn* is "heart" or "mind" and the original meaning of *dān* is "carry on a shoulder pole". Thus *dānxīn* "to shoulder the heart, to have the heart (mind) suspended--to worry". The opposite is *fàng-xīn*, literally "to set the heart down", meaning "rest assured, relax".

2. *Cài* means "vegetable" in the ordinary sense of broccoli, cabbage, spinach, etc. (You learned it in *shēngcài* "salad" in II.3.2.) But here it is used with a different meaning. Chinese meals consist of a staple food, like cooked rice (*fàn*) or noodles (*miàn*), plus various prepared dishes of meat and/or vegetables. These dishes are also called *cài*. When you learn Chinese cooking you *xué zuò Zhōng.guó-cài*. (Don't say *xué zuò-fàn*. *Zuò-fàn* means either "cook rice", which is nothing remarkable, or "prepare meals" in a very general sense.) To compliment a host(ess) you have to say *Nín.de cài* (not *fàn*) *zuò .de zhēn hǎo!* "Your food is great!".

3. You have learned *jiào* as "call" or "be called". Here it means "ask or tell (someone to do something)". *Tā.mén jiào .wǒ jiāo .tā.mén* "they asked me to teach them". The polite form of *jiào* is *qǐng* "to invite". If a man asks his teacher to write a few characters for him, you describe the action as *tā qǐng lǎoshī xiě jǐ.ge zì*. If he asks his son, you say *tā jiào ér.zi xiě jǐ.ge zì*.

4. *Bó.x*, literally "father's elder brother", is also used by children to refer to any male friends of one's father who are older than the father. When used in this latter way, the family name (*xìng*) is usually added at the front--thus *Wáng Bó.x* "'Uncle' Wáng". The same general principle holds for *shū.x* "father's younger brother--younger friends of one's father". One's mother's sisters are *yí* or *yímā*, and female friends of one's parents are called *āyí*, again usually prefixed with the family name: *Chén Āyí* "'Auntie' Chén". Ways of referring to relatives are more complex in Chinese than in English. For details see Culture Note 18, below.

5. *Lùyǐngdài* "record-image-ribbon" means "videotape" in Chinese communities abroad as well as in Taiwan and Hong Kong. In the People's Republic, *lùxiàngdài* "record-likeness-ribbon" is more common. You should learn both terms. A video player-recorder is a *lùyǐngjī* or *lùxiàngjī* "record-image/likeness-machine". Remember that you have learned *lùyīndài* "audiotape" in V.2. An audio recorder is *lùyīnjī*.

6. *Kěn* "willing to" is an auxiliary verb like *néng* "can" or *yào* "want to" or "will". *Kěn* should be compared with *yuàn.yì*, which appeared in the last lesson. *Yuàn.yì* is more positive, sometimes equivalent to "be glad to" or "wish" in English. *Kěn* simply indicates absence of aversion, closer to ordinary "willing to" in English.

7. *.Shém.de* "and so forth". Cf. English "what not".

8. "*Jì.de Dāngshí Nián.jì Xiǎo*" is the first line of a song entitled *Běnshì*. *Dāngshí* "at the time (in the past that I am talking about)"; *nián.jì* "age".

9. *Má.fán* here is an adjective meaning "troublesome". It can also be 1) a transitive verb "put (someone) to trouble--bother (someone)", as it was in VI.2; 2) a noun "trouble, irritating tasks"; or 3) an exclamation: *Zhēn má.fán!* "what a nuisance!". *.Kě* in this sentence is used for emphasis.

10. *Hú-shuō* "nonsense". *Hú* as an adverb means "wildly, stupidly, confusedly". Thus *hú-chī* "eat crazily", *hú-nào* "cause a ruckus for no reason", *hú-lái* "do (something) recklessly".

11. It is obvious that the mother is irritated because of the way she says *zàijiàn* "good-bye". It is normal, and more gentle, to repeat the two syllables in quick succession *.zài.jiàn vx*, all in neutral tones, or to add *.ah* with a glottal stop: *.zài.jiàn, .ah!*. A plain *zàijiàn*, in full fourth tones, is abrupt and a bit harsh. It goes well with the mother's raised voice.

Culture Note 18:   **Kinship Chart**

Paternal side

Grandparents

Zǔfù   Zǔmǔ

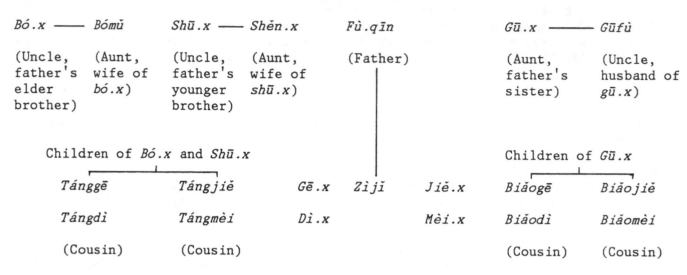

Bó.x —— *Bómǔ*   *Shū.x* —— *Shěn.x*   *Fù.qīn*   *Gū.x* —— *Gūfù*

(Uncle,   (Aunt,   (Uncle,   (Aunt,   (Father)   (Aunt,   (Uncle,
father's   wife of   father's   wife of   father's   husband of
elder   *bó.x*)   younger   *shū.x*)   sister)   *gū.x*)
brother)   brother)

Children of *Bó.x* and *Shū.x*   Children of *Gū.x*

Tánggē   *Tángjiě*   *Gē.x   Zìjǐ   Jiě.x*   *Biǎogē*   *Biǎojiě*

Tángdì   *Tángmèi*   *Dì.x*   *Mèi.x*   *Biǎodì*   *Biǎomèi*

(Cousin)   (Cousin)   (Cousin)   (Cousin)

Maternal side

Grandparents

Wài-zǔfù   Wài-zǔmǔ

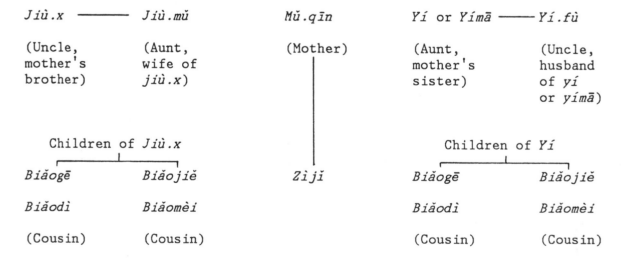

Jiù.x —————— *Jiù.mǔ*   *Mǔ.qīn*   *Yí* or *Yímā* ——*Yí.fù*

(Uncle,   (Aunt,   (Mother)   (Aunt,   (Uncle,
mother's   wife of   mother's   husband
brother)   *jiù.x*)   sister)   of *yí*
                                                               or *yímā*)

Children of *Jiù.x*   Children of *Yí*

Biǎogē   *Biǎojiě*   *Biǎogē*   *Biǎojiě*

Biǎodì   *Biǎomèi*   *Zìjǐ*   *Biǎodì*   *Biǎomèi*

(Cousin)   (Cousin)   (Cousin)   (Cousin)

Note:
1.   Cousins of the same family name are called *táng* whereas cousins of different
      family names are called *biǎo*.

2.   For uncles, aunts, siblings, and cousins, if there are more than one, you can
     number them according to age: *Dà* (eldest), *èr* (second), *sān* (third), e.g., *dà-bó*,
     dà-bómŭ, *sān-shū*, *sān-shĕn*, *wŭ-gū*, *wŭ-gū.fù*, *qī-jiù*, *qī-jiù.mŭ*, *sì-yí*, *sì-yí.fù*,
     dà-biăogē, *èr-biăojiĕ*, etc. Also note that the eldest (first) is not *yī* but *dà*.
3.   Terms of address, if different from above:
     Zŭfù = yé.x; *zŭmŭ = năi.x*; *wài-zŭfù = wàigōng*; *wài-zŭmŭ = wàipó*; *fù.qīn = bà.x*;
     mŭ.qīn = mā.x.
     For cousins *táng* is not used for direct address; one calls his *tánggē* and *tángjiĕ*
     dà-gē, *èr-jiĕ*, etc. For *tángdì* and *tángmèi*, one calls them by their given names.
     Biăo can be used for direct address, hence, *dà-biăojiĕ*, *sān-biăogē*, etc., but it
     is often dropped.

Exercises

In-class exercises:

1.   Answer the following questions in Chinese.

     A.   Xiăo Zhēn yào qĭng mā.x bāng .tā shém máng?
     B.   Wèishém mā.x duì Xiăo Zhēn shuō "Nĭ .kĕ zhēn má.fán?"
     C.   Xiăo Zhēn tīng tā mā.x shuō "Nĭ.de jīnyú sĭ .le" yĭhòu, tā shuō, "Wŏ zhēn
          dānxīn." Tā dānxīn shém.me?

2.   Fill in the blanks with either *jiào* or *qĭng*.

     A.   Lăoshī ... .wŏ bă jiàoshì zhĕng.lĭ gān.jìng.
     B.   Xiăo Zhēn ... tā mŭ.qīn bă lùyīndài jì .gĕi .tā.
     C.   Lăo Wáng, nĭ mŭ.qīn ... .nĭ dào jiē.shàng .qù măi .diănr dōng.xī .qù.
     D.   Wŏ xiăng ... .nĭ bāng wŏ.de máng.
     E.   Míng.tiān shàng.wŭ wŏ méi kòngr, kĕ .bù.kĕ.yĭ ... .nĭ xià.wŭ zài lái?

Homework:

1.   Translate the following sentences into Chinese.

     A.   This afternoon I saw the doctor for the last time, and he said that my hand
          had completely healed.
     B.   There's going to be a China Night here next month. The students are going
          to sing Chinese songs, make Chinese food, write Chinese calligraphy, and do
          Chinese painting.
     C.   Please help me by recording a videotape with all those things on it:
          singing, cooking, calligraphy, and painting. Can you have it done by next
          week?

2.   You've come to China to study. Today you are making your first call home from
     China. Write out in Chinese the telephone conversation between you and your
     family.

3.   Explain the following words in Chinese, giving examples to illustrate the meaning:
     (1) *wănhuì*, (2) *tán.de-lái*, (3) *héchàng*, (4)· *băihuò gōngsī*, (5) *yī.shēng*, (6)
     má.fán.

4.   Review exercise. Translate into Chinese the following dialogue, which is entitled
"Beyond Repair".

A: Xiǎo Lǐ, Mr. Wáng said something to me that I didn't understand. Maybe you
    can help me to guess what he meant.

B: What did he say?

A: He said that he wanted to "repair" me. Automobiles, computers, and
    phonographs can be repaired, as far as I know (I only know). I have never
    heard that a human being can be repaired. I simply cannot figure out (think
    out) what he meant.

B: I think what he means is that he is going to beat you up.

A: My Gosh! Then what shall I do?

B: When did he say this to you?

A: He told me three days ago.

B: How did he tell you? Did he tell you over the phone or did he write you a
    letter (to tell you)?

A: I went to see him and he told me himself.

B: Where did you see him?

A: I saw him at his home.

B: Do you know why he wants to beat you up?

A: He asked me to paint a landscape painting for him. I did (painted) one for
    him and gave it to him last Friday. Probably he didn't like my painting.
    After he looked at it, he asked, "Where is the beef?". I was very unhappy. I
    yelled at him (said to him in a loud voice), "You stupid egg! The beef is in
    the restaurant. Do you mean to say that you don't know?" His face (turned)
    red. He asked me to apologize to him. I said, "You ought to apologize to me,
    you rotten egg!" He stood up and walked out. Before he walked out of the
    door, he said to me, "Be careful, I am going to repair you."

B: So now he wants to fix you up.

A: Mr. Wáng is really a rat. I really want (think) to repair him.

B: In a society like this, I am afraid you have no way to repair him. He has
    many relatives and friends. All the people here are afraid of (pà) him. You
    have only a few schoolmates who are just students. I don't think they can
    help you.

A: Can you help me?

B: If you just want me to quarrel with Mr. Wáng, maybe I can help. If you want me to fight with Mr. Wáng, I am sure he will win and I will lose.

A: Since you can't help me, the only thing I can do is to figure out a way by myself.

B: This evening you had better stay home and not go out. Tomorrow morning you should first drive to Chicago, then fly to California. In California you will have to live in a place where nobody knows you.

A: This evening I originally wanted to treat my girlfriend to a movie and then a big meal in a Chinese restaurant. Now I can't go. Could I bother you to give her a call? Please also tell her that the reason I can't go is that Mr. Wáng wants to repair me.

B: Please rest assured. I'll definitely call her and explain everything to her. I hope everything goes well with you on the road.

A: Good-bye.

B: Bye.

(*A calls his girlfriend, Xiǎo Zhēn*).

A: Hello, is this Xiǎo Zhēn? This is Rúsī.

Z: Oh, Rúsī. How are you now? Why haven't I had any news from you for two days? I have been waiting extremely impatiently (nervous to death). I have been so nervous that I can neither eat nor sleep.

A: I am sorry. Did Xiǎo Lǐ call you?

Z: Yes, he did; he told me everything. It's another of Mr. Wáng's good deeds. He really is a rat. Where are you now? Are you okay? Why didn't you call?

A: I am calling from Cleveland. Yesterday I drove for twenty hours. I was extremely (life-demandingly) tired. I was so tired that I couldn't even keep my eyes open. How can I have any energy left for making a phone call? But don't worry, Xiǎo Zhēn. Last night I had sufficient rest. Today I'm in good shape (my spirit-energy is good).

Z: I know this is your first time driving on a long trip. You must be very nervous (tense). Actually, driving on long trips is not really difficult. So long as you pay attention to driving, it will be okay (it will do). However, you have a bad habit which should be corrected. You always sing while you drive. I feel that when you don't have enough energy, you had better not sing.

A: I'll certainly (definitely) remember what you say. I'll be very careful and pay close attention (properly pay attention) to driving.

Z: This time Mr. Wáng made (let) you suffer a big loss (eat a big loss). You had to leave home and go alone to California. But it's good for you, too, because

on the one hand Mr. Wáng can't find you, and on the other hand you can go
visit (take a look at) the University of California's Chinese Department. The
University of California's Chinese Department is famous all over the world.
Sometimes a department may be famous (all right), but the teachers aren't
necessarily good, so (you) definitely have to go yourself and attend class.
Only then can (you) know whether it really (after all) is good or not.

A: Calling long distance in the daytime is really expensive. I have already put
     in more than twenty quarters. I don't have any more money. I have to hang
     up. Good-bye.

Classroom/Homework exercises:

1.   Answer the following questions using "... *shém.me.de*".

     Example: Nǐ.de wū.zi.lǐ yǒu shém.me?
               Wǒ.de wū.zi.lǐ yǒu zhuō.zi, yǐ.zi, shū, hái.yǒu
                    shūjià.zi, diàndēng, shém.me.de.

     A.   Shàng Zhōngwén-kè .de shí.hòur lǎoshī yào xué.shēng zuò shém.me?
     B.   Zuó.tiān Xiǎo Zhēn .dào bǎihuò gōngsī .qù .le; tā mǎi.le shém.me dōng.xī?

2.   Fill in the blanks with the appropriate complement.

     A.   Tā shuō nèi.ge gēr hěn hǎotīng, suǒ.yǐ tā jiào .wǒ bǎ nèi.ge gēr yě lù ... .
     B.   Tā kuài bì-yè .le, suǒ.yǐ děi cóng sùshè bān ... .le.
     C.   Diànhuà shēng.yīn huài-jí.le, wǒ tīng ... shi shéi dǎ-lái .de.
     D.   Zuó.tiān wǎn.shàng wǒ.de tóngwūr dǎ-hū dǎ .de hěn xiǎng, wǒ yì.diǎnr yě shuì
          ... .
     E.   Tā kùn .de lián yǎn.jīng dōu zhēng ... .

3.   Translate the following sentences using the construction "*bié zài* V ... *.le*".

     A.   Don't come late anymore.
     B.   Will you two people stop arguing? (You two people, please don't argue any
          more.)
     C.   This is the last time I will teach you how to write this character. Don't
          write it incorrectly anymore.

4.   Translate the following sentences into Chinese using the construction "*zǎo.diǎnr*
     V".

     A.   Next week I have three exams. I have to start studying a little earlier.
     B.   You should have told him this good news earlier.
     C.   Although there is still half a year before my graduation, I'd better start
          looking for a job a little earlier.

UNIT VII

LESSON 1

Vocabulary

kàn.fǎ	看法	viewpoint		kètīng	客廳	'guest hall', living room
kǎo	考	to examine		shāfā	沙發	(transliteration of sofa), armchair or sofa
xiū.xí	休息	to rest				
huí-jiā	回家	return home		zhāo-jí	着急	nervous, anxious
fāng.biàn	方便	convenient		.ng	嗯	interjection of agreement
				jié-hūn	結婚	get married

Vocabulary Classified by Type

	Nouns		xiū.xí		zhāo-jí	
kàn.fǎ					jié-hūn	
kètīng			**Adjectives**			
shāfā			fāng.biàn			**Interjection**
					.ng	
	Verbs			**V-Os**		
kǎo			huí-jiā			

Grammar Notes

1. *Fǎ* "law, method, way" can be attached to many verbs as a suffix meaning "way or manner of [verbing]": *kàn.fǎ* "way of looking at--viewpoint, opinion"; *xiǎng.fǎ* "way of thinking"; *xiě.fǎ* "way of writing"; *shuō.fǎ* "way of talking--(linguistic) usage"; *qiē.fǎ* "manner of slicing", etc. (The word *fá.zi* "method, way" was introduced in II.1. *Fá* is the same character as *fǎ*, but is pronounced in the second tone because *.zi* is an abbreviation for third-tone *zǐ*.)

2. *Xiū.xí* and *xiē* are both verbs meaning "rest" or "take a rest," and are frequently repeated as *xiū.xí vx* or *xiē.x*. *Xiē* is more colloquial than *xiū.xí*. Only *xiū.xí* can be used in formal written contexts, such as in announcing an intermission on a

printed program. *Xiū.xí* is, moreover, used everywhere in China, whereas *xiē* (or *xiē.zhe*) is common only in the Běijīng area.

3. *Zhāo-jí* "feel anxious" or "get impatient" is similar to *dānxīn* "worry" (VI.4.1) and *jǐn.zhāng* "tense" (III.3.16). In some contexts, the three terms are interchangeable, but sometimes only one is appropriate. (By this point in your study, you should begin to distinguish nuances and finer points of usage among similar terms. It is seldom the case that corresponding terms in English are reliable guides.)

   Zhāo-jí, *dānxīn*, and *jǐn.zhāng* could be used interchangeably when, for example, you have a big Chinese test the next day and have not yet begun to review. You might say *wǒ hěn zhāo-jí* "I am anxious, nervous" or *wǒ hěn dānxīn* "I'm worried (about the result)" or *wǒ hěn jǐn.zhāng* "I'm tense, nervous." But there are other times when only one of the three will do. For example:

   (1) When something tries your patience, but does not really cause worry or fear, *zhāo-jí* is appropriate but not the other two. If you've been waiting a long time for a bus that does not arrive, you might say *wǒ děng .de hěn zhāo-jí* "I got impatient waiting".

   (2) *Zhāo-jí* and *dānxīn* refer only to specific instances of being upset or worried. But *jǐn.zhāng* can also describe a person's general disposition (*tā zhèi.ge rén hěn jǐn.zhāng* "he is a nervous type") or a general state of affairs (*Zhōng-Měi guān.xì yǒu .diǎn jǐn.zhāng* "Sino-American relations are a bit tense").

   (3) In all the above usages, we are discussing *zhāo-jí, dānxīn* and *jǐn.zhāng* as adjectives. But *dānxīn* (and not the others) can also be a transitive verb that takes a clause as object: *tā dānxīn lóngxiā búgòu* "He's worried there won't be enough lobster"; *wǒ dānxīn tā tīng.bù-dǒng* "I'm afraid she won't understand".

4. *Dōu*...[verb]....*le* "all (the way to)—already". (The *.le* here indicates "new discovery of an existing situation".) A clause that uses "*dōu* Verb *.le*" is often followed by a second clause (whether stated or implied) that expresses a "but" or asks a question. Examples:

Wǒ dōu lái.le sān.ge lǐbài .le, kě.shi hǎo.xiàng shi zuó.tiān gāng dào .de.	I've already been here three weeks, but it seems as if I just arrived yesterday.
Xiànzài dōu shí'èr-diǎn .le, kě.shi tā hái méi huí.lái.	It's already 12 o'clock, but she hasn't come back yet.
Zhèi-běnr shū dōu zèm jiù .le, nǐ zěm bù mǎi yì-běnr xīn .de .ne.?	This book's already so old—why don't you buy a new one?
Nǐ mèi.x dōu liù-suì .le; zěm hái.bú shàng-xué?	Your sister is already six years old; how come she's not going to school yet?

Note that this *dōu* is often in the neutral tone.

5. *Hǎo* "on good terms, close".

6. *Tán.dào* "talk about". Similarly, *shuō.dào* "speak about", *xiǎng.dào* "think about".

7.   Review III.3.25 on *zài shuō*. *Děng*, literally "wait", here has the sense of "wait until" in English. Another example:

Děng .nǐ shàng dàxué nǐ jiù   Wait until you go to college, and then
dǒng .le.·   you'll understand.

Exercises

In-class exercises:

1.   Fill in the blanks with *zhāo-jí*, *dānxīn*, or *jǐn.zhāng*

A.   Měi-yí-cì kǎo-shì .de shí.hòur wǒ dōu hěn ... , yǒu shí.hòur lián zuì jiǎndān .de zì dōu wàng.le zěm xiě.
B.   Zǎo.shàng wǒ děng bā-diǎn .de chē qù xuéxiào. Wǒ děng.le bàn.ge zhōngtóu chē dōu méi lái, wǒ děng .de hěn ... .
C.   Dào.le xuéxiào, tóngxué yí kàn.dào .wǒ jiù shuō, "Wǒ.mén dōu ... nǐ huì chídào."
D.   Lǎoshī lái .le, gēn .wǒ.mén shuō, "Bié ... , zhèi-cì kǎoshì hěn róng.yì, wǒ xiāngxìn nǐ.mén yídìng kǎo.de-hǎo."

Homework:

1.   Translate the following sentences into Chinese.

A.   You sound tired. I'm sure you haven't been sleeping well. When are you coming home?
B.   Oh, you have a boyfriend, wonderful. Your dad and I were worrying (about this) yesterday. We were saying that you were about to graduate from college and still didn't have a boyfriend. Are the two of you close yet?
C.   Uh-huh. We have already talked about getting married. Mom, I'll bring him home the day after tomorrow. You will be seeing him pretty soon.
D.   Your elder sister and your elder brother are coming to live with us. I will have to put another desk in your room. I also want to put another bed in your younger sister's room.
E.   I would like to come to see you at half past three this afternoon. I wonder if that's convenient for you.
F.   Please don't bother to prepare a bed for me. Let me sleep on the sofa in the living room. I am only staying one night.
G.   You want to give me a watch? Why don't you wait until my graduation to give it to me?

Classroom/Homework exercises:

1.   Oral Substitution

A.   Given: Yǐ.jīng sān-yuè .le, tiān hái.shi zěm lěng (cold).

Response: Dōu sān-yuè .le, tiān hái.shi zěm lěng.

A.   Yǐ.jīng bàn-yè shí'èr diǎn .le, nǐ zěm hái.bù huí-jiā?

B.   Yǐ.jīng kuài yào kǎo-shì .le, nǐ zěm hái.bú yù.bèi gōngkè?
C.   Shíjiān guò .de zhēn kuài, wǒ mèi.x yǐ.jīng bǐ wǒ gāo .le.
D.   Tā yìzhí (all along) jiǎng, wǒ yǐ.jīng kuài shuì-zháo .le tā hái .zài jiǎng.
E.   Tiān yǐ.jīng hēi .le, tā hái.bù kāi-dēng.

LESSON 2

Vocabulary

tīng.jiàn	聽見	hear		bómǔ	伯母	aunt (wife of father's older brother; polite form to address parents' friends)
diànshì	電視	television				
zhòngyào	重要	important; sig-nificant				
jiè.shào	介紹	to introduce		wǔfàn	午飯	lunch (same as zhōngfàn)
lǎobó	老伯	polite form to address parents' friends or friend's father (see bó.x in VI.4.4)		fēijī	飛機	airplane

Vocabulary Classified by Type

Nouns	Verbs	Verb-RCs
diànshì	jiè.shào	tīng.jiàn
lǎobó		
bómǔ	**Adjectives**	
fēijī	zhòngyào	

Grammar Notes

1. *Kàn.le liǎng.ge zhōngtóur .de diànshì .le* "have watched two hours of television as of now--have been watching TV for two hours". Review II.2.4 on the use of a "completed action" *.le* together with a "new situation *.le*" with a time expression intervening: for example, *wǒ xué.le yì-nián Zhōngwén .le* "I've been studying Chinese for one year". The only difference in the example here is that an optional *.de* is added after *zhōngtóur*. The *.de* could also be added in such sentences as: *tā xué.le liǎng-nián .de Zhōngwén* "He took two years of Chinese"; *wǒ dǎ.le sān.ge zhōngtóur .de bīngbāng qiú* "I played ping pong for three hours". If a final particle *.le* is added to the above two examples, then the meanings will be "He has been taking Chinese for two years (and is still taking it)", and "I have been playing ping pong for three hours (and am still playing)".

2. Both *Zhòngyào* and *yàojǐn* mean "important", but the two terms have somewhat different connotations, and often are not interchangeable. *Zhòngyào* is closer to "major" or "significant" in English, as in *zhòngyào .de gòng.xiàn* "significant contribution" or *zhòngyào .de fāzhǎn* "major development". In both cases, *zhòngyào*

cannot be replaced by *yàojǐn*. *Yàojǐn* is closer to "urgent" or "pressing", as in: *wǒ jīn.tiān yǒu yàojǐn shì.qíng, bùnéng kàn diàn.yǐng .le, duì.bùqǐ* "I have something urgent today, so I can't go to the movie. Sorry." In general, *zhòngyào* is also a more formal term than *yàojǐn*.

3.   *Jiù.shi* "simply is" sometimes implies that a thing rather stubbornly stays the way it is. *Tā.de xìng.qíng jiù.shi zèm tèbié* "Her disposition just **is** peculiar like that (and there's no changing it)"; *tā jiù.shi zèm bù xǐ.huān shuō-huà* "he's just that way—doesn't like to talk", etc.

4.   Here is another double negative used to express an emphatic positive (review III.4.18). *Nǐ yě bú.shi bùzhīdào* "it's not that you don't know—of course you know!".

5.   *Bó.x*, "paternal uncle (older than one's father)" was introduced at VI.4.4 as a respectful term of address for older male friends of one's father. *Lǎobó* is the same as *bó.x* except: (1) *lǎobó* implies a somewhat more advanced age, and thus more honor for the person referred to; (2) *lǎobó* is never used to address actual family; it is always "uncle" in the honorific sense.

6.   Review Culture Notes on personal names. *Méiyīng*, literally "plum flower", is another typical feminine name. *Yīng*, which can also mean "hero", is sometimes used in men's names as well.

7.   *Chī-guò.le* "have finished eating". Review III.2.9.

"Zhè.shi wǒ péng.yǒu Lǐ Wénxīn."

Exercises

Homework:

1.   Translate the following sentences into Chinese.

   A.   She said she had finished her exams. She is coming home with her boyfriend
        the day after tomorrow. She invited him to stay with us for a few days.
        They are pretty close already—even talked about getting married.
   B.   Let me introduce you, Dad. This is my friend Lǐ Wénxīn.
   C.   Have you had lunch yet? You must be hungry.
   D.   We're not hungry. We ate on the plane. We want to rest first.
   E.   You are about to get married. Do you mean to say that you haven't talked
        about where you are going to live?
   F.   The sky is very dark. It surely is going to rain in the afternoon.
   G.   In the beginning, the two of them were very polite. Later on when they
        talked about American social problems during the Vietnam War (Yuèzhàn)
        period, both of them became upset (got mad), and they began to quarrel.
        This was because what the two of them thought was entirely different. (For
        the last sentence use the emphatic adv. *suǒ* and the "*shì ... .de yuán.gù*"
        construction.)

   H.   A: Did you hear that?

        B: It's not that I didn't hear, it's just that I don't want to know.

2.   Write a short dialogue to introduce your parents to your schoolmates.

Classroom/Homework exercises:

1.   Explain the following words in Chinese: *zhòngyào*; *wǔfàn*; *zhāo-jí*; *xiū.xí*; *kěn*;
     dānxīn; *zhùyì*; *jiǎndān* ; *mǎshàng*; *méi guān.xi*.

2.   Answer the following questions. Your answer should be no less than 25 words.

   A.   Nǐ xǐ.huān .bù.xǐ.huān kàn diànshì? Wèishém.me?
   B.   Kàn diànshì gēn rén .de shēng.huó yǒu shém guān.xì (relation)?
   C.   Kàn Zhōngwén diànshì gēn xué Zhōngwén yǒu shém guān.xì?

3.   Oral Substitution

   Given: xué Zhōngwén; yì-nián

   Response: Wǒ.mén yǐ.jīng xué.le yì-nián .de Zhōngwén .le.

   A.   kàn diànshì; liǎng.ge zhōngtóu
   B.   kāi-chē; liù.ge zhōngtóu
   C.   tīng lùyīndài; sān.shí-fēn zhōng
   D.   shuì-jiào; liǎng.ge bàn zhōngtóu
   E.   tīng diànchàngjī; yí.ge bàn zhōngtóu

LESSON 3

Vocabulary

huǒchē	火車	train	dī	低	low
fēijīchǎng	飛機場	airport	méi.máo	眉毛	eyebrow
jīchǎng	機場	airport	cháng	長	long
shàng	上	to board	duǎn	短	short
nán	南	south	zuǐ	嘴	mouth
běi	北	north	yàng.zi	樣子	shape
tóu.fà	頭髮	hair	xiǎoshēng	小聲	in a low voice, "hush"
huī	灰	grey	tán-huà	談話	to talk, to chat
ěr.duǒ	耳朵	ear	péi	陪	keep company, accompany

Vocabulary Classified by Type

Nouns		**Verbs**		cháng
huǒchē		shàng		duǎn
fēijīchǎng		péi		
jīchǎng				**Adverbs**
tóu.fà		**Adjectives**		xiǎoshēng
ěr.duǒ		nán		
méi.máo		běi		**V-Os**
zuǐ		huī		tán-huà
yàng.zi		dī		

Grammar Notes

1. Review V.4.3 on the use of *shì....de* to emphasize the time, place, or manner of a past action. This important pattern recurs in several of the sentences that follow in the text.

2. Review V.4.4 on the alternate positioning of *.de* in *shì....de* constructions. *Shàng .de fēijī* is equivalent to *shàng fēijī .de*.

3. *Tóu.fà bàn huī bàn huáng* "with half-grey half-brown hair". If completely spelled out, the sentence would be *tóu.fà yí-bàn shì huī .de yí-bàn shì huáng .de*; but it

is common to contract such expressions to *bàn* A *bàn* B, where A and B usually have opposite or contrasting meanings. A and B can be adjectives, as in *bàn xīn bàn jiù* "half-new half-old", or verbs, as in *bàn xǐng bàn shuì* "half-awake half-asleep".

4. *Ěr.duǒ* "ear" in Běijīng Mandarin is actually pronounced *ěr.dōu* or *ěr.tóu*. But *duǒ* is the formal reading, and *ěr.duǒ* is standard outside Běijīng. *Ěr* does not change to second tone even though *.duǒ* is originally a third-tone word.

    Like *bàn* A *bàn* B in the previous note, *yì(yí)* A *yì(yí)* B means "one A and one B". In this contracted usage it is all right to omit the normal ANs, which, if included, would make the sentence in the text: *tā.de ěr.duǒ yí.ge gāo yí.ge dī, méi.máo yì-gēn cháng yì-gēn duǎn, yǎn.jīng yí.ge dà yí.ge xiǎo.*

5. *Shì búhuì tīng.jiàn .de* "is (most) unlikely to hear". *Huì* is used with *shì....de* to express confident predictions by the speaker. *Tā shì huì lái .de* "he's likely to come"; *jīn.tiān shì búhuì xià-yǔ .de* "it's not going to rain today". As in other uses of *shì....de*, the *shì* is sometimes omitted: *tā huì lái .de*; *jīn.tiān búhuì xià-yǔ .de.*

6. *Kě shuō .de* "worth saying". This *kě*, an abbreviation for *kě.yǐ*, also conveys the sense of "worth [verbing]". Other examples:

    kě chī .de   worth eating
    kě tīng .de   worth listening to

Exercises

Homework:

1. Translate the following sentences into Chinese using the "*shì ... .de*" construction.

    A.   We left the dorm at nine o'clock this morning.
    B.   He came from New York by train yesterday.
    C.   It was Xiǎo Dīng who thought of a way to paint your nose.
    D.   It must have been you who wrote this note.
    E.   My parents came to see my sister yesterday afternoon.
    F.   At which train station did you board the train? Was it at the south station or at the north station? (station: zhàn)
    G.   We boarded at the south station.

2. Arrange the following into an order that makes sense.

    A.   měi-tiān chú.le chī-fàn, shuì-jiào, kàn diànshì yǐwài
    B.   díquè, diànshì zài zhèi-xiē rén .de shēng.huó.li fēicháng zhòngyào
    C.   diànshì kě.yǐ suàn.shi tā.mén.de ěr.duǒ gēn yǎn.jīng
    D.   yǒu rén jué.de diànshì shì rén zuì hǎo .de péng.yǒu
    E.   shém bié.de shì dōu bú zuò
    F.   ràng tā.mén kàn.dào, tīng.dào shì.jiè.shàng .de shì.qíng
    G.   tā.mén yì-tiān-dào-wǎn kàn diànshì

3.   Translate the following sentences into Chinese.

        A.   This is the first time I have ridden on an airplane. I'm a bit frightened.
                That's why I asked my daughter to keep me company.
        B.   A: The character *chǎng* is in both *qiúchǎng* and *fēijīchǎng*. Exactly
                    (after all) what does this character mean?
                B: It means a large piece of empty ground.
        C.   There are often many birds flying in the vicinity of airports. Sometimes
                the birds bump into the front of an airplane and may cause (make) the
                airplane to fall down.
        D.   The teachers at world-famous universities are not necessarily all good ones.

Classroom/Homework exercises:

1.   First describe Xiǎo Zhēn's boyfriend, then answer the following questions.

        A.   Xiǎo Zhēn .de fù-mǔ xi.huān .bù.xi.huān Lǐ Wénxīn?
        B.   Nǐ jué.de tā.mén liǎng.ge rén jié-hūn héshì .bù.hé.shì? Wèishém.me?

2.   Explain the following words in Chinese: *shēng-qì*; *hǎotīng*; *guì*; *xi.huān*;
        cōng.míng; *dì.xià*.

UNIT VIII

LESSON 1

Vocabulary

yìzhí	一直	all along	Běijīng	北京	'north-capital', Peking
wèntí	問題	question	Shànghǎi	上海	Shanghai
lǎo	老	always	Nánjīng	南京	Nanking
jī.huì	機會	opportunity, chance	Xī'ān	西安	Sian, Xi'an
zhènghǎo	正好	happen to; by coincidence; just at the right time	Guǎngzhōu	廣州	Canton, Guang-zhou
			Xiānggǎng	香港	Hong Kong
			Táiwān	台灣	Taiwan
dāngchū	當初	at the outset; in the first place	gāi	該	should, ought to
			kàn.dào	看到	similar to kàn.jiàn
huídá	回答	answer; to answer	chēng.hū	稱呼	to address
yǒu.de	有的	some	bié.rén	別人	other people
tài.x	太太	Mrs.; wife	xiān.shēng	先生	Mr.; teacher; husband
ài.rén	愛人	spouse (PRC usage); lover	rúguǒ	如果	if
qù.nián	去年	last year	shóu	熟	'cooked', famil-iar

Vocabulary Classified by Type

Nouns
wèntí
jī.huì
huídá
tài.x
ài.rén
bié.rén
xiān.shēng

Proper Nouns
Běijīng
Shànghǎi
Nánjīng
Xī'ān
Guǎngzhōu

Xiānggǎng
Táiwān

Verbs
huídá
chēng.hū

V-Resultative Complements
kàn.dào

Auxiliary Verbs
gāi

Adjectives
yǒu.de

shóu

Adverbs
yìzhí
lǎo

Sentential Adverbs
(Moveable Adverbs)
zhènghǎo

Conjunctions
rúguǒ

Time Words
dāngchū
qù.nián

Grammar Notes

1. *Ài.rén*, originally meaning "lover", now means "spouse" in the People's Republic of China. (See Culture Note 7, Unit II, Lesson 2.)

2. *Yìzhí*, literally "one-straight", means "all along" in time, or "keep (verb)-ing". *Yìzhí xiǎng wèn* "all along have been wanting to ask" or "keep meaning to ask". *Yìzhí* can also be used in its literal, spatial sense: *yìzhí zǒu* "go straight".

3. When *.zhèr* is in the neutral tone, *zài.zhèr* simply means "to be present", with no emphasis on location. *Zài zhèr*, by contrast, means "to be **here**". The same distinction holds between *zài.nàr* "**to be** there" and *zài nàr* "to be **there**".

4. *.Lái* preceding a verb indicates an intention or suggestion of the speaker's. *Wǒ .lái wèn.x .ni.mén* "I'll ask you". *Nǐ .lái chàng .ge gēr .ba* "How about a song from you?"; *Nǐ qù mǎi dōng.xī, wǒ .lái zuò-fàn* "You go shopping and I'll cook". The *.lái* can be omitted with very little change in sense. Sometimes *lái*, in its full tone, substitutes for the whole verb: *wǒ chàng-wán.le, xiànzài nǐ lái .ba* "I'm finished singing; now it's your turn".

5. *Yǒu.de*, literally "there are those which", means "some". You may think of *yǒu.de* as a modifier before a noun: *yǒu.de Zhōng.guórén* "some Chinese"; *yǒu.de shū* "some books"; etc. If the noun is understood, *yǒu.de* becomes a substantive: *yǒu.de hǎo, yǒu.de huài* "some are good and some are bad".

6. In the 19th century, the names of China's provinces and major cities were given English equivalents, somewhat arbitrarily, for use in the international postal system. Some of these terms, such as Peking for *Běijīng*, Canton for *Guǎngzhōu*, and Hong Kong for *Xiānggǎng*, are still common today. Others, such as Chekiang for *Zhè.jiāng* and Hopeh for *Hé.běi*, are less common but still occasionally used. Increasingly, the standard spellings of the *pīnyīn* system are being adopted: Běijīng, Guǎngzhōu, Zhèjiāng, Héběi, etc. The *pīnyīn* system is not used at all in

Taiwan, where a combination of the old postal spellings and Wade-Giles romanization is used. In Taiwan, moreover, Peiping (pronounced *Běipíng* and meaning "northern peace") is used in preference to Peking (*Běijīng*), because *Běipíng* was the name of the city when the Nationalist government left the mainland in 1949. The name Peking (*Běijīng*), which had been used in the Ming and Ching dynasties, was re-adopted by the Communists when they made the city their capital (*jīng* = "capital").

Most two-syllable Chinese place names can be pronounced with an optional neutral tone for the second syllable. Thus: *Guǎngzhōu* or *Guǎng.zhōu*, *Shànghǎi* or *Shàng.hǎi*, *Nánjīng* or *Nán.jīng*. But certain place names, such as *Běipíng*, cannot use the neutral tone.

7.   Review I.5.26 on *bùzhīdào* followed by a question to mean "I wonder...". *Bùzhīdào tā zài nǎr* "I wonder where he is"; *bùzhīdào shālā.lǐ yǒu méi.yǒu xiǎo fānqié* "I wonder if there are any cherry tomatoes in the salad"; etc.

When *hǎo* is added at the end of such sentences, the sense is "I don't know (or I wonder) who/what/where/etc. would be best". *Bùzhīdào zěm jiào hǎo* "wonder how to call best--I wonder what the best mode of address would be". *Bùzhīdào gěi shéi hǎo* "I wonder whom I should give it to"; *bùzhīdào shuō shém.me hǎo* "I didn't know (couldn't decide) what would be appropriate to say". When *bùzhīdào* has no subject in such sentences, it is assumed to be *wǒ*. But other subjects can be specified: *tā bùzhīdào mǎi něi.ge hǎo* "she couldn't decide which it would be best to buy".

8.   *Rúguǒ* "if" is slightly more formal than *yào.shi*. It is also more common in Southern Mandarin, while *yào.shi* is used more in the North.

9.   *Shóu* "cooked" is the opposite of *shēng*, which you learned in I.3 as "raw" (*jī tài*
        shēng "the chicken was too raw"). In II.3 you learned *shēngcài*
        "raw-vegetable—salad". *Shēng* also has the extended meaning of "unknown,
        strange", and *shóu* the corresponding meaning of "known, familiar". Thus *shēngrén*
        "strangers"; *shóurén* "familiar people". Other common terms are *shēng zì* "new
        vocabulary" and *shēng dì.fāng* "strange places".

Exercises

In-class exercises:

1.   Answer the following questions in Chinese.

        A.   Wèishém Lǎo Wáng yào yòng "wife" zhèi.ge zì?
        B.   Lǎo Wáng dào.guò něi.xiē dì.fāng? Nǎr .de rén guǎn "wife" jiào ài.rén?
        C.   Nǐ kě .bù.kě.yǐ guǎn Zhāng .Xīan.shēng Lǐ .Xīan.shēng .de ài.rén jiào Zhāng
                ài.rén Lǐ ài.rén? Wèishém.me?

Homework:

1.   Translate the following sentences into Chinese.

        A.   There's a question I've always wanted to ask the two of you, but I've never
                had the chance.
        B.   Now that both of you are here, I'll ask you: "Why did you study Chinese in
                the first place?"
        C.   My answer is simple. I wanted to study Chinese because my "wife" is
                Chinese.
        D.   It's fine when you use "wife" for your own wife, but there are problems when
                you use it to address somebody else's wife.
        E.   I would like very much to teach Chinese in your school (I very much desire
                to go to your school to teach Chinese). Do you think there is a chance?
        F.   He seemed to be very familiar with Mrs. Wáng. Actually that was the first
                time they met. He called her "*Xiǎo Wáng*" and she seemed to be quite
                unhappy. She must have found him very rude.
        G.   There are more than thirty Americans who can speak Chinese living in this
                dormitory. So, I believe that Chinese is really not that difficult to
                learn.

2.   Write a dialogue in which you use the following words and expressions: *yìzhí*;
        rúguǒ; *zhènghǎo*; *jiè.shào*; *zhǐ hǎo*; *bǎ*; *cái*; *jiù*; *dānxīn*

Classroom/Homework exercises:

1.   Draw a map of China and locate on it the cities introduced in this lesson. Write
        down anything you know about these cities, and present it in your class.

LESSON 2

Vocabulary

duì	對	(speaking) to	hú.tú	糊塗	indistinct, muddled, confused
nǔ.ér	女兒	daughter	bī	逼	compel, to force
guān.xì	關係	relation	gōng.píng	公平	fair, just

Vocabulary Classified by Type

Nouns		Verbs	gōng.píng
nǔ.ér	bī		
guān.xì			**First Position Verbs**
		Adjectives	duì
		hú.tú	

Grammar Notes

1. *Shì* here is an emphatic *shì*, used to reinforce something that has been said earlier. It is always pronounced in the full fourth tone. *Tā shì huì shuō Yīngwén* "She **can** speak English". Without this emphatic *shì*, a sentence stands on its own perfectly well, but is not emphatic: *tā huì shuō Yīngwén* "she can speak English". The emphatic *shì* is added before verbs with or without auxiliary verbs or adverbs: *Tā shì dǒng Zhōngwén* "He **does** understand Chinese"; *wǒ shì xǐ.huān chī-táng* "I **do** like candy"; *Lǎo Wáng shì méi shàng túshūguǎn .qù* "Lǎo Wáng **didn't** go to the library". It can also be inserted before adjectives: *zhèi-zhāng zhuō.zi shì hěn guì* "this table **is** expensive"; *nǐ shì tǎoyàn* "you **are** disgusting". Be careful not to misunderstand this *shì* as the English verb "to be", which you might do if you try to translate word by word. The normal way to say "this table is expensive" is *zhèi-zhāng zhuō.zi .hěn guì*.

    Also be sure to distinguish this *shì* from the *shi* in *shi....de*: *zhèi-zhāng zhuō.zi shi hěn guì .de* is less emphatic than the same sentence without *.de*.

2. *Duì*, originally meaning "to face toward", means "to" in phrases like *duì nǔ.ér shuō* "say to daughter". In this use it is similar to *gēn* "with" or "to", although *gēn* implies two-way communication while *duì* is only one-way. *Gēn .tā shuō-huà .kě zhēn lèi* (VII.3) "Talking with him is really tiring"; but *Wǒ duì .tā shuō: "Nǐ .kě zhēn lèi-rén"* "I told him, 'You really tire a person out'". (*Gēn* could be used for *duì* in the second example, but *duì* could not substitute for *gēn* in the first.)

3.   *Zhōngwén xuéxiào* "Chinese school". Chinese communities in America often run
      Chinese schools on weekends. Using classrooms at colleges, schools, or churches,
      they usually meet Saturday or Sunday for two or three hours and teach culture in
      addition to language. The students are mostly Chinese-American children, or the
      children of Chinese immigrants, but American children from other backgrounds are
      beginning to attend as well. Some schools also have classes for adults.

Exercises

In-class exercises:

1.   Answer the following questions.

      A.   Nǐ wèishém yào xué Zhōngwén? Shi nǐ zìjǐ juédìng .de .hái.shi nǐ fù-mǔ bī
            .nǐ xué .de?
      B.   Wèishém nǔ.ér bú yuàn.yì dào Zhōngwén xuéxiào qù? Rúguǒ nǐ shi tā, nǐ
            yuàn.yì .bú.yuàn.yì qù? Wèishém.me?
      C.   Nǐ jué.de zhèi-wèi fù.qīn (father) ràng nǔ.ér xué Zhōngwén .de fá.zi hǎo
            .bù.hǎo? Wèishém.me? Nǐ yǒu méi.yǒu gèng hǎo .de fá.zi?

Homework:

1.   Translate the following sentences into Chinese.

      A.   Your wife went to college in America. I remember you were classmates. Of
            course she can speak English.
      B.   My wife can speak English, but my daughter is unwilling to speak Chinese.
      C.   My wife has always forced our daughter to learn Chinese, but our daughter
            really doesn't want to.
      D.   If she really doesn't want to learn Chinese, there is no point forcing her.
      E.   An elementary school student once told me that her father is Japanese
            (Japan: Rìběn) and her mother is Chinese. One day her parents said to her,
            "You ought to be able to speak both Chinese and Japanese and to read both
            Chinese and Japanese books. We have already decided to send you to Chinese
            school on Saturdays and Japanese school on Sundays. Are you willing to go?"
            She replied, "Sorry, Daddy and Mommy. No way. It won't do because I want
            to have some good solid recreation on the weekends."
      F.   Later on, the parents of that child began to quarrel because, when the
            father forced the child to study Japanese, the mother felt it was unfair and
            when the mother forced the child to study Chinese, the father felt it was
            unfair. So they decided that, other than English, their daughter didn't
            have to study any other language (wén). The child was finally free.

Classroom/Homework exercises:

1.   Fill in the blanks.

      A.   Wǒ ... tā shuō, "Qǐng .nǐ bié zuò zài wǒ.de yǐ.zi.shàng."
      B.   Xiǎo Yīng, bié nào, wǒ zài ... Wáng Āyí dǎ-diànhuà.
      C.   Zuó.tiān wǒ ... wǒ mǔ.qīn dǎ.le yí.ge diànhuà. Mǔ.qīn wèn .wǒ wèishém dào
            xuéxiào yǐhòu yìzhí méi ... tā xiě-xìn.

D.   Zhèi-jiàn yī.fú tài duǎn .le, ... wǒ bútài héshì.
E.   ... wǒ, ... Yīngwén xiě-xìn hěn róng.yì.
F.   Qǐng .nǐ ... wǒ.mén jiè.shào yí-xià.
G.   Dú-shū ... zuò-rén yíyàng yàojǐn.
H.   Tā shi ... Bōshìdùn lái .de.
I.   Wǒ.mén yào qù wánr, nǐ yào .bú.yào ... wǒ.mén yíkuàir qù?
J.   Tā ... rén hěn bú kè.qì, suǒ.yǐ rénx dōu tǎoyàn .tā.

LESSON 3

Vocabulary

mǔ-nǚ	母女	mother and daughter	zhèi.ge	這個	word used as "filler-in"
xìng.qù	興趣	interest	ss	嘶	interjection of hesitation
shǔqī xuéxiào	暑期學校	summer school	yì-shí	一時	for the moment
Táiběi	台北	Taipei	xiǎng.qǐ.lái	想起來	recall
...yǐhòu	以後	after...	búdàn...yě...	不但…也…	not only...but also...
jì.xù	繼續	to continue	guójì	國際	international
.ne.me....ne?	那麼…呢	(see Grammar Note 4)	zhèng.zhì	政治	politics
bǐjiào	比較	comparative	Yǎzhōu (Yàzhōu)	亞洲	Asia
wénxué	文學	literature	lìshǐ	歷史	history
ménr (mén)	門兒, 門	AN for course	tóngshí	同時	at the same time
dú	讀	to read	Zhōng-Měi	中美	Sino-American
shǒu	首	AN for poem, song	piān	篇	AN for articles
fānyì	翻譯	to translate, translation	dào.lǐ	道理	principle, reason, argument
shī	詩	poem	bùguǎn	不管	no matter (what)
dǎ-chà	打岔	to make an interruption	wúlùn	無論	no matter (what)
jù	句	sentence	chuī-niú	吹牛	to brag
			duō-nián	多年	many years; long-lasting

Vocabulary Classified by Type

Nouns	Adjectives	Interjections
mǔ-nǚ	bǐjiào	ss
xìng.qù	guójì	
shǔqī xuéxiào	Zhōng-Měi	**V-Directional Complements**
wénxué	duō-nián	xiǎng.qǐ.lái
fānyì		
shī	**ANs**	**Time Words**
zhèng.zhì	ménr (mén)	...yǐhòu
lìshǐ	shǒu	yì-shí
dào.lǐ	jù	tóngshí
	piān	
Proper Nouns		**Sentential Modifiers**
Táiběi	**V-Os**	bùguǎn
Yǎzhōu (Yàzhōu)	dǎ-chà	wúlùn
	chuī-niú	
Verbs		**Idiomatic Expressions**
jì.xù	**Conjunctions**	.ne.me....ne?
dú	búdàn...yě...	
fānyì		

Grammar Notes

1. This *.le* is a "completed action *.le*". Review II.1.20, and especially the point that a "completed action *.le*" by no means indicates past tense. In the text we have *yào.shi wǒ xué-huì.le* "if I **were** to learn (some day)..." referring to a **projected** action, not now completed but to-be-completed. In such cases it is quite possible for the "completed action *.le*" to refer to the future.

2. *Xìng.qù* is a noun meaning "interest". To say someone is "interested in X", you say that that person *duì X yǒu xìng.qù*. Do not use *yǒu xìng.qù* to mean "interesting"; use *yǒu yì.sī* (introduced in the next lesson). *Zhōngwén hěn yǒu yì.sī* "Chinese is very interesting". *Wǒ duì Zhōngwén hěn yǒu xìng.qù* "I am very interested in Chinese".

3. *Shǔqī xuéxiào* "summer school". "Summer", which is *xià.tiān* in spoken Chinese, is *shǔ* in literary Chinese. *Qī* "period" is also a literary word, but the combination *shǔqī* "summer-period", is commonly spoken. Similarly, "summer vacation" is *shǔjià*, where *jià* is "holiday, time off".

4. *.Ne.me* "well, in that case, then" usually introduces a follow-up question, and is usually accompanied by *.ne* at the end of the question. *.Ne.me X .ne?* "Then how about X?". The same effect is achieved by simply saying *X .ne?* "And X?". But *.ne.me* at the beginning strengthens the connotation of follow-up.

5. *Bǐjiào* "comparative, comparatively" can also be pronounced *bǐjiǎo* or *bǐ.jiào*. *Bǐjiào wénxué* is "comparative literature". When used as an adverb meaning "comparatively", *bǐjiào* usually precedes an adjective: *Zhèi.ge wèntí bǐjiào dà* "This is a comparatively big problem." *Gēn nǚ.ér shuō Zhōng.guó-huà bǐ.jiào hǎo* "It's better to speak Chinese with your daughter." When you want to compare one thing with another, you use the A *bǐ* B pattern (III.1.7): *Ná kuài.zi chī-fàn bǐ*

ná chā.zi fāng.biàn "Eating with chopsticks is more convenient than with a fork." But if you don't have a specific second thing to compare to, or if that thing is so obvious it doesn't need to be mentioned, you can use *bǐjiào*: *Ná kuài.zi chī-fàn bǐ.jiào fāng.biàn* "Eating with chopsticks is more convenient (than unspoken alternatives)."

6. *Ménr* or *mén* "door" serves as an AN for courses of study. *Yì-mén kè* "a course of study". Distinguish this from *yì-táng kè* (see I.4.4), which means "one class" in the sense of "one class-hour during the day".

    "To take" a course is *xuǎn* (literally, "select") or *niàn* (study), and the verb "to go to" class is *shàng* (see III.4). Thus:

Wǒ jīn.nián xuǎn.le (or niàn) sì-mén kè.	I'm taking four courses this year.
Wǒ jīn.tiān shàng.le liǎng-táng kè.	I went to two classes today.

    WARNING: On American campuses you may hear *ná-kè* for "take courses" and *ná-jià* for "take vacation". For example: *Nǐ ná shém.me kè?* "What courses are you taking?"; *wǒ xià .ge yuè ná-jià* "I'm taking vacation next month". These are non-standard usages that you should avoid. They are based on literal borrowings from English and are not used in China.

7. *Lǐ Bái*, one of the greatest Chinese poets, and one of the most translated into English, lived in the 8th century A.D. Formerly his name was pronounced *Lǐ Bó*, or Li Po in the Wade-Giles romanization system, and this spelling is sometimes still used. But *Lǐ Bái* (or Li Pai in Wade-Giles) has become more common.

8. *Zài méi.yǒu bǐ Lǐ Bái .de shī gèng hǎo .de* "There's no better poetry than Lǐ Bái's". In general, *zài méi.yǒu bǐ X gèng* Adj. *.de* means "there's nothing more Adj. than X". *Shì.jiè.shàng zài méi.yǒu bǐ .tā gèng tǎoyàn .de rén .le.* "There is no one in the world more annoying than he".

9. *Dǎ-chà* "strike digression—to interrupt" is a Verb-Object compound like *shuō-huà*. *Dǎ yí.ge chà* or *dǎ .ge chà* "make an interruption". If you want to say **whom** one is interrupting (for example "I am interrupting you"), you must say either (1) *wǒ dǎ nǐ.de chà* or (2) *wǒ gēn .nǐ dǎ-chà*.

10. *.Zhèi.ge* or *.nèi.ge*, usually repeated one or more times, is a common filler-in, used during hesitations or to hold the floor while thinking of what to say next. It is similar to "um", "ah", or "well, let's see..." in English. *.Zhèi.ge* is more common than *.nèi.ge*.

11. *Ss*, pronounced by sucking in air between the teeth, expresses hesitation or thinking over. It is different from the Japanese sucked in *ss*, which is pronounced very long and expresses politeness.

12. *Yì-shí* "one moment—for the moment".

13. *Xiǎng.bù-qǐlái*, literally "can't think (and have the recollection) come up", means "can't recall". *Xiǎng-qǐ.lái* "recall" is grammatically a verb plus directional complement.

14.   *Yăzhōu* "Asia" can also be pronounced *Yàzhōu*.   *Zhōu* can be neutral tone as well: *Yă.zhōu*, *Yà.zhōu*.

15.   *Dào.li* "principle, reason".   *Dà dào.li* "major principle, great truth" is used sarcastically here.   *Piān* is an AN for compositions or articles.   *Liăng-piān wénzhāng* "two articles".   *Yì-piān dà dào.li* "a composition(ful) of major principles—a lot of pompous talk".

   .Lái here is the second part of the directional complement *chūlái*, which is split.   (Review IV.4.8).

16.   *Bùguăn* "not care-about" and *wúlùn* "without discussing—no matter" mean "no matter (or regardless of)...[whom, where, what, why, when, how, whether, etc.]".   The two terms are similar except that *wúlùn* is slightly more formal than *bùguăn*.

   Bùguăn and *wúlùn* must be followed by clauses that contain either (a) question words:

Bùguăn (or wúlùn) tā zài năr...	No matter where he is... (wherever he is...)
Wúlùn (or bùguăn) shi shéi...	Regardless of who it is... (whoever it may be...)
Bùguăn (or wúlùn) nǐ gēn .ta zěm shuō...	No matter what you say to her... (whatever you say to her...)

Or (b) choice-type questions (see I.1.9):

Bùguăn tā dŏng .bù.dŏng...	Regardless of whether he understands or not...
Wúlùn nǐ qù .bú.qù...	Whether you go or not...

Note that in the *next* clause after one containing *bùguăn* or *wúlùn*, it is common (but not required) to use a word like *dōu* "in all cases" or *zŏng* "always, in any case":

Bùguăn nǐ wèn .tā shém shì, tā dōu gěi .nǐ yì-piān dà dào.li.	No matter what you ask him about, he always gives you a crock of great truths.
Wúlùn nǐ qù .bú.qù, zŏng děi gào.sù .tā.	Whether you go or not, you should be sure to tell her.
Bùguăn dŏng .bù.dŏng, wŏ dōu yào qù tīng.	I'm going to go listen whether I understand or not.

Another word that is commonly used in the same way is *suíbiàn* "follow convenience—as you like":

Suíbiàn nǐ gēn .tā shuō shém shì, tā dōu bú yuàn.yì tīng.	Whatever you talk to her about, she never feels like listening.
Suíbiàn nǐ xǐ.huān .bù.xǐ.huān, wŏ.mén yǐ.jīng juédìng măi zhèi-suŏ fáng.zi .le.	Whether you like it or not, we've already decided to buy this house.

17.   *Chuī-niú* "blow cow" or *chuī niú pí* "blow cow's skin" means "to brag". Euphemisms
      in Chinese, the latter is the less decorous.

Exercises

Homework:

1.   Translate the following sentences into Chinese

      A.   Once I began studying Chinese I got very interested, and so I have just kept
           on studying.
      B.   I saw Sino-American relations getting better day by day, so I decided to
           study Chinese.
      C.   No matter what you ask him—whether big questions or little questions—he
           always gives you a lot of baloney (big principles).
      D.   There is nothing better on the weekend than to spend it sleeping. That is
           really the best way in the world.
      E.   A: How many courses have you taken this semester (xuéqī)?
           B: I took three: Translation, International Relations and Comparative
               Literature.
      F.   I am interested in both history and literature. I don't know whether I
           should enroll in (enter) the Department of Chinese Literature or the
           Department of Asian History.
      G.   My eyesight is extremely bad. Although they put the newspaper right in
           front of my eyes, I still can't read (it).
      H.   He always has liked to play politics. I never trust him.
      I.   A: My roommate has lived in America for eight years, but he can't even
               drive. (Use the "*lián ... dōu ....*" pattern.)
           B: What does that have to do with you?
           A: It has a lot to do with me. Because he can't drive, he rides in my car
               every day to go to school and to buy groceries. I can't pay attention
               to driving because he talks too much. One day my car bumped into a tree
               and I bumped my head and was injured. I had to see the doctor and pay
               him five hundred bucks. Do you mean to say that my roommate's inability
               to drive has nothing to do with me?

Classroom/Homework exercises:

1.   Answer the following questions in Chinese.

      A.   Wèishém mǔ-nǚ .de guān.xì hěn jǐn.zhāng?
      B.   Yào.shi Lǎo Wáng gēn .tā tài.x zài jiā.li shuō Zhōngwén, tā.mén.de nǚ.ér shi
           .bú.shi hěn kuài jiù huì shuō Zhōngwén .le?
      C.   Lǎo Dīng jué.de shéi .de shī shi shì.jiè.shàng zuì hǎo .de shī?

2.   Fill in the blanks.

      A.   Tā ... nǎr? Tā ... chuáng.shàng shuì-jiào .ne.
      B.   Zǎo.shàng bā-diǎn zhōng tài zǎo .le, ... wǒ bútài fāng.biàn.
      C.   Wǒ bān-jiā .le, bān .dào ... xuéxiào bǐjiào jìn .de dì.fāng.
      D.   ... lǎoshī suǒ jiǎng .de, zhèi-yí-kè .de gù.shì hěn yǒu yì.sī.

E.   Tā suírán xīn bùhǎo, kě.shi yě ... bǎ tā dì.x gěi dǎ-shāng.le.
F.   Tā ... shém dōu yǒu xìng.qù.
G.   Ni zěm.le? Zěm lián wǒ ... bú rèn.shì .le.
H.   ... wǒ yígòng yǒu sì.ge rén yào qù kàn diànyìng.

3.   Oral Substitution

      Given: "Lǐ Bái .de shī zuì hǎo" shi shém yì.sī?

Response: "Lǐ Bái .de shī zuì hǎo" .de yì.sī shi wúlùn shéi.de shī dōu méi.yǒu Lǐ Bái
          .de nèm hǎo; yě jiù.shi shuō zài méi.yǒu bǐ Lǐ Bái .de shī gèng hǎo .de .le.

      A.   Tā.de nüpéng.yǒu zuì hǎokàn.
      B.   Zhèi.ge xuéxiào .de xué.shēng zuì duō.
      C.   Zhèi.ge fànguǎnr .de lóngxiā zuì yǒumíng.
      D.   Shì.jiè Mào.yì Zhōngxīn shi Niǔyuē zuì gāo .de lóu.
      E.   Wǒ jué.de Zhōngguó cài shi shì.jiè.shàng zuì hǎochī .de cài.
      F.   Zuò fēijī shi dào wài.guó .qu zuì fāng.biàn .de fá.zi.
      G.   Zài bié.rén shuì-jiào .de shí.hòur, huà bié.rén .de bí.zi shi zuì kěwù .de
            shì.qíng.

LESSON 4

Vocabulary

gù.shì	故事	story		chūn	春	spring (not used alone in spoken Chinese)
měi	美	beautiful				
miáo.xiě	描寫	to describe		yǒu yì.sī	有意思	interesting
chūn.tiān	春天	spring		nǎ.lǐ	哪裏	used in polite denials of compliments
bèi	背	to recite				
tóu	頭	the first		shàng-bān	上班	go to work

Vocabulary Classified by Type

Nouns	**Adjectives**	**Determinatives**
gù.shì	měi	tóu
chūn.tiān	yǒu yì.sī	
chūn		**Idiomatic Expressions**
		nǎ.lǐ
Verbs	**V-Os**	
miáo.xiě	shàng-bān	
bèi		

Grammar Notes

1. *Bèi*, originally meaning "back", also means "to recite by heart". This is because, in old China, the way a student showed that he had memorized a text was to turn his back to his teacher (so that he could not see his books) and recite by heart. *Bèi-shū* eventually came to be a verb-object compound meaning "to (turn one's) back (to the teacher and recite from) books--to recite texts".

2. *Tóu* "head" can be used before a number and AN (with or without a following noun) to mean "the first": *tóu-liǎng-jù* "the first two sentences"; *tóu-yi-huí* "the first time"; *tóu-sān.ge zì* "the first three characters".

3. *Shém.me* is here used in an indefinite meaning, similar to "something" in English. It is often elongated to indicate uncertainty.

4. *Yǒu yì.sī* "having meaning" means "interesting". Although a V-O construction, it behaves like any other adjective. *Hěn yǒu yì.sī* "very interesting"; *yǒu yì.sī jí.le* "extremely interesting"; etc. The negative is *méi.yǒu yì.sī* or *méi yì.sī*, which also can be modified: *fēicháng méi yì.sī* "extremely boring". Review note 2 in the last lesson on the important difference between *yǒu yì.sī* and *yǒu xìng.qù*.

Another useful adjective that is similar to *yǒu yì.sī* is *hǎowánr* "fun, amusing". *Zhōngwén hěn hǎowánr* "Chinese is lots of fun".

5.   *Nǎ.lǐ nǎ.lǐ* here is a case of the "polite denial" described in the Culture Note 16 (VI.2). But the "polite" language in this case is itself sarcastic.

Exercises

Homework:

1.   Translate the following sentences into Chinese.

   A.   Well, um... ah... the first two lines I've forgotten. I don't quite remember the third line, either. The fourth line seems to be something... something... something... "spring".

   B.   Your point is that I am like the guy in the story, right? In fact, you are completely wrong.

   C.   At least he came up with one word--"spring." I couldn't even get a single word out, so he's way ahead of me.

   D.   This Chinese Summer School is a very special school. Students are not allowed to speak even a word of English. We speak Chinese all the time. We even speak Chinese in our dream talk, and grind our teeth in Chinese when we are asleep. Teachers and students live in the same dormitory and have meals together. There is ample opportunity to practice Chinese. The language lab is the best in the world. We enjoy very much sitting in the lab listening to audiotapes and watching videotapes. It may be that I am learning more now than the summer I was in China. In China there was no teacher forcing me to study. There was a work schedule, to be sure, but the demands were not very high. In this summer school the work is indeed formidable (lì.hài). Almost every day there is a quiz (small exam) and every week an exam. Therefore you have to study hard (use the pattern "*fēi....bùkě*"). They force you to memorize a lot of Chinese, and what you learn in class you can immediately practice in conversation outside the classroom with your teachers and schoolmates. After you say something several times, you will never forget it. Moreover (érqiě), the teachers spend a lot of time to help the students. If you don't study hard, you feel ashamed.

2.   Summarize the story of this Unit in Chinese.

Classroom/Homework exercises:

1.   Make one sentence using each of the following expressions: *yǒu yì.sī*; *yǒu xìng.qù*; *yǒumíng*; *yǒu dào.lǐ*; *yǒuyòng*; *yǒu qián*; *yǒu jīng.shén*; *yǒu xīwàng*; *yǒu wèntí*

GRAMMAR CHECKLIST

bàn "half"   III.4.8|

bàn "manage, handle" (compared   V.3.2|
  with *zuò*)

bié

    "don't"   I.3.25|

    "other"   I.5.33|

bìng [*bù*(*bú*)/*méi*] "really [not]"   II.4.1|

búdàn... érqiě... "not only...   III.2.5|
  but also..."

bùdéliǎo (adj..*de bùdéliǎo*)   III.2.8|

bùguǎn... [*wúlùn...*] "no   VIII.3.16|
  matter..."

bú.shi... jiù.shi...   V.2.13|

bùzhīdào   I.5.26|

  (followed by a question to   III.1.7|
    mean) "I wonder... "

cái (adv.)   II.3.12|
                                              III.3.21|
                                              III.4.10|

  "later than expected"   III.3.18|

cáixíng   III.3.6|

Chinese time and place order   II.1.6|
  (large units to small ones)

chū.lái (extended meaning of di-   IV.4.7|
  rectional complement) "make out
  by [seeing; hearing; etc.]"

  split complement   IV.4.8|

chú.le... yǐwài   V.2.7|

Comparisons

  A *bǐ* B adj.   III.1.7|

  A *méi.yǒu* B *nèm.me* adj.   III.1.11|

A *yǒu méi.yǒu* B *nèm.me* adj.   III.1.22|
  (choice type question)

A *gēn* B *chà.bùduō* (about   III.1.12|
  the same)

A *gēn* B *yíyàng*; *yíyàng* adj.   III.1.13|
  (same)

A *gēn* B *bùtóng* (different   III.1.23|
  from)

A adj. *.yi.diǎnr* (implicit   III.1.9|
  comparison with *bǐ* B   III.1.21|
  understood)

adj. *duō.le*; or, adj. *.de duō*   III.1.10|
  "is much more adj."

yì-AN bǐ yì-AN adj.   III.2.2|
  (*yí-AN bǐ yí-AN* adj.)
    (*yì-tiān bǐ yì-tiān luàn*)

compare verbs (*nǐ xiě-zì*   III.2.29|
  xiě .de bǐ .wǒ hǎo)

compare with someone (*gēn*   III.3.9|
  hǎo.de bǐ)

Complements

  Bound-phrase Complements   II.2.35|
  (*fàng.dào shūjià.zi.shàng*)   III.2.15|
                                              III.2.27|
                                              IV.2.12|
                                              IV.3.3|

  Directional Complements   IV.2.8|

    .qǐ.lái (extended use: III.3.10|
      begin to)

    .shàng.lái   III.3.11|

    huí.lái; *lái*; *qù*   III.4.11|

    simple complement   IV.2.8|

    compound complement   IV.2.8|

    potential directional   IV.2.9|
      complement

    V.*shàng.lái* vs. V.*shàng.qù*   IV.3.2|

240 CHINESE PRIMER

Zěm huí shi?	III.4.9		
		zhāojí vs. *dānxīn* vs. *jīn.zhāng*	VII.1.3
Ni zěm.me .le? "What	VI.3.8,9		
happened?"; "What's wrong		*.zhe* See progressive action	
with you?"			
		zhǐ hǎo	III.4.2
zěm jiào & *shém jiào*	V.2.11		
		zhǐ yào... jiù... "as long as...	II.4.2
zèm & *nèm*	I.3.11	then..."	
	II.1.22		
	II.2.23	*zhōngjiànr* between A and B	IV.3.5
zhào "according to"	IV.1.7	*zhòngyào* vs. *yàojin*	VII.2.2
"to reflect"; "look into	V.3.8	*zui hǎo* "had better"	III.2.25
mirrors"			V.3.7

List of Warnings

Glosses vs. "equivalents"	I.1
yě vs. "me too"	I.1.10
.ma question vs. V-not-V question	I.1.13
dōu vs. "all"	I.1.18
gēn vs. "and"	I.1.19
	I.3.7
yǒu yìdiǎnr vs. *yìdiǎnr*	I.3.5
hěn vs. "very"	I.3.7
gòu ying vs. "hard enough"	I.3.8
yǒu vs. "have"	I.4.3
Omission of "if"	I.4.15
	II.1.15
yi(yí).... jiù... vs. "as soon as"	I.4.22
yào.shí vs. "if"	II.1.16
Completed action vs. past tense	II.1.20
	II.3.14
Omission of "your", "my", "his"	II.2.22
jìrán vs. *yīn.wèi*	II.3.5